JN441371

ADVER-TISING AND CULTURE

: Theoretical Challenges and Future Directions

ADVERTISING AND CULTURE
: THEORETICAL CHALLENGES AND FUTURE DIRECTIONS

SANGPIL HAN

—

Published by **HANYANG UNIVERSITY PRESS**
Tel. +82.2.2220.1432
Web. http://press.hanyang.ac.kr
Email. presshy@hanyang.ac.kr

—

This work was supported by the Ministry of Education of the Republic of Korea and the National Research Foundation of Korea (NRF-2022S1A6A4045931).

—

ISBN **978.89.7218.859.9 [93320]**

ADVER-TISING AND CULTURE

: Theoretical Challenges and Future Directions

SANGPIL HAN

HANYANG UNIVERSITY PRESS

Preface

In an era where globalization and digital transformation are reshaping the way businesses communicate, cross-cultural advertising stands as both a vital opportunity and a formidable challenge. The fusion of diverse cultural values, traditions, and consumer behaviors presents unique opportunities for brands to craft messages that resonate on a global scale. However, navigating the nuances of cultural sensitivity, consumer expectations, and emerging technologies requires a nuanced understanding of both the art and science of advertising.

This book, Advertising and Culture : Theoretical Challenges and Future Directions, is a comprehensive examination of the theories, methodologies, and practical applications that define cross-cultural advertising in the 21st century. Designed for a wide audience, including scholars, students, and professionals in the fields of marketing, advertising, and global business, it offers a balanced approach that bridges academic rigor with real-world relevance.

The chapters in this book provide a multi-dimensional exploration of cross-cultural advertising. Starting with foundational discussions in "The Growth of Cross-Cultural Business and Advertising" and "Advertising and Culture," this two chapters establish the theoretical underpinnings that frame this dynamic field. Subsequent chapters delve into practical challenges and solutions, such as "Coordinating and Controlling Cross-Cultural Advertising" and "Cross-Cultural Advertising Blunders." These discussions are supplemented with empirical insights, case studies, and methodological advancements, including detailed analyses of global advertising markets and cultural variability.

A distinctive feature of this book is its emphasis on future-forward thinking. The final chapter "Theoretical Challenges and Future Directions in Global Consumer Psychology" reflects on the evolving interplay between cultural norms and technological advancements. This exploration extends to emerging areas, such as the role of artificial intelligence in cross-cultural advertising and the ethical considerations it entails. By combining a retrospective evaluation with forward-looking perspectives, this book aims to equip readers with the knowledge and tools necessary to navigate an increasingly interconnected and culturally complex global marketplace.

The motivation for this book stems from a recognition of the critical role cross-cultural advertising plays in fostering global understanding and economic integration. This book addresses gaps in existing literature while providing actionable insights for practitioners. This endeavor would not have been possible without the collaborative efforts of a dedicated team of scholars and industry professionals who brought their expertise and passion to every stage of this project.

I am deeply grateful to the researchers, practitioners, and educators whose work has inspired this book. Special thanks are due to many scholars and contributors, whose diverse perspectives and innovative ideas have enriched the content of this volume. I also acknowledge the unwavering support of Korea National Research Foundation, who ensured the clarity and coherence of writing.

It is my hope that this book will serve as both a foundational text and a source of inspiration for those engaged in the field of cross-cultural advertising. Whether you are a student seeking to understand the basics, a researcher exploring uncharted territory, or a practitioner striving to craft impactful campaigns, I believe this book offers valuable insights and practical guidance.

As the boundaries between cultures continue to

blur and the pace of technological innovation accelerates, cross-cultural advertising will remain a dynamic and evolving field. I invite readers to join me in this ongoing exploration, contributing to a deeper understanding of how cultural diversity can enrich global communication and drive meaningful connections.

Sangpil Han, Ph.D.

Professor, Department of Advertising and PR, Hanyang University

Table of Contents

Chapter 1

The Growth of Cross-cultural Business and Advertising

Structural Changes in the Global Advertising Industry

World Advertising Market

The global advertising market is showing 5% growth every year. The growth rate of global advertising spending has been growing continuously, except for 2020, when Corona19 began. 2021 and 2022 are forecast to rebound to 5.8% and 6.9%. In contrast, Korea is expected to stop at a growth rate of 4% in 2021, which is less than the average of the global advertising growth rate (reflecting the base effect following a sharp decline in 2020).

According to data from five companies estimating global advertising expenses, global advertising expenses in 2024 are estimated to be between $750 billion and $1 trillion. Among the five companies, WARC predicts that global advertising spending will be the highest at $1.0439 trillion, while Dentsu predicts a conservative assumption of $750 billion. In comparison, Group M, Magna, and Zenith predict that it will exceed $900 billion. According to these data, the size of the global advertising market is growing at about 5% to 7% every year. The media that is leading the growth of the global advertising market is digital media, and the sales of traditional media such as television, newspapers, and magazines are plummeting.

Table 1 Estimated Global Advertising Spending (Unit : 100 million dollar. growth rate %)

Company	2023	2024	2025
Dentsu	7,198 (2.7%)	7,528 (4.6%)	7,846 (4.2%)
Group M	8,890 (5.8%)	9,360 (5.3%)	-
Magna	8,530 (5.5%)	9,144 (7.2%)	-
Zenith	8,742 (5.2%)	9,164 (4.8%)	9,569 (4.4%)
WARC	9,634 (4.4%)	10,429 (8.2%)	-

* Source : Advertising Yearbook, Cheil Worldwide, 2024.

Compared to the United States, where the share of advertising spending in GDP accounts for more than 1.4%, Korea's share has been steadily declining since 2000, remaining at the 0.6% - 0.7% level. While the ratio of advertising expenditure to GDP in developed countries such as the United States and Japan is maintained at 1.4% to 1.5% even during economic recessions, Korea's advertising industry has been gradually declining since peaking at 1.25% just before the IMF in the 1990s. Even worse, it is showing a growth rate that is less than the economic growth rate.

As of 2018, per capita advertising expenditure is $783 in the US, $492 in France, $387 in the UK, and $354 in Japan, compared to $252 in Korea. Advertising expenditure per capita is only 32% of the US, 51% of France, and 71% of Japan.

Comparing the growth rate of advertising expenditures by continent over the past 10 years, North America, including the United States and Canada, holds the top spot in terms of scale, but the recent growth rate is relatively high in Asia/Pacific and Eastern Europe. The countries leading the growth of the Asia/Pacific advertising market are China, India, Indonesia, Thailand and Vietnam. In the Asia/Pacific region, China has the world's second largest advertising market and Japan has the world's third largest advertising market. Recently, India and Indonesia are growing into the world's top 10 advertising countries, and Southeast Asian countries such as Vietnam and Thailand have very high growth rate of advertising spending. In Eastern Europe, the share of advertising expenditure in GDP was low in the past, but the recent development of the advertising industry is noteworthy.

Table 2 **Top 10 Global Advertising Market Rankings by Year (Unit : US$ million)**

Rank	2018		2019		2020		2021		2022	
	Coutnry	Ad expern diture	Coutnry	Ad expern diture	Coutnry	Ad expern diture	Coutnry	Ad expern diture	Coutnry	Ad expern diture
1	USA	229,680	USA	242,718	USA	225,790	USA	268,448	USA	281,612
2	China	87,077	China	90,969	China	105,25	China	95,343	China	101,704
3	Japan	45,135	Japan	46,037	Japan	42,671	Japan	48,840	Japan	50,033
4	England	27,469	England	28,364	England	26,842	England	31,146	England	32,675
5	Germany	24.917	Germany	24,779	Germany	19,983	Germany	25,146	Germany	25,217
6	Brazil	13,463	France	13,903	France	12,520	France	15,086	France	15,681
7	France	13,262	Brazil	13,846	Brazil	11,895	Brazil	14,809	Brazil	15,404
8	Korea	12,891	Korea	13,471	Canada	10,870	Korea	14,683	Korea	15,289
9	Australia	12,429	Australia	12,781	Australia	10,820	Australia	13,125	India	14,354
10	Canada	10,781	Canada	11,020	Korea	8,890	India	12,748	Australia	13,385

* Source : Park Jong-gu et al. (2021)., *Korea Broadcast Advertising Promotion Corporation Research Report.*

Comparing global advertising expenditures by major media, digital media's advertising expenditures are growing rapidly, while broadcast media and print media,

**Figure 1 Global Advertising Spending (2021 – 2026)
(Unit : million dollars)**

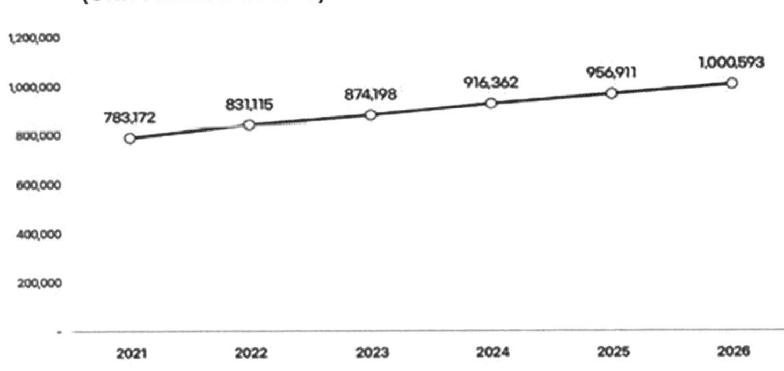

* Source : ZenithOptimedia (2023).

which are traditional media, are growing slowly in line with the growth of digital media. Global advertising spending has increased by 39% from $442.5 billion in 2010 to $615.8 billion in 10 years. During this period, newspapers, the representative of traditional media, grew by 45% from USD 93 billion to USD 442.5 billion, while digital advertising expenditures, a new medium, increased by 451% from USD 70.4 billion to USD 317.7 billion.

In 2020, advertising expenditures in major media decreased in all but digital media. Digital advertising spending showed solid growth of 21.2% despite COVID-19, while television advertising, which is a traditional medium, was 3.2%, newspaper advertising 26.3, magazine advertising 22.1%, outdoor and theater advertising 32.6%, and radio advertising 23.7%. showed a decrease in %. Even in 2021, advertising spending by media is summarized by the growth of digital media and the sluggishness of other media.

Table 3 World Advertising Spending by Medium (unit : 100 million dollars, %)

Media	Ad Experditure			Year-over-Year Growth		
	2019	2020	2021	2019	2020	2021
Digital	3,177	3,467	3,966	21.2	9.4	14.1
TV	1,607	1,428	1,472	-3.2	-11.2	3.1
Radio	314	240	260	-0.1	-23.7	8.3
Outdoor/Cinema	417	280	335	-0.1	-32.8	19.6
Magazine	217	169	163	-8.3	-22.1	-3.7
Newspaper	425	313	315	-8.6	-26.3	0.8
Total	6,158	5,906	6,511	7.8	-4.1	10.2

* Source : Ad Age (2021). Advertising Marketing Fact Book.

Looking at the advertising expenditures by media in Korea in 2023, digital media accounted for the largest share at 57.2%, followed by broadcast media (including terrestrial TV, radio, cable TV, IPTV, satellite TV, and

DMB) at 23.3%, and print media (including newspapers and magazines). In 2020, the proportion of advertising expenses for these three media is expected to be 47.6%, 28.9%, and 13.5%, respectively.

The print media, which accounted for more than 50% of the total advertising cost in the 1990s, and the broadcast media advertising market, which accounted for more than 50% of the total advertising cost in the early 2000s, have recently been replaced by digital media advertising. Since 2015, when digital advertising expenditures began to be officially counted, digital advertising expenditures, which have consistently shown a high growth trend every year, have generated sales of more than 5 trillion won and are expected to record a high growth of more than 10% compared to the previous year in 2022. Digital advertising, which started in the early 2000s as Internet advertising, has taken up more than half of the entire advertising market in just 20 years.

Table 4 Advertising Market by Medium in Korea (unit : 100 million won, %)

Media		Ad Expenditure			Growth rate		Ratio	
		2021	2022	2023	2022	2023	2022	2023
Brocast	Terrestrial TV	13,795	13,987	11,303	1.4	-19.2	9.4	7.7
	Radio	2,291	2,276	1,968	-0.7	-13.5	1.5	1.3
	Cable	21,825	21,529	18,597	-1.4	-13.8	14.5	12.7
	IPTV	1,071	961	871	-10.3	-9.4	0.6	0.6
	Satellite TV	330	307	274	-7.0	-10.7	0.2	0.2
	DMB	18	13	7	-2,7	-47.4	0.0	0.0
	SO	1,113	1,122	1,071	-0.8	-4.0	0.8	0.7
	Total	41,438	40,195	34,096	-0.6	-15.2	27.0	25.3
Print	Newpaper	14,170	14,652	14,394	3.4	-1.8	9.8	9.8
	Magazine	2,439	3,022	2,997	23.9	-0.8	2.0	2.0
	Total	16,609	17,674	17,391	6.4	-1.6	11.9	11.9
Digital	Search	36,165	39,494	42,040	9.2	6.4	26.5	28.7
	Exposure	38,953	41,640	41,770	6.9	0.3	28.0	28.5
	Total	75,118	81,134	83,810	8.0	3.3	54.5	57.2
OOH	Total	8,161	9,968	11,316	22.1	13.5	6.7	7.7
Total		140,325	148,971	146,613	6.2	-1.6	100.0	100.0

* Source : Cheil Worldwide (2024). Advertising Yearbook.

With the growth of digital advertising spending in the advertising market, the sales of digital advertising companies are overwhelming those of traditional advertising companies in the United States. In Korea, traditional advertising agencies still occupy the top ranks in sales.

Looking at the sales data of the US digital advertising agency, the top 1 to 4 companies are not traditional advertising companies. They are IT and consulting parent companies that have newly entered the market since 2000. Acenture Interactive, which ranked first with $4.6 billion in advertising billings in 2020, Deloitte Digital, PwC Digital Service, and IBM pc, ranked 4th, are not

Figure 2 Advertising Industry where Data, Network, and AI are Concentrated

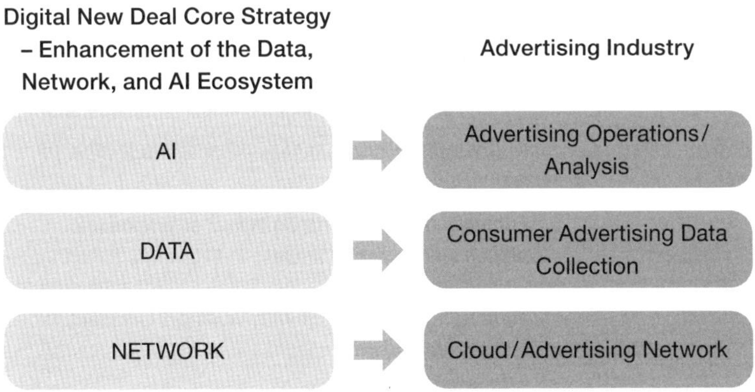

Digital New Deal Core Strategy – Enhancement of the Data, Network, and AI Ecosystem		Advertising Industry
AI	→	Advertising Operations/ Analysis
DATA	→	Consumer Advertising Data Collection
NETWORK	→	Cloud/Advertising Network

* Source : Korea Digital Advertising Association internal data, 2021.

companies that started out as advertising companies, but are tech companies based on IT and consulting. It is a representative company that has expanded its business into the advertising field. Top 10 digital advertising companies in the US 5th to 9th are traditional advertising companies such as Publicis, WPP, Interpublic, Ominicom, etc.

Table 5 Top 10 US Digital Advertising Companies for 2023 based on Advertising Spending

Rank	Company	Key Highlights
1	Google	Dominates in digital advertising with platforms like Google Ads and YouTube
2	Meta (Facebook)	Strong presence with Facebook and Instagram advertising solutions
3	Amazon	Gaining market share rapidly with its e-commerce and Prime ad platforms, Adbeat and The Social Shepherd
4	Microsoft	Includes LinkedIn advertising as a key component of its offering
5	Verizon Media	Known for Yahoo and AOL advertising platforms
6	Adobe	Focuses on marketing software solutions like Adobe Experience Cloud
7	Walmart	Increasing its footprint with Walmart Connect for retail advertising Adbeat

Rank	Company	Key Highlights
8	Spotify	Rapid growth in audio advertising through its streaming platform
9	TikTok	Popular among younger demographics for video advertising
10	Snapchat	Significant focus on AR and location-based advertising

* Source : Ad Age (2024). Ad Agency Report.

Unlike the United States, Korea's advertising agency sales rankings are still dominated by general advertising agencies based on traditional media, based on conglomerates, almost monopolizing the top 10 advertising agencies. In-house advertising companies, large corporations leading the advertising industry, are showing limitations in not being able to quickly adapt to the new advertising environment despite a drastic increase in digital advertising costs and a decrease in advertising costs in traditional media. The profitability of the digital advertising field is lower than that of the traditional media field, because it relies on subcontracting rather than direct investment in technology development.

In the United States, a new digital advertising company with IT and consulting as its parent company is occupying the top spot in advertising companies through AdTech technology development and is focusing on entering the global market. In Korea, as general advertising companies focus on increasing sales through subcontracting rather than technology development, the subordination of AdTech technology is deepening, and it is approaching as an obstacle to entering the global market. For the advancement of the advertising industry, it is urgently required to expand the digital business of large advertising companies and enter the AdTech technology development field.

Table 6 Digital Advertising Expenditure by Year in Korea (unit : 100 million won, %)

	Ad expenditure										
	2013	2014	2015	2016	2017	2018	2019	2020	2021	2022	2023
Expen diture	24,630	27,065	30,018	33,825	38,402	43,935	50,532	57,106	75,118	81.134	83,810
Rise rate	13.8	9.9	10.9	12.7	13.5	14.4	15.0	13.0	31.5	8.0	3.3

* Source : Cheil Worldwide (2024). *2024 Advertising Yearbook.*

Table 7 Trends in Advertising Expenditure by Major Media in Korea

	Ratio							
	2016	2017	2018	2019	2020	2021	2022	2023
Broadcast	39.3%	37.4%	35.6%	32.7%	28.9%	28.3%	27.0%	23.3%
print	18.1%	16.8%	15.7%	14.7%	13.5%	12.6%	11.9	11.9
Digital	32.8%	36.3%	39.4%	43.6%	47.6%	49.4%	54.5	57.2
OOH	9.8%	9.5%	9.3%	9.0%	6.3%	6.1%	6.7	7.7

* Source : Cheil Worldwide (2024). *2024 Advertising Yearbook.*

If the business model of advertising companies in the past consisted of advertisers - advertising companies - media companies, in the digital media era, the structure of the advertising industry is expanding to advertisers - DSP - DMP - SSP - Ad Network - media companies. As changes are made to the AdTech ecosystem based on programmatic buying, it is a technology-based ecosystem that maximizes advertising sales revenue through advertising exposure through the selection of precise target consumers.
In the case of Korea, small and medium-sized digital advertising companies that depend on subcontracting from large advertising companies have limitations in being competitive with global tech companies due to lack of capital and technology development experts.

Figure 3 **Digital Advertising Ecosystem**

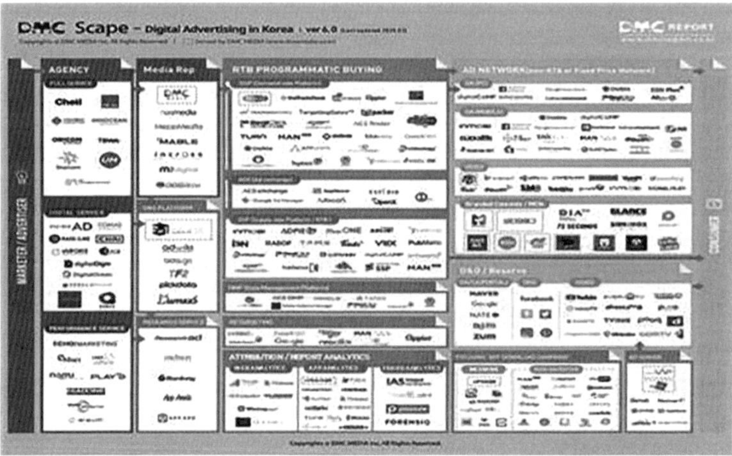

* Source : ZenithOptimedia (2023).

Global Advertising Industry in the Age of Data Economy

Acquiring and utilizing data serves as a catalyst for the development of all industries. In the era of industrialization, natural resources such as coal and oil were closely related to national power, but now data is in the limelight as a key resource. The data economy drives the growth of the hardware industry and service industry. Infinite data produced every day becomes the basic economic asset of all industries and a key resource for creating added value (IT Terminology Dictionary, Korea Information and Communication Technology

Association).

Global companies that didn't even exist before 2000 are at the top of the market capitalization rankings. Apple, Microsoft, Amazon, Google and Meta (formerly Facebook) are companies where data is a major asset. The advent of the data economy is establishing a new economic order and emerging as a key area of national competitiveness.

In the data economy, Korea's conditions are not so easy. The US dominates the global market with digital platforms such as Google, Meta (Facebook), Amazon and Netflix. Based on a population of more than 1 billion, China maintains its second-largest position in the world after the United States, preparing for the era of the data economy through national policies that restrict the movement of data abroad.

Korea is limited in terms of linguistic, regional, and demographic structure in acquiring global competitiveness only with domestic data. Korea, which had global competitiveness in some areas of the manufacturing industry, is a key data trading destination in Asia, South America, Africa, and Europe to become a data powerhouse and take another leap forward in the era of the data economy. The data economy is a prerequisite for protecting data sovereignt, and is a key field for national competitiveness in the future.

In the era of the data economy, Korea needs to prepare to survive in the competition for global platform supremacy. The digital territory is classified into three areas: digital tech, digital platform, and digital content. The digital tech area is a technology field such as 5G, 6G, AI, cloud, big data, and the Internet of Things. The digital platform area is a distribution field such as a search platform, shopping platform, portal platform, and SNS platform. The digital content area is service products such as advertisements, movies, games, music, dramas, fashion, beauty, food, and books.

Korea does not have an edge in global competition in the digital tech and platform areas in the global platform supremacy competition, but in the digital content area, it has competitiveness in areas such as music, movies, dramas, games, and webtoons. Content such as Squid Game and Hell produced by Korea were evaluated as Netflix's best works in 2021. However, depending on the supply of content centered on the global OTT platform, most of the proceeds go to global companies. In the future, it is expected that the majority of media consumers will consume content through digital platforms, and the need to become the top predator in the digital realm is on the rise.

Figure 4 Expansion of the Digital Realm

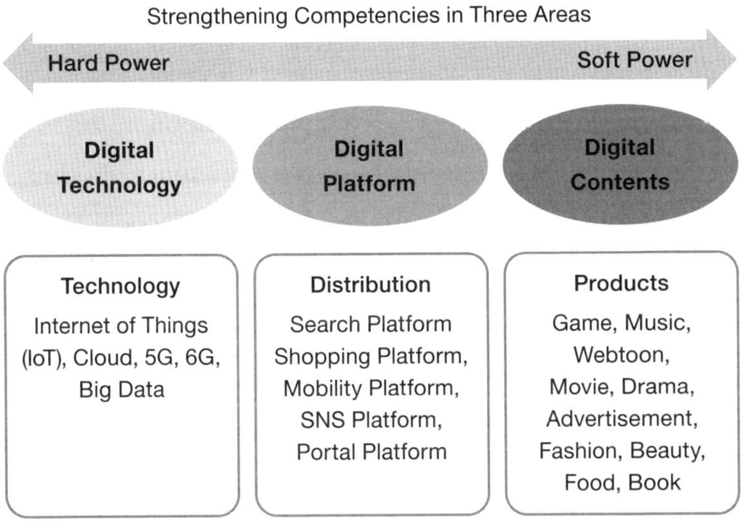

Technology	Distribution	Products
Internet of Things (IoT), Cloud, 5G, 6G, Big Data	Search Platform Shopping Platform, Mobility Platform, SNS Platform, Portal Platform	Game, Music, Webtoon, Movie, Drama, Advertisement, Fashion, Beauty, Food, Book

There is a need to foster digital platforms responsible for the balanced development of hard power and soft power, as well as global distribution.

* Source : Internal data of the Korea Digital Advertising Association (2022).

Advertising plays a role in pioneering overseas markets by standing at the forefront of Korean digital content services entering overseas markets. Advertising can support manpower in all fields of Korea's content industry, and it is the most promising leading industry. Professionals who grew up in the fields of games, movies, webtoons, and music show limitations in demonstrating their expertise by moving to other content fields. In contrast, professionals with rich experience in the advertising industry can adapt to any industry of digital content and play an important role in leading new innovations.

Advertising personnel equipped with soft digital power competency has a high contribution to strengthening the soft digital power competency of other content industries. For example, Yeo Min-soo, co-CEO of Kakao, and Kim Dae-sun, the first representative of Yahoo Korea, can be cited. These are successful examples of advancing into the largest platform company in Korea and a global platform company based on the digital capabilities of an advertising agency. Minsoo Yeo, a co-CEO from HSAd, is currently working as a co-CEO of Kakao after working at NHN eBiz, eBay Korea, and LG Electronics. Starting with advertising at Cheil Worldwide, CEO Kim Dae-seon served as CEO of Saerom Technology, Overture Korea, Yahoo Korea, Inmony Korea, and Chunjae Education. In addition to these, many advertising professionals are active in platforms such as Google, Facebook, Naver, and Kakao. Advertising professionals in the IT ecosystem prove that they have the optimal capabilities to lead innovation in the digital content industry.

Table 8 Global Advertising Industry in the Data Economy Era

Category	Key Issues
Data Economy & Industry	Data is a key asset for all industries and acts as a catalyst for industrial development
Key Companies in the Data Economy	Companies like Apple, Microsoft, Amazon, Google, and Meta lead the global market with data-driven business models
Korea's Competitiveness in the Data Economy	Compared to the U.S. and China, Korea faces challenges in global competitiveness due to population and language limitations
Classification of the Digital Domain	Divided into digital tech (5G, AI, etc.), digital platforms (search, shopping, etc.), and digital content (advertising, movies, etc.)
Korea's Strength in Digital Content	Strong competitiveness in areas such as music, movies, dramas, games, and webtoons
Role of Advertising	Advertising plays a key role in pioneering overseas markets and supporting digital content industry professionals
Influence of Advertising Experts	Advertising professionals can drive innovation in various digital content industries
Advertising & IT Ecosystem	The two main business models sustaining the IT ecosystem are advertising and commerce; ads enable free content consumption
Changes in the Advertising Market	Previously divided into online and offline, now all media are integrated into the online sphere
Competition in the Advertising Industry	Shift from regional competition to simultaneous domestic and global competition due to the growth of global platforms

Category	Key Issues
Korea's Strength in the Advertising Industry	Well-equipped digital infrastructure makes Korea a test-bed market for global companies

The two main business models that sustain the IT ecosystem are advertising and commerce. While commerce allows consumers to use services after paying for them, advertisements allow them to use content services such as movies, dramas, sports, webtoons, and music for free without paying for them. The advertising market was divided into online and offline in the past, but now all media are integrated online. Offline media such as television, radio, newspapers, and magazines are in a difficult situation to survive unless they develop new business models through onlineization to overcome the difficult market environment.

In the era before digital media, competition in the advertising industry was regionally separated between domestic and overseas advertising companies. However, with the recent growth of global platforms, competition is changing from local competition to simultaneous competition between domestic and foreign companies. Korea has a suitable market size for test beds and is well-

Figure 5 Reorganization of the Global Media Market and Advertising Industry

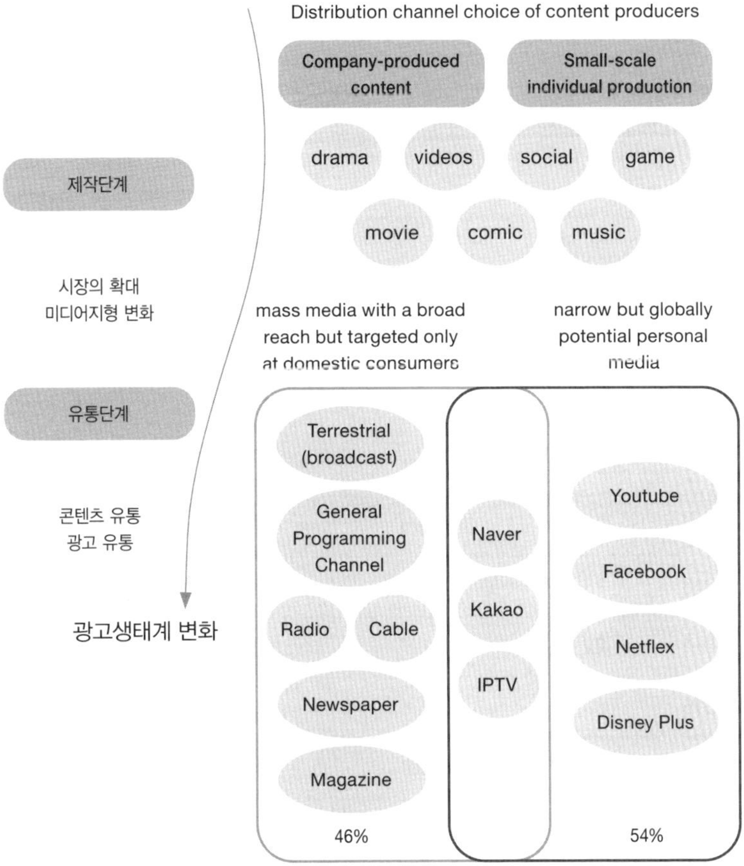

Distribution channel choice of content producers

Company-produced content

Small-scale individual production

drama
videos
social
game
movie
comic
music

제작단계

시장의 확대
미디어지형 변화

mass media with a broad reach but targeted only at domestic consumers

narrow but globally potential personal media

유통단계

콘텐츠 유통
광고 유통

광고생태계 변화

Terrestrial (broadcast)
General Programming Channel
Radio
Cable
Newspaper
Magazine
46%

Naver
Kakao
IPTV

Youtube
Facebook
Netflex
Disney Plus
54%

* Source : Internal data of the Korea Digital Advertising Association (2022).

equipped with digital infrastructure, making it a test bed market for companies around the world. In addition, the advertising industry is expanding its market due to competition with domestic and foreign platform companies, and telecommunication companies.

Figure 5 Google, Facebook's Ad Revenue Growth and U.S. Newspaper Ad Revenue Decline (unit : a billion dollars)

연도	Advertising Revenue	Subscription Revenue	Google Advertising Revenue	Facebook Advertising Revenue
2009	27.5	10.06	21.3	2.5
2010	25.8	10.04	30.2	3.1
2011	27.1	9.9	30.1	4.0
2012	25.3	10.4	39.4	5.4
2013	23.5	10.6	58.5	9.6
2014	22.1	10.7	64.3	13.3
2015	20.3	10.8	67.9	18.2
2016	18.2	10.9	79.5	26.6
2017	16.4	11.2	95.6	39.7
2018	14.3	10.9	116.6	54.9

Over the past 10 years, advertising revenue in the U.S. newspaper industry has been cut in half. Subscription revenue has seen little change, as digital subscribers have offset the decline in print newspaper subscribers. Meanwhile, Google and Facebook have shown revenue increases of over 500% during the same period.

Chapter 2

Advertising and Culture

When we commonly think of advertising, we tend to view it as persuasive communication by companies to sell goods. However, upon closer examination of the impact advertising has on our society, it becomes evident that advertising serves not only the economic function of promoting products or services but also much more (Guang and Trotter, 2012; Han, 2021).

Today, we are living amidst a deluge of advertisements. From the moment we wake up until we go to bed at night, we are exposed to hundreds or even thousands of advertisements throughout the day. Advertising exerts a tremendous influence on the daily lives of everyone, especially children and adolescents who, while learning how to navigate traditional social institutions such as schools, families, and religions, are also socialized through advertising, a particular institution of capitalism. Advertising impacts the values, behaviors, and language of individuals across all cultural spheres

(Abuhashesh et al., 2021; Barton, 1970; Hofstede, 2001).

The cultural formation function of advertising is more important than its economic function. Beyond its original economic functions of providing information to consumers, enabling mass production to lower prices, and promoting mass consumption, thus contributing to the maintenance and development of capitalist society, advertising should be recognized as a cultural mechanism that becomes part of our lives, strengthening or changing existing lifestyles and cultural norms (Mooij and Hofstede, 2011). It is essential to have a correct understanding that advertising exists within culture and serves as a cultural apparatus that both exists within and shapes culture (Glenn, Witneyer and Stevenson, 1977; Guang and Trotter, 2012).

Culture is closely related to the social habits and lifestyles of the people within a society. To successfully conduct global advertising marketing, it is important to understand the social habits and lifestyles of overseas regions (Diehl, and Terlutter, 2006). Culture, which influences individual habits and ways of living, is crucial in marketing and becomes a significant factor in the form of products and advertising marketing strategies.

Cultural factors influencing consumer behavior include culture, subculture, social class, and these factors have a broad and profound influence on consumer behavior. Culture shapes the fundamental value system of consumers in society, familiarizing them with preferences and providing standards for how consumers should behave (Ford, Mueller and Mueller, 2023). For this reason, differences in consumer behavior due to cultural differences and the complexity of culture have emerged as important research topics in global advertising (Cheng, 2014; Mooij and Hofstede, 2011; Van de Vijver and Leung, 2021).

Social habits and taboos vary greatly across cultural regions. For example, whether or not to remove outdoor shoes when entering a home differs between Eastern and Western cultures. People in Eastern cultures typically remove their shoes before entering indoors, while Americans do not. Such differences in social customs also influence marketing promotion methods even among countries within the same Western culture (Lau-Gest and Loraine, 2023).

For instance, the practice of individual sales representatives visiting consumers' homes for sales promotion may be successful in the United States but met with resistance from Europeans. Europeans consider uninvited home visits as an invasion of privacy since they have not granted prior permission. The cultural environment, encompassing family systems, religious institutions, educational systems, language, values, and more, is a significant factor in global advertising marketing communication (Cheng, 2014; Diehl, and Terlutter, 2006; Taylor, 2023).

Table 1 Cultural Influences on Advertising

Cultural Aspect	Details
Cultural Influence	Culture shapes value systems, preferences, and behavioral standards in society and influence on advertising contents
Cultural Differences	Consumer behavior varies by culture due to complex cultural elements, critical for global advertising
Social Customs	Eastern vs. Western habits (e.g., removing shoes indoors) influence behaviors and advertising approaches
Regional Variations	Advertising strategies (e.g., home visits) succeed in the U.S. but face resistance in Europe due to privacy norms
Cultural Environment	Family, religion, education, language, and values are key factors in global marketing and advertising communication

Does advertising simply reflect culture like a mirror? What influence does advertising have on different cultures? Why must advertising reflect culture? How is advertising changing in the face of a new era?

Advertising is certainly a mirror of the times, but it is also a mirror that reflects culture. In hard-sell advertisements that persistently appeal to consumers with logic and numbers, we can see the cultural characteristics of competition-driven Western societies. However, in contrast to Westerners, people in Korea, Japan, and China are more influenced by emotions than by logic and reason. Therefore, in Eastern cultures, soft-sell advertisements that convey images are often more effective than hard-sell advertisements. This contrast is a point that inevitably comes to mind when discussing Western and Eastern advertisements (Gudykunst and Ting-Toomey, 1988; Rhee, Alexandre and Powell, 2020; Terpstra, 1980).

In this chapter, we will examine the relationship between advertising and culture, compare the characteristics of Eastern and Western advertising, and finally, explain how advertising is changing within culture in response to the changes of the times.

Advertising and Culture

Advertising occupies a significant portion of content in mass media and plays a crucial role in modern society due to its substantial influence on individuals' socialization processes. Advertising is not merely about providing information and persuading consumers to promote the sale of products and services; it also serves a socio-cultural function by reflecting and shaping the consciousness, values, and ideologies of a society. Therefore, advertising is recognized as a social institution and cultural tool that influences various aspects of our daily lives. Thus, systematically identifying the societal values that advertising reflects and creates can not only help us understand our current culture but also serve as an important indicator for predicting future cultural trends (Martinez and Fieulaine, 2015; Sharma and Bumb, 2020).

Culture is a human-made environment. Culture is defined as the shared patterns of behaviors, beliefs, customs, norms, values, and symbols that are learned and transmitted within a society or group from one generation to another. It encompasses various aspects of human social life, including values, norms, language, religion, social structures, and ways of thinking. Culture shapes individuals' identities, influences their perceptions of the world, and guides their interactions with others. It is dynamic and constantly evolving, influenced by social, economic, and environmental, political factors (Han and Shavitt, 1994).

Advertising and culture are closely related. There's a saying that advertising is born from culture and becomes a part of culture. This means that advertising not only reflects current cultural values but also significantly influences the creation of future cultural values.

One of the reasons we have a particular interest in the relationship between advertising and culture, as mentioned above, is the mutual interdependence between advertising and culture. In particular, advertising reflects and influences popular culture rather than high culture, thereby exerting significant influence in creating new popular culture. Every aspect of advertising, from the attire and behavior of celebrities such as actors, singers, models, athletes, and influencers depicted in ads to the language used in advertisements, is influenced by popular culture. This, in turn, guides trends in our society and leads young people to form values regarding what to think, what they need, what is important, and what to aspire to in life, thereby driving changes in popular culture (Ford, Mueller and Mueller, 2023; Mooij and Hofstede, 2011).

From this perspective, it is evident that advertising should be perceived not only as serving its original economic function of providing information to consumers, enabling mass production to lower product prices, and promoting mass consumption, thereby contributing to the maintenance and development of capitalist society. It should also be recognized as a cultural apparatus that becomes part of our lives, strengthening or changing existing cultural values and norms (Desmaras, 2017). Research on advertising is necessary as it exists within culture, reflects culture, and serves as a cultural mechanism for both reflection and creation.

Cultural values reflected and created by advertising

Figure 1 Culture and Consumer Behavior

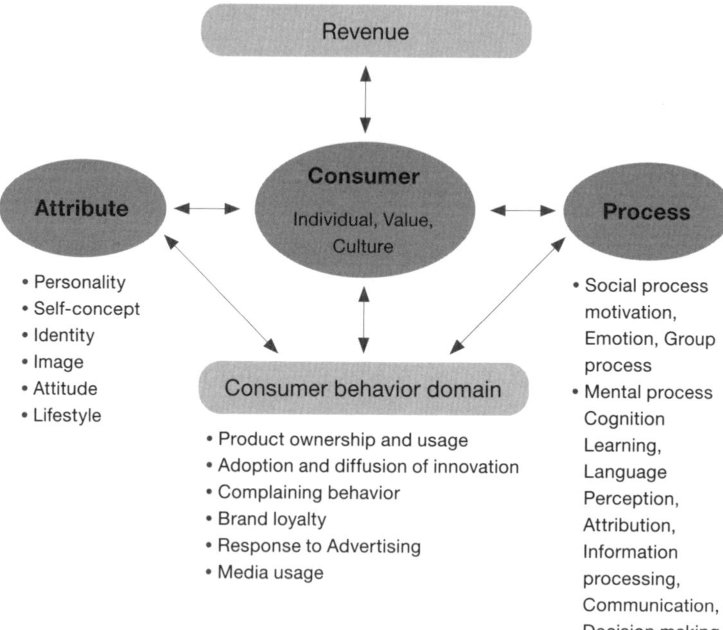

* Source : de Mooij (2004)

change over time. Korean society has shown a dual structural characteristic of coexisting traditional and modern values due to rapid economic development over the past 40 years and the influence of Western culture. Some values in Korean society are experiencing confusion amidst the conflicting traditional and modern values. Lim recently argued that social and cultural changes in Korea over the past few decades have led to conflict and confusion between traditional values, modern values, and foreign values, as well as discrepancies between

Figure 2 **Individualism, Collectivism, and Power Distance by Country**

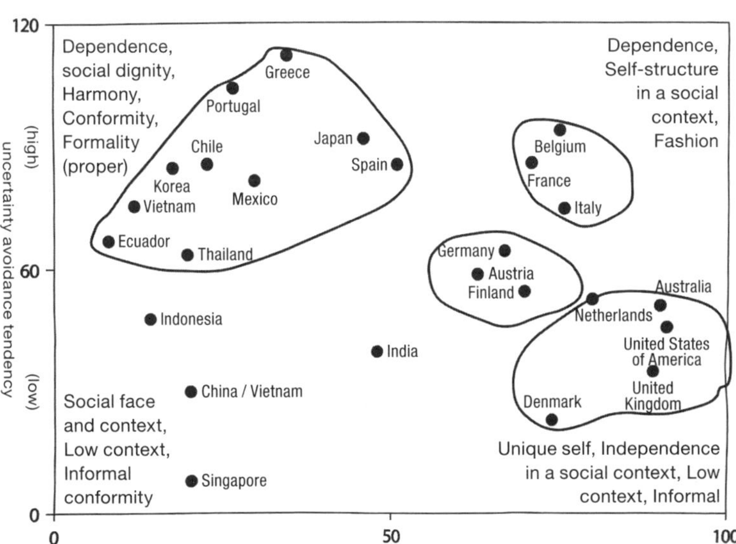

* Source : de Mooij (2004)

value systems and social structures, differences in values among generations, regions, and social classes, which are interpreted as a kind of anomie phenomenon (Guang and Trotter, 2012; Han, 2024).

These changes in cultural values in Korean society can be easily observed in advertising. Recently, Korean advertisements coexist with ads that use indigenous culture and traditions (such as filial piety, hometown, traditional customs, holidays, Pansori, mask dance, collectivist values, etc.) and ads that utilize Western values and customs (such as American basketball players, individualistic values, sensationalist thinking, conquest of nature, etc.). It is known that young people in Korea psychologically prefer advertisements with traditional elements, but their actual behavior is influenced by advertisements that lean towards Western values). This fact can also be found in criticisms that advertisements with traditional values tend to merely incorporate traditional themes or emotions as a scene in the advertisement rather than truly reflecting our traditional values.

Many scholars study the cultural values depicted in advertisements because advertising influences our values and norms, and the values and norms formed by society through advertising influence human behavior and ways of life. In particular, because advertising tends to selectively emphasize certain values such as materialism, sensationalism, individualism, modernism while ignoring others, it has become a subject of criticism for its cultural role of reflecting and creating culture (Taylor, 2023; Triandis, 1995).

Korean society has undergone rapid changes since the 1960s, 1970s, and 1980s due to economic growth, the influence of foreign cultures, and the adoption of democratic ideals and institutions, and these changes are still ongoing. This process of social change inevitably leads to changes in values.

Trends in Existing Research on Advertising and Culture

The influence of advertising on culture and the influence of culture on advertising have been the subject of heated debate among scholars, with two main opposing perspectives coexisting. One argument suggests that advertising serves the function of reflecting culture, while the other argues that advertising creates culture. Therefore, much of the research in this field has employed content analysis methods to conduct empirical studies on the aforementioned debate by examining the cultural values depicted in advertisements.

In particular, numerous papers have been published on the differences in advertising content across cultures, and some studies aimed to explore how the values portrayed in advertisements change over time.

The hypotheses of existing research have been set from two contrasting perspectives (Han and Shavitt, 1994; Liamputtong, 2008). One hypothesis is from the perspective that advertising reflects culture. This hypothesis suggests that since humans tend to maintain existing lifestyles and values rather than adopting new ones psychologically, advertising can only be effective when it reflects reality. Therefore, advertising is seen as merely reflecting culture like a mirror, refuting the arguments of some advertising critics who claim that advertising brings about conflicts in societal values and value systems. Advocates of the cultural reflection hypothesis emphasize that advertising only reflects existing culture, lifestyles, and values. In other words, scholars supporting the cultural reflection hypothesis emphasize that advertising only reflects society and culture, without significantly influencing changes in values and social structures. Thus, they stress that advertising does not have a negative impact on society or culture (Mai, Ketron and Yang, 2020).

In contrast to the cultural reflection hypothesis, the second hypothesis suggests that advertising creates new cultures different from existing ones, thereby encouraging members of society to adopt the newly created culture. The cultural creation hypothesis stands in direct opposition to the cultural reflection hypothesis. It posits that because humans psychologically aspire for something new rather than adhering to existing lifestyles and values, advertising tends to create new lifestyles and values rather than simply reflecting existing ones to persuade consumers. Particularly, this perspective views advertising as potentially causing conflicts and confusion between existing and new values, thereby promoting changes in values and societal structures, ultimately leading to the destruction of traditional culture and fostering over consumption.

In addition to these two extreme hypotheses, some scholars argue for the duality of advertising. They suggest that while advertising sometimes reflects culture, in other cases, it also creates culture, implying a mutual influence between advertising and culture. According to their logic, advertising is fundamentally based on existing culture but can play a crucial role in shaping entirely new cultures by showcasing new lifestyles and values depending on the characteristics of the advertised products (Han, 2024; Westjohn, Magnusson, Franke, and Peng, 2022).

On the other hand, a minority of scholars claim that advertising and culture are unrelated. They argue that despite advertising being a significant part of our daily lives with considerable influence, advertising and culture operate independently without any interaction.

As observed, various scholars have proposed and researched different hypotheses to elucidate the relationship between advertising and culture. However, due to the challenges in conducting empirical studies to validate these hypotheses, it remains difficult to determine which of the three perspectives (cultural reflection of advertising, cultural creation of advertising, or the cultural duality of advertising) is more valid than the others. Nonetheless, most scholars agree that advertising is closely related to culture, whether it reflects or creates it.

Table 2 Trends in Existing Research on Advertising and Culture

Trends	Contents
Cultural Sensitivity	Focus on how cultural nuances affect message interpretation and consumer preferences
Localization vs. Standardization	Debate on adapting ads to local cultures vs. creating globally uniform campaigns
Cross-Cultural Consumer Behavior	Examination of how cultural values like individualism/collectivism influence ad effectiveness
Role of Language and Symbols	Importance of language and visual elements in cross-cultural communication

Trends	Contents
Technology and Globalization	Impact of digital platforms in merging or highlighting cultural differences in advertising

Advertising's Mirror Reflection Theory

The cultural reflection hypothesis posits that advertising reflects culture, while culture, in turn, influences advertising. This issue has been debated by scholars for a long time, with two opposing perspectives coexisting. One perspective argues that advertising merely reflects culture, while the other contends that advertising creates culture. Previous research has predominantly focused on setting one of these two opposing views as a hypothesis and conducting studies accordingly (Manrai, 2018; Mueller, 1987).

According to the cultural reflection hypothesis, humans tend to maintain and reinforce existing lifestyles and values rather than adopt new ones psychologically. Therefore, advertising is believed to be effective only when it accurately reflects reality. Proponents of this hypothesis argue that advertising serves as a mirror that perfectly reflects culture. They refute the claims of some advertising critics who argue that advertising exacerbates societal value conflicts and confusion. Advocates of the cultural reflection hypothesis emphasize that advertising merely reflects existing culture, lifestyles, and values. They argue that advertising does not significantly influence changes in values and societal structures; thus, it does not have a detrimental impact on society or culture (Mueller, 1987).

Advertising's Cultural Creation Theory

The cultural creation hypothesis suggests that advertising influences the creation of new cultures that differ from existing ones, thereby compelling members of society to accept the new culture created by advertising. In contrast to the cultural reflection hypothesis, the cultural creation hypothesis posits that humans have dreams and desires to achieve something new through change rather than strictly adhering to existing cultures, lifestyles, or values. Therefore, advertising tends to create new lifestyles and values rather than merely reflecting existing ones, aiming to persuade consumers. This perspective argues that advertising can be a cause of conflict and confusion between existing and new values, ultimately promoting changes in values and societal structures (Han, 2024). Critics of advertising view it as having a negative function, leading to the destruction of traditional cultures and promoting over consumption (Han, 2021).

The Ambiguity of Advertising: Cultural Reflection and Cultural Creation

The duality of advertising is argued by a minority of scholars who suggest that advertising sometimes reflects culture and, at other times, plays a role in creating culture, thereby influencing each other. According to their logic, advertising is generally based on existing cultures but depending on the nature of the advertised product, it can also play a significant role in shaping entirely new cultures by showcasing new lifestyles and values. On the other hand, a few scholars argue that advertising and culture are unrelated. They claim that despite advertising being a significant part of our daily lives and exerting considerable influence, advertising and culture operate independently without any interaction.

Table 3 **Trends in Existing Research on Advertising and Culture**

Theory	Key Hypothes is	Human Behavior Assumption	Role of Advertising	Criticism
Advertising's Mirror Reflection Theory	Advertising reflects existing culture, lifestyles, and values.	Humans tend to maintain and reinforce existing lifestyles and values.	Serves as a mirror reflecting culture without causing societal or cultural harm.	Critics argue that advertising does not exacerbate societal value conflicts or confusion.
Advertising's Cultural Creation Theory	Advertising creates new cultures, lifestyles, and values, influencing societal change.	Humans aspire to achieve new dreams and desires through change.	Acts as a force promoting changes in values and societal structures, potentially leading to conflict.	Critics see advertising as destructive to traditional cultures and a promoter of overconsump tion.
The Ambiguity of Advertising	Advertising reflects and creates culture depending on the product or context.	Advertising is influenced by culture and, in turn, influences cultural shifts.	Dual role: reflects existing culture and shapes new cultures.	Some scholars argue that advertising and culture might operate independently without interaction.

Changes in Cultural Values of Koreans and Evolving Advertising Contents

Korean society has undergone significant changes in the past 50 years, including rapid population growth, the adoption of democratic ideals and institutions, economic growth driven by industrialization, urban population concentration, the popularization of formal education, widespread access to mass media, the introduction and utilization of modern science and technology, the emergence of various social organizations, and bureaucratization. Consequently, the consciousness and values of Korean citizens have also undergone significant transformation.

A synthesis of the perspectives of several scholars who have deeply studied the evolution of Korean societal values reveals that Korean values have transitioned from collectivist to individualistic, from moral (humanistic) to materialistic, from authoritarian to egalitarian, and from a fatalistic view of nature to a conquest-oriented view of nature. Additionally, there is a sense of confusion experienced between these contrasting values. Such changes and ambiguities in Korean societal values are well-reflected in advertisements. For instance, research on family values in television advertisements conducted by a Korean researcher found that Korean advertisements currently express traditional and modern values in similar frequencies.

Combining the theories of cultural reflection and cultural creation in advertisements, it can be concluded that advertisements not only reflect current cultural values but also significantly influence the creation of future cultural values. Therefore, it can be assumed that advertising content is sensitive to changes in the zeitgeist. Consequently, longitudinal analysis of domestic advertising content over an extended period could provide insights into how values expressed in advertisements evolve in response to changes in societal values.

For example, a research paper published in 1990s analyzed advertising content published in women's magazines from 1962 to 1992, examining trends in advertising appeal types (technical, pleasurable, functional, compositional, diversity, corporate image), changes in consumer values (functional, social, emotional, intrinsic, situational), and variations in product benefit themes (luxury/enjoyment, functional/practical, beauty/attraction). Summarizing their findings, they concluded that there is a consistent trend emerging from the research: advertisements appearing in Korean women's magazines are increasingly adopting emotional and pleasurable consumer values. Korean consumers are showing a tendency to prioritize emotional and pleasurable consumer values over rational and utilitarian ones.

In addition to these changes in values, other significant issues extensively researched in the advertising field include family values expressed in advertisements and the dichotomy between traditional and Western advertising appeals.

Differences Between Eastern and Western Advertising

Advertising is a reflection of the human brain's thinking process. Geographically separated for a long time, Eastern and Western societies have formed distinct and differentiated cultures. Easterners and Westerners also demonstrate differences in brain usage. Easterners primarily use the left hemisphere, while Westerners mainly engage the right hemisphere. Psychological and brain research has found that when engaging in creative thinking and tasks, Easterners and Westerners tend to use the opposite hemisphere of their brains (Maheswaran and Shavitt, 1994; Mooij and Hofstede, 2011; Triandis, 1995).

Such differences in brain usage also influence

advertising production. In Eastern cultures, there is an emphasis on soft-sell advertising, whereas in Western cultures, the focus is on hard-sell advertising. Soft-sell advertisements, reflecting the characteristics of Eastern cultures, are categorized as image ads, whereas hard-sell advertisements, reflecting Western culture, are classified as product quality ads. The reason behind this divergence in advertising direction between Eastern and Western cultures lies in the emphasis on sensibility, style, and form in Eastern cultures, while logic and rationality are emphasized in Western cultures. In Eastern cultures, advertisements often convey images and styles without directly selling the product, allowing consumers to infer the product's advantages based on the emphasized images and styles. However, in Western countries like the United States and Europe, hard-sell advertising has traditionally dominated. Advertisements emphasizing logic, based on realistic evidence, and highlighting product quality are more effective in Western cultures (Han and Shavitt, 1994).

One successful advertising campaign in South Korea is the Orion Chocopie cookie advertisement, which has been widely recognized for its warm image that resonates with the public's emotions. The Chocopie cookie advertisement effectively conveys the idea of sharing affection, resonating with the emotions of the Korean people. Instead of emphasizing the characteristics of the snack product, the advertisement stimulates the emotions of Koreans. This Chocopie marketing strategy can also be analyzed as emotional marketing, which stimulates customer emotions. Orion Chocopie cookie successfully establishes a warm image by conveying warmth, showcasing a successful case of emotional marketing and illustrating how culturally reflective advertising can be successful.

In Eastern cultures, comparative advertising that compares the strengths and weaknesses of one's own brand with competing brands is considered impolite and unethical. Emphasizing that one's own brand is better than competitors is not only unsuccessful but also criticized in Eastern cultures.

In contrast, comparative advertising is actively conducted in Western cultures. Comparative advertising refers to advertisements that appear in one's own advertisements, comparing one or more specific brand names belonging to the same product or service category. In the United States, since the Federal Trade Commission (FTC) directly permitted comparative advertising in 1972, there has been much debate and research on comparative advertising, and it has been widely used in advertising practice. The main reason the FTC encourages comparative advertising is to provide consumers with more information by comparing different brands, thereby helping them make rational purchasing decisions and, on a macro level, promoting competition among brands to stimulate product improvement. In other words, in a competitive business environment, companies need to dig into the weaknesses of competing companies to secure relative superiority.

Comparative advertising directly compares two or more brands, prompting consumers to seek out the superior brand among them. Ultimately, inferior brands may fade away from the market, prompting companies to focus on quality improvement to survive. Thus, comparative advertising encourages healthy competition among companies and helps consumers make product choices. Such comparisons, where one's own brand is considered superior and the competing company's brand is deemed inferior, are effective in Western cultures, where logic and rationality are valued.

One famous example of Pepsi Cola's (number brand) comparative advertising against Coca-Cola (leading brand) is the "Pepsi Challenge" campaign. This campaign was initiated in the 1970s and continued through the 1980s and 1990s, and there have been iterations of it over the years. The Pepsi's comparative advertising challenge involved blind taste tests where participants were given sips of both Pepsi and Coca-Cola without knowing which was which, and then asked to choose which one they preferred.

In these taste tests, Pepsi often came out on top, with more participants preferring its taste over Coca-Cola's. Pepsi heavily promoted the results of these taste tests in its advertising, directly comparing the preference for Pepsi over Coca-Cola among consumers.

The comparative advertising strategy employed by Pepsi-Cola as described above is widely recognized in academia and industry as a very effective approach for the second or third brand to compete against the leading brand. It is a frequently used tactic in advertising within Western cultures, where competition and evidence-based claims are highly valued.

The advertising characteristics described for Eastern and Western cultures may not apply in all cases, as there are instances where hard-sell advertising in the East and soft-sell advertising in the West may be effective. Advertising appeals and techniques can transcend cultural barriers. Just as soft-sell advertising types may fail to resonate with Easterners in countries like South Korea, Japan, and China, hard-sell advertising types that emphasize factual evidence and logic may fail to persuade Westerners in countries like the United States, the

United Kingdom, and France. Similarly, product quality advertising may succeed in Eastern cultures, while soft-sell advertising may capture the interest and empathy of consumers in Western cultures (Mueller, 1987).

The characteristics of advertising in the East and the West described earlier may not apply in all cases, and there are instances where hard sell advertising in the East or soft sell advertising in the West can be effective (Baek, Kim and Kim, 2024; Vignali, 2001). Types of advertising appeals and techniques can sometimes transcend cultural barriers. Just as soft sell advertising types in East Asia like Korea, Japan, and China can fail with Eastern audiences, similarly, hard sell advertising types emphasizing factual reasoning and logic in the West such as the United States, the United Kingdom, and France can fail to persuade Westerners. Likewise, there are cases where product quality advertising succeeds in East Asia while soft sell advertising captures the interest and empathy of consumers in the West.

From a cultural and advertising perspective, it holds true that image advertising in the East and product quality advertising in the West are more persuasive, as explained earlier. However, advertisements with unexpectedness and dynamism that do not necessarily align with culture can pique consumer interest and show positive effects. Cases where product quality advertising succeeded in the

East and image advertising succeeded in the West can be illustrated as follows (Han and Shavitt, 1994).

Brand image is the holistic perception consumers have of a brand. To increase the value of brand assets, it's essential to maintain a consistent and strong brand image. Due to the importance of brand image, many companies in both East and West are running image advertising campaigns regardless of cultural differences. For example, we can look at Adidas' sports spirit campaign. Adidas has always lagged behind Nike in terms of recognition and brand image. Nike appealed to consumers by sponsoring top athletes in marathon competitions held worldwide. In response, Adidas interpreted marathons from a new perspective, emphasizing that it's not about competing with others but with oneself. Consequently, they sponsored the oldest participant in marathon races who struggled the most with self-competition, rather than focusing on winning. Typically, marathon winners finish within 2 hours and 10 minutes, but Adidas created an image advertisement praising an elderly participant who took over 5 hours, saying, "We applaud this elderly person who won the battle against themselves. That's the sports spirit." With this fresh perspective, Adidas managed to resonate with consumers, surpassing Nike, which had invested heavily in top athletes.

Another successful example of image advertising in the West is McDonald's campaign featuring disabled individuals. This advertisement visually portrayed a child ordering food using a braille menu, highlighting McDonald's consideration for visually impaired individuals. It's a successful advertising case where image, rather than product quality, was emphasized in the Western context.

Introducing a highly regarded product quality advertising case in the East, we can look at the following example. Product quality advertising can be expressed in various ways, but one of the most commonly used techniques is to concretely present the advantages of the advertised product. To convey the unique selling point of our company's product, it's crucial to provide concrete evidence of its benefits to gain trust above all else. This is a representative expression technique in Western advertising. Abstractly and ambiguously delivering the advantages of a product not only fails to differentiate it from competitors but also undermines trust in the product.

Let's examine successful product quality advertising cases in the West. Pringles potato chips emphasized their freshness due to their unique packaging and boasted the ability to be stored in households for a long time. Crest toothpaste focused on being certified by the American

Dental Association for its quality. M&M's chocolate discovered that consumers find it inconvenient when chocolate melts and sticks to their hands while eating, so they advertised that their chocolate doesn't melt in your hands and succeeded. Attributes expressed in such advertisements were specific and easily understandable for consumers, making them highly effective.

Another method of expressing product quality advertising, besides providing specific evidence, is through numerical appeals. Utilizing numbers is an effective way to convey the attributes of a product. People are naturally drawn to numbers; they find them intriguing and trustworthy. This method is commonly used, especially when comparing product attributes with those of competitors.

Airbus, a European aircraft manufacturing company, effectively utilized numerical advertising. Initially aiming to introduce the relatively unknown company to the world, Airbus is a consortium formed by four European countries: the UK, France, Germany, and Spain, along with hundreds of directly or indirectly associated companies from 16 European countries, including the Netherlands and Belgium. The advertising copy "Four nations partnering on aircraft manufacturing programs" effectively captured consumers' attention.

Volkswagen automobiles claimed to be the most fuel-efficient car in the world by providing specific numbers, stating, "32km on a liter of kerosene lamp oil," to convey the message of energy-saving vehicles.

Product quality advertising is a commonly used technique in the West. However, despite cultural disparities, there are many successful cases of product quality advertising appeals in the East as well. One such example is the brand 'Morning Juice,' which emerged like a comet in the beverage industry about a decade ago. They emphasized maintaining oranges at the most suitable temperature of 5 degrees Celsius by inserting a thermometer directly into the oranges and discussing the temperature that oranges prefer. While it's typical to talk about orange juice in terms of concentrate or its refreshing taste, this brand introduced a new topic in the beverage industry by focusing on temperature as a number for morning juice, quickly establishing itself as a leader in the industry (Akaka and Alden, 2010; Han and Shavitt, 1994).

Another example is Baeksul Cooking Oil, which emphasized being 100% made from soybeans and highlighted its 0% cholesterol content, garnering attention by presenting these points as numbers.

Hite Beer succeeded as a dominant player in the fiercely competitive beer industry by emphasizing that it is made from 100% natural bedrock water drawn from 150 meters underground.

These examples demonstrate how product quality advertising, although more commonly associated with Western advertising practices, has been effectively utilized in the East as well.

Table 4 **Comparison of Eastern and Western Advertising**

Aspect	Eastern Advertising	Western Advertising
Brain Usage	Primarily use the left hemisphere.	Primarily use the right hemisphere.
Advertising Style	Soft-sell, focusing on image and emotional appeal.	Hard-sell, emphasizing product quality and logic.
Cultural Values in Advertising	Emphasis on sensibility, style, and form. Comparative advertising is seen as impolite and unethical.	Emphasis on logic, rationality, and evidence-based claims. Comparative advertising is actively practiced.
Comparative Advertising	Rarely used; considered impolite and unethical.	Widely used; promotes healthy competition and informed consumer decisions.
Emotional Advertising Examples	Orion Chocopie: warm image and emotional resonance with Korean values.	McDonald's: braille menu for visually impaired; Adidas: marathon spirit emphasizing personal struggle.

Aspect	Eastern Advertising	Western Advertising
Product Quality Advertising Examples	Hite Beer: natural bedrock water; Morning Juice: optimal temperature for oranges.	Crest Toothpaste: ADA certification; M&M's: chocolate doesn't melt in hands.
Numerical Advertising Examples	Baeksul Cooking Oil: 0% cholesterol; Morning Juice	Volkswagen: fuel efficiency; Airbus: multinational partnership in aircraft manufacturing.

The Change of the Times and the Change of Advertising

The advertising industry, like a chameleon, changes according to the times and circumstances. Multinational companies formulate advertising strategies tailored to market conditions when executing global advertising campaigns. In actuality, advertising is currently in harmony with society and often anticipates the trends. Just as toys provide novelty and enjoyment to children, advertising also offers novelty and enjoyment to consumers. Advertising that fails to engage consumers' interest and provoke emotions will not succeed in the market (Hilton, 2022).

Modern individuals spend time across various platforms such as YouTube, Instagram, blogs, television, and magazines. These platforms not only provide entertainment with diverse content but also serve as the primary sources of recreation. Effective and efficient advertising depends not only on providing information to consumers but also on offering enjoyable content that resonates with them.

Modern individuals are exposed to thousands or even tens of thousands of advertisements from morning until bedtime. However, among these numerous advertisements, only a limited number have a positive impact on consumers. The success of advertising is not merely determined by whether consumers have seen it or not. Advertising must surprise, amuse, or shock consumers to leave a lasting impression. Regardless of the emotions evoked, advertising must include empathy and novelty to be successful.

The statement that empathy and novelty are important factors for advertising success implies that the cultural values reflected in advertisements are not always consistent but change with the times. Culture encompasses the possibility of change. Therefore, one method of verifying the relationship between advertising and culture, in addition to cross-cultural comparative studies between Eastern and Western cultures, is to conduct longitudinal analyses of advertising within a single cultural context.

While cross-cultural comparative studies may encounter methodological challenges such as linguistic equivalence, functional equivalence, conceptual equivalence, sample equivalence, and measurement equivalence, longitudinal studies within one culture have the advantage of controlling for these issues.

In the following section, we will summarize research findings on the cultural reflection and creation of advertising to elucidate the relationship between advertising and culture.

A Study on How Product Characteristics Influence Advertising and Culture

The relationship between advertising and culture has been the subject of significant academic inquiry. While considerable progress has been made in understanding this dynamic, the diversity of consumer behaviors and the complex nature of advertising pose challenges to generalizing findings. Advertising strategies are influenced by multiple factors, including product characteristics, consumer preferences, market conditions, and cultural values. Among these, product characteristics have emerged as a critical element in understanding how culture shapes advertising effectiveness (Han, 2024).

Cultural values such as individualism and collectivism, first introduced in cross-cultural research during the 1970s, remain fundamental in examining societal and occupational systems. These dimensions influence ethical norms, communication strategies, and advertising practices (Hofstede, 2011; Lau-Gesk & Loraine, 2023). Individualism is characterized by a focus on personal independence, achievement, and self-expression, while collectivism emphasizes group harmony, interdependence, and social hierarchy. These values manifest in various consumer behaviors, such as self-perception, decision-making, and responses to persuasive communication (Abuhashesh et al., 2021; Gudykunst and Ting-Toomey, 1988).

Understanding how these cultural orientations interact with advertising appeals is essential for developing effective strategies. This study investigates the differential impact of individualistic and collectivistic advertising appeals, particularly when moderated by product type, to provide new insights into culturally adaptive marketing.

Based on the interplay between culture and product characteristics, two hypotheses are proposed: First is cultural alignment. In individualistic cultures, advertising appeals emphasizing personal benefits and independence will demonstrate higher effectiveness, while in collectivistic cultures, appeals highlighting group benefits and harmony will be more persuasive. Second is product type moderation. The effectiveness of individualistic and collectivistic advertising appeals will vary depending on product type. Shared products are expected to amplify cultural differences, whereas personal items will mitigate them (Han and Shavitt, 1994).

The study sampled 120 participants, divided equally between the United States and South Korea, representing individualistic and collectivistic cultural orientations, respectively. To minimize cultural variations within generational shifts, Korean participants were aged 60 and above from rural areas, while US participants were urban residents. Gender was balanced within both groups to eliminate bias.

Two product categories were chosen to test cultural and advertising appeal inter-actions. Personal Items were chewing gum and sneakers, which are typically associated with individual usage. Shared Products were detergent and iron, frequently used within households or groups.

Advertisements were developed to represent individualistic and collectivistic appeals. These were validated by 33 advertising professionals, achieving a 96.9% agreement on appeal classification. Ads featured headlines and visuals only, using personal photos for individualistic appeals and group photos for collectivistic appeals to control for extraneous influences.

Participants evaluated four pairs of advertisements, representing personal and shared products with individualistic and collectivistic appeals. A Latin-square design was employed to balance presentation order. Responses were measured on three dimensions—attitude toward the advertisement, brand perception, and purchase intention—using a 5-point Likert scale.

Cultural alignment significantly influenced advertising effectiveness. US participants rated individualistic appeals higher than collectivistic appeals. Conversely, Korean participants rated collectivistic appeals more positively than individualistic appeals.

Product characteristics moderated cultural differences. For personal Items, individualistic appeals were universally more effective, with US participants scoring them at $M = 4.36$ and Korean participants at $M = 4.15$. For shared products, cultural contrasts were more pronounced. In South Korea, collectivistic appeals outperformed individualistic appeals, while in the US, the differences were less significant.

The findings affirm the importance of cultural alignment in advertising. Individualistic appeals resonated more with personal items due to their inherently self-oriented nature. Conversely, shared products—designed to benefit groups—enhanced the salience of cultural differences, with collectivistic appeals performing better in South Korea.

These results highlight the role of product type as a moderator in the cultural applicability of advertising strategies. While personal items limit the scope for cultural differentiation due to their individual use, shared products provide greater opportunities for culturally resonant messaging.

This study underscores the necessity for marketers to consider cultural orientations and product characteristics when crafting advertising strategies. For shared products, leveraging culturally consistent messages can enhance persuasion. Personal items, however, may require less cultural adaptation given their universal appeal to individual benefits.

Table 5 **Summary of Study on How Product Characteristics Influence Advertising and Culture**

Category	Key Issues
Research Purpose	Explore how individualistic and collectivistic advertising appeals differ in effectiveness, focusing on the influence of product types (personal vs. shared).
Research Methods	Participants from the US and South Korea evaluated print ads with individualistic or collectivistic appeals. Products were classified via pilot surveys; reliability and attitudes were measured.
Research Results	1. US participants preferred individualistic appeals; Koreans preferred collectivistic appeals. 2. Shared products showed stronger cultural differences. 3. Personal items were effective with individualistic appeals across cultures.
Research Conclusion	Cultural values influence ad effectiveness. Personal items show less cultural impact, while shared products amplify cultural differences. Further studies on media and longitudinal effects are needed.

CHAPTER 3

GLOBAL ADVERTISING MARKET AND CROSS-CULTURAL ADVERTISING COMMUNICATION

Formation of the Global Advertising Market

After the Second World War, many colonial countries gained independence and emerged as newly formed nations. These newly formed nations, based on a common understanding of their historical experiences, began to form a single power bloc in the international community. The concept in international politics that refers to these newly formed nations is the Third World, which emerged as a single power bloc in the international community through the non-aligned movement. From the late 1950s, Third World countries began to actively participate in various international organizations such as the United Nations and UNESCO to increase their voices (Sampson, 2014).

Third World countries argued that the existing international order existed only for the sake of the sacrifices of Third World countries. Therefore, they have strived to find their fair share through compensation for past sacrifices and concrete, active participation. Third World countries advocate for a new international order that ensures sovereignty and fair distribution equal to that of developed countries.

At the 6th UN Special Session, all UN member states agreed to cooperate to eliminate the widening economic disparities between developed and developing countries based on mutual cooperation for the overall economic and social development of all countries worldwide and to revise the current unequal order, which is the legacy of past colonial domination.

Debates on a new international information order began in the early 1970s. UNESCO, particularly since its 16th General Conference, has shown significant interest in the issue of information order and has served as a platform for international discussions on the matter. The non-aligned movement also became interested in communication issues following the 1973 Algiers Summit and advocated for the decolonization of mass media. Since the 1970s, this movement has manifested as a fierce struggle between Western superpowers and Third World countries in the arena of international politics, with the central issue summarized as the confrontation between the principle of free flow of information advocated by developed countries and the balanced and free flow advocated by Third World countries.

The free flow of information is a principle that has acted as a dominant ideology during the rise of the United States as the world's leading superpower following the end of World War II. It is rooted in the philosophical principles of 19th-century liberalism, following the ideologies of Adam Smith and John Stuart Mill (Mehra, 1986).

The principle of liberalism requires that all participants have equal opportunities and conditions to participate. Without this premise, freedom merely represents the freedom of the powerful nations. In reality, the dominance of the principle of the free flow of information since the end of World War II has resulted in a unilateral and imbalanced information order in terms of both quantity and quality in international social information exchange. This imbalanced information order has become the basis for the imbalance in international economic relations and has served as a means to perpetuate these relations.

Criticism of the free flow of information serves as the logical starting point for the New International Information Order Movement. Third World countries criticize the free flow of information as a means of cultural imperialism and advocate for the establishment of a new order, promoting ideologies such as "cultural sovereignty." They demand the structural revision of the existing international information order, which can be described as the domination of developed countries, to establish a mutually cooperative information order guaranteeing free and balanced flow (Mehra, 1986).

The logical background of the New International Information Order Movement advocated by Third World countries is constituted by the theory of cultural imperialism. The existing unequal international information order ultimately leads to the increased dominance of Western superpowers over the culture of Third World countries (Silver, 1993). Cultural imperialism is argued to be a mechanism that controls and dominates human consciousness through ideological or psychological means, far more potent and comprehensive than direct control through political or military power (Mowlana, 1986).

Communication scholar Herbert Schiller defines cultural imperialism as a comprehensive process in which a society is induced or coerced into fitting its social institutions into the values and structures at the center of the world system, and is suppressed and forced in the process.

As evident from this conceptual definition, modern

cultural imperialism is a phenomenon occurring within the framework of the reconfigured global capitalist system after World War II. Third World countries, as they began their journey as independent nations after the end of World War II, were incorporated into the capitalist economic system, forming a vast market known as the "world capitalist system," introduced through economic institutions of Western advanced capitalist countries. This economic dependency process led to the adoption of Western advanced capitalist culture as well (Mowlana, 1986). The acceptance of Western commercial mass culture by Third World countries implies the adoption of a culture generated from entirely different historical backgrounds, threatening the existence of traditional cultures in these regions.

This adoption of Western commercial mass culture results in the domination of Third World countries by foreign cultures, or cultural imperialism, leading to the replacement of indigenous cultures and the adoption of Westernized lifestyles and consciousness. In this process, mass communication and advertising play a central role (Mehra, 1986).

Mass communication and advertising have facilitated the massive influx of Western culture into third world countries. Today's international information exchange is characterized by a serious imbalance where Western developed countries almost entirely dominate every aspect. This imbalance in information exchange is evident across all fields of mass media, including advertising, movies, TV programs, records, news, books, magazines, and more (Norris, 1980; Sampson, 2014).

Analyzing the international exchange of mass media and advertising reveals two key characteristics. Firstly, there's the unilateral nature of international media exchange. For instance, vast amounts of media content are exported from the United States to various Asian countries, but very little or almost none is exported in return. Secondly, a handful of advanced Western countries, such as the United States, the United Kingdom, France, and Germany, predominantly occupy the international media and advertising industry's influence worldwide. These countries possess individualistic cultural characteristics (Triandis, 1995).

Many third world countries in Asia and Latin America are merely recipients of the influence of these Western countries. For example, today, four major Western communication agencies—namely, AP and UPI from the United States, Reuters from the United Kingdom, and AFP from France—monopolize the supply of world news. Similarly, in the realm of TV programs, a few dominant countries like the United States sell their programs to almost every country globally, with the majority being entertainment content. In the advertising industry, large advertising companies from the US and UK dominate the global market (Ad age, 2024), requiring new strategies for communication between different cultures in the East and West (Norris, 1980).

Through the unilateral domination of advertising markets and mass media, Western superpowers continue to profit significantly while continuously introducing Western culture into third world countries. Third world countries become subjected to domination by the ongoing influx of Western culture through advertising and mass media. The international activities of mass media prominently feature the operations of multinational corporations (MNCs). The fundamental economic units of the world capitalist economy are increasingly becoming MNCs. Several hundred corporations from a few countries, centered around the United States, use their vast capital to dominate the production and distribution of goods, services, communication, and cultural products worldwide.

The international flow of advertising communication has a unilateral nature, transferring content from advanced Western countries to developing countries in the East. In reality, it is the giant multinational corporations from the West that wield this influence. Thus, under cultural imperialism, the role of multinational corporations is significant (Mowlana, 1986).

Supporting the global activities of these corporations are multinational advertising companies. They play a crucial role in creating the image and message of global corporations, disseminating information about their products and services, and cultivating a positive image of these corporations, facilitating their international operations (Norris, 1980; Sampson, 2014)..

Advertising is sometimes referred to as the vanguard of imperialism. This phrase implies that multinational advertising companies create conditions for Western capital and products to penetrate new markets in third world countries. For example, consider indigenous peoples in Africa who traditionally do not wear shoes. To sell shoes to them and make a profit, a shift in cultural norms towards wearing and buying shoes is necessary. Advertising can play a role in introducing this new cultural norm. Multinational advertising companies enable new market expansion for multinational corporations and the expansion of sales in existing markets (Wells, Burnett and Moriarty, 1995). The advertising content of these global advertising companies spreads Western culture to developing countries in Asia, Latin America, and Africa.

In conclusion, the activities of multinational advertising companies play a significant role in the development of cultural imperialism. In other words, multinational advertising companies are responsible for importing Western individualistic and commercial cultural values to dominate culture under cultural imperialism (Mowlana, 1986). They directly support the international activities of mass media and global corporations, contributing to the transmission of Western culture from Western superpowers to developing countries.

Table 1 **Impact on the Advertising Industry**

Period	Impact on the advertising industry
Post-War Global Context	Post-WWII, many colonies gained independence, forming the Third World, which advocated for sovereignty and fair economic and social systems
Third World Advocacy	Third World nations sought a new international order through global organizations to address economic disparities and promote equitable resource distribution
Criticism of Free Flow of Information	Criticized as cultural imperialism by Third World nations, the 'free flow of information' was seen as perpetuating Western dominance and an unequal information order
Cultural Imperialism	Cultural imperialism replaces indigenous cultures with Westernized values, facilitated through mass communication and advertising

Period	Impact on the advertising industry
Role of Mass Communication and Advertising	Advertising and media imported Western mass culture into Third World countries, replacing traditional values and influencing consumer behavior
Key Characteristics of Media Exchange	Media exchanges are unilateral, with content flowing from the US and Europe to Asia, Latin America, and Africa. Few Western agencies dominate global news and advertising.
Role of Multinational Corporations (MNCs)	MNCs dominate global production and distribution, leveraging advertising to expand markets and profits by reshaping cultural norms in developing countries
Impact of Multinational Advertising Companies	Multinational advertising companies serve as cultural imperialism's vanguard, spreading Western cultural values and facilitating MNC operations in Third World markets

Growth of Global Advertising Companies

Growth of Global Corporations and Global Advertising Companies

During the 1940s, Henry Luce, the editor-in-chief of the American magazine Life, set out to make the United States the most powerful and significant nation in the world, urging the mobilization of appropriate means to exert

American influence worldwide. He argued that the United States would play a central role in producing and supplying goods and services to all of humanity (Min, 1993a; Norris, 1980). This can be seen as a declaration that "the time has come for the United States to lead the world's markets and cultures."

During World War II, with Europe in ruins, the United States was able to become the dominant capitalist power in the world without any competing nations. During Europe's reconstruction, when the United States played a major role, American companies greatly increased investment in recovering Europe, securing significant portions of its markets, and expanding into markets in Asia and Africa, even beyond Europe's former colonies. The United States penetrated the Middle East, once a stronghold of British capital, and deployed troops to several countries, including Greece, becoming a global economic power (Sampson, 2014).

After World War II, the United States surpassed traditional capitalist powers such as Britain, France, and Germany, rising as the world's most powerful economic nation. In the process of establishing the new empire of capitalism worldwide, the United States provided various forms of assistance to several European countries, as well as to newly independent nations in Asia and Africa. However, this aid from the United States was more reflective of America's ideological necessity for the reproduction of the pre- and post-capitalist structure, rather than meeting the needs of recipient countries. Ultimately, it also played a role in influencing Eastern cultures with Western culture (Sampson, 2014).

Furthermore, the United States introduced individualistic and commercial mass media and advertising systems to third-world countries, selling various hardware and software products and spreading its popular culture. In the post-World War II capitalist society, the process of expanding American influence economically and culturally ultimately served as the backdrop for the international expansion of the American advertising industry.

The Overseas Market Expansion of Global Advertising Agencies

The development of the advertising industry in the United States began in the 1700s, but the modern development and establishment of advertising started in the 1810s. Professor Sandage of the Advertising Department at the University of Illinois summarized notable aspects of the development of American advertising from around 1840 to before World War I as follows: The beginning of advertising agency business, The Industrial Revolution, Emergence of patented medicine advertising,

Commencement of nationwide advertising, Competition between wholesalers and retailers, Development of mass media such as newspapers, magazines, and catalogs, Emergence of the advertising industry as an institution, Growth of advertising agencies, Establishment of advertising agency commission systems, Emergence of full-service advertising agencies, Development of advertising theory, Self-regulation and growth of the advertising industry (Min, 1993b, Kim and Lee, 2001).

The expansion of the overseas network of American advertising agencies began modestly in the early 20th century, reaching only a few countries (Norris, 1980). However, after the end of World War II, the development of the American advertising industry underwent a remarkable transformation. Between the 1940s and 1960s, advertising expenditure in the United States tripled, and total advertising expenditure grew faster than GNP or national income (Sampson, 2014). During this period, the annual growth rate of total advertising expenditure exceeded an average of 10% each year.

Expansion of American advertising agencies' overseas networks until the early 20th century had only reached a few countries abroad (Leslie, 1995). However, following the end of World War II, the development of the American advertising industry progressed dramatically. Between the 1940s and 1960s, advertising expenditure within the United States tripled, and total advertising spending showed a faster increase than the GNP or national income. During this period, the annual growth rate of total advertising spending exceeded an average of 10% each year.

In the 1960s, American advertising agencies began significant international expansion. Over a span of 45 years between 1915 and 1959, the top 15 multinational advertising agencies in the United States established a total of 50 overseas branches. In contrast, within just a decade from the 1960s to the 1970s, they set up 210 overseas branches, a fourfold increase compared to the previous 45 years.

The expansion of overseas branches signifies the increased international activities of American advertising agencies and their direct entry into the advertising industries of the countries where branches were established. Since the 1960s, American advertising agencies have established branches not only in Europe but also in Latin America, Asia, and Africa (Sampson, 2014).. This international expansion was driven not only by the expansion of the advertising industry but also by the higher profit margins offered by overseas markets. In the 1960s, overseas branches recorded profits twice as high as those in the domestic US market, as overseas markets had lower wage levels and advertisers demanded fewer complex services such as market research. Another advantage of this international expansion was the freedom it provided from the direct impact of changes in the conditions of the US domestic market. For instance, in 1970, when the US domestic market experienced a temporary downturn, the total domestic sales of the top 10 advertising agencies decreased by $13.4 million compared to the previous year, while their total overseas market sales increased by $27.23 million in the same year.

This phenomenon stems not only from the inherent benefits within the industry but also from its close relationship with the overseas expansion of other sectors. This is due to the essential nature of advertising, which provides consumers with information about productive goods, thereby creating demand and enabling the consumption of those goods. In other words, for various products from the US manufacturing sector to be sold in overseas markets, the function of advertising, which markets these products, is essential (Lee, 2001; Monthly Advertising, 1999).

Historically, the overseas expansion of the US manufacturing sector preceded the international expansion of US advertising agencies ((Leslie, 1995; Wells, Burnett and Moriarty, 1995). Early overseas manufacturing companies contracted with local advertising agencies in the markets where their products were produced or distributed, managing all related tasks from their headquarters in the US. However, these companies faced difficulties due to lack of control over agency relationships, accounting issues related to agencies, and various pricing policies, as well as a lack of consumer and media research methods. In other words, there were no integrated advertising strategies available at that time (Ad age, 2024; Cheil worldwide, 2024).

Therefore, multinational companies in the US manufacturing sector needed local advertising agencies in their home countries to address the challenges of overseas operations. For this reason, the overseas expansion of US global advertising companies accelerated further (Down, 2000; Lee, 2002).

Between the 1960s and the early 1970s, US multinational advertising companies established extensive networks of overseas branches in Europe, Canada, Central and South America, and Asia. During a similar period, television emerged as a mass medium in major consumer markets worldwide. The formation of international organizations by US global advertising companies coincided with television's penetration into major consumer markets, providing the underlying structure of communication necessary for global advertising activities for expanding corporations. As a result, these companies were able to control their global image, integrate campaigns, reduce costs, and apply the same advertising techniques to markets worldwide.

The development of international communication networks and advertising activities enabled global campaigns to be conducted. Global advertising campaigns have been used by many global companies for a long time as they help enhance marketing efficiency and reduce costs (Mowlana, 1986). This allowed for the development of worldwide campaigns using visual symbols through television. In the majority of countries worldwide, the market share of US global advertising companies exceeded that of local advertising agencies.

As US global advertising companies established and operated overseas branches, they began researching cross-cultural advertising communication strategies in markets with different cultures from the US (Leslie, 1995).

The first US advertising company to attempt internationalization was J. Walter Thomson (JWT), which had its headquarters in New York and opened an office in London in 1899. As the 20th century progressed, multinational advertising companies based in New York's Madison Avenue began spreading globally along with the expansion of the world capitalist market system. They started to play a significant role in promoting the global operations of multinational corporations. However, the true commencement of multinational advertising companies' overseas activities occurred after World War II, when multinational corporations began expanding their markets globally (Ad age, 2021).

The first reason US advertising companies ventured into overseas markets was the expansion of the industry itself. After World War II, US companies faced uncertain market conditions due to excessive production capacity, saturated market penetration, rising production costs, and increased competition among domestic companies. In such a situation, US companies began investing in rapidly growing foreign markets in terms of advanced technology or product demand. As US companies expanded globally, advertising agencies began opening overseas branches at the request of advertisers. The expansion of both industries simultaneously signifies the need for a global communication system as industries venture overseas. As large US companies established production and distribution systems in overseas markets, the need for communication and marketing tools to handle business activities efficiently became apparent.

The overseas expansion of advertising companies can be seen as supporting the local marketing activities of multinational corporations and serving as a repository of knowledge about foreign markets for multinational corporations (Korea Broadcasting Advertising Corporation, 1996; Lee, 2001; Sampson, 2014).).

The 1960s were a challenging time for the US advertising industry. As many companies expanded abroad, many advertising agencies began seriously considering opportunities overseas. Faced with fierce competition among advertising agencies due to the growth of the US advertising market, market saturation in the US consumer market, and declining profits, advertising agencies began turning their attention to the growing advertising industries in overseas markets, particularly in Western European countries.

Thus, US advertising companies actively pursued overseas expansion to compensate for the slowdown in the domestic market. In fact, these multinational advertising companies recorded higher growth rates and profit margins overseas, particularly in Europe and the developing world, compared to the United States.

The expansion of these US multinational advertising companies into overseas markets is seen as having made a significant contribution to overcoming the difficulties in the domestic market during the 1960s.

Multinational advertising companies, like multinational corporations, primarily expanded into countries such as the UK and Europe, but later expanded into third-world countries. A study conducted by the UN in 1979 found that multinational advertising companies reported earning over 85% of their total revenue from activities in developed countries, with revenue from activities in developing countries being less than that earned in developed countries. While the economies of developing countries were much smaller in scale compared to those of developed countries, they had a significant economic and cultural impact on those countries (Korea Commercial Film Production Association, 1995; Sampson, 2014).

Furthermore, overseas expansion was pursued to diversify the risk burden through the expansion of operational areas. In other words, by operating in different regions, companies could avoid significant risk burdens even if difficulties arose in one region. Against the backdrop of these reasons, the overseas expansion of US advertising companies has expanded more and more over time, now exercising overwhelming influence in almost all countries worldwide (Leslie, 1995).

Types of Global Advertising Agency Overseas Expansion

The entry into the global market by multinational advertising agencies commonly coincides with the globalization of advertisers. Through various types of overseas expansion, global advertising agencies can expand their business worldwide, enhance international competitiveness, and grow. Multinational advertising agencies provide marketing communication services to satisfy the needs of advertisers in the markets they operate in, while also gaining additional sources of revenue. Additionally, this process influences advertising messages, content strategies, and production, thereby impacting how Western culture influences Eastern culture (Jung, 2004; Kim, 1990; Korea Foundation of Advertising Associations, 2001; Mooij, 1994).

The methods and processes by which multinational advertising agencies enter foreign advertising markets are chosen based on the political, economic, social, and cultural conditions and characteristics of the regions they seek to enter. There are four types of entry modes for multinational advertising agencies into domestic markets

(Jung, 2004; Min, 1994).

| Business partnership

Multinational advertising agencies exert influence on the advertising activities of multinational advertisers by forming business partnerships with local advertising agencies in target countries for overseas expansion. This involves seeking to enhance the quality of services provided to advertisers already present in the domestic market, ensuring that services offered are of the same standard as those provided in markets around the world, and implementing globally consistent brand strategies. To achieve this, multinational advertising agencies collaborate with domestic advertising agencies deemed capable of handling the advertising activities of multinational advertisers or those with the potential to do so in the future. Additionally, they provide employee training, market insights, and advertising-related information to these domestic agencies while offering advisory services on advertising in exchange for compensation. Through this process, multinational agencies secure a foothold for future entry into the domestic market.

| Equity participation

In countries where capital participation in the advertising

market is permitted, one method is to inject capital into advertising companies in that country to obtain a certain percentage of equity. This approach allows multinational advertisers to exert significant influence by securing a position as shareholders. It also minimizes the risk of failure when establishing branches due to lack of information and experience in the advertising market of the respective country. Additionally, there is an advantage in observing the domestic market and applying their policies and strategies accordingly.

| Joint Venture

The method involves establishing a joint venture advertising agency with advertising companies in the target country for overseas expansion. In some cases, participation may involve small shareholders contributing to management, while in others, majority shareholders may control management rights. There are instances where individuals initially participate as small shareholders but later become majority shareholders, depending on changes in the advertising market conditions and business environment of the target country.

| Direct Investment

Establishing a branch independently without forming any kind of relationship with advertising companies in the target country. This method is employed when a multinational advertising agency has secured a sufficient number of clients in the market and has thoroughly prepared information and plans in advance. While many multinational advertising agencies have succeeded by attempting to participate in the target country's advertising companies or establishing joint ventures, there have also been cases where business partnerships were terminated or relationships severed after equity participation (Jung, 2004).

Table 2 Types of Global Advertising Agency Overseas Expansion

Types of Expansion	Characteristics of advertising
Business Partnership	Collaborating with local agencies to enhance service quality, implement global brand strategies, and provide training and market insights for mutual benefit.
Equity Participation	Investing capital into local advertising companies to gain equity, minimize risks, and influence advertising strategies as shareholders.
Joint Venture	Forming joint venture agencies with local companies, with varying shareholder involvement, from small stakes to majority control based on market conditions.

Types of Expansion	Characteristics of advertising
Direct Investment	Independently establishing branches in target markets when sufficient clients, information, and plans are secured, without relying on local partnerships.

The Transformation of the Korean Domestic Advertising Industry due to the Globalization of Advertising Agencies.

After the advertising market was liberalized, our country's advertising industry underwent tremendous changes. Representative phenomena of the changes brought about by the opening of the advertising market include (Kumkang Planning and Hyundai Research Institute for Economic and Social Studies, 1991): Changes in policies regarding the introduction of foreign involvement in advertising, Changes in the capital structure of advertising agencies, Increase in foreign-produced advertisements, Acceleration in the movement of advertising personnel, Intensification of excessive competition within the advertising industry, Deepening of shifts in advertisers, Changes in the advertising production environment, Shifts in perception within the advertising industry regarding marketing (Mooij, 1994)

The Opening of the Advertising Market and Changes in the Advertising Industry

| Changes in Foreign Investment Policies Related to Advertising

With the decision to open the advertising market, the government had to amend policies related to foreign investment in advertising to allow for the domestic expansion of foreign advertising agencies. Until 1987, the Korean government strictly prohibited the establishment of branches of foreign advertising agencies. However, in 1988, it announced the permission for the establishment of subsidiaries and branches of foreign advertising agencies. The transition from absolute prohibition to full authorization regarding foreign investment in advertising took just over a year (Park, 1989; Cho and Jang, 1987; Sampson, 2014).

The opening of the advertising market also led to changes in the Korean Standard Industrial Classification system. Previously categorized under a subcategory (other service industries excluding machinery and equipment), the advertising industry was elevated to a separate subcategory. While falling short of the industry's desired reclassification to a higher category, this elevation from a subcategory to a separate one laid the foundation for recognizing the advertising industry as an independent sector. Such changes eventually facilitated improvements in credit rating criteria for companies and institutional enhancements in financial transactions.

| Changes in the Capital Structure of Advertising Agencies

The encroachment of the domestic market by foreign advertising agencies continued persistently. Foreign advertising agencies entering the domestic market leveraged the characteristic division of the Korean advertising industry into affiliates and non-affiliates to attract advertisers. Additionally, in cases of joint investment by foreign advertising agencies, there was a tendency to seek independence from domestic joint venture companies in attracting advertisers, striving for their own independent path. One significant reason why joint investment foreign advertising agencies could grow in the domestic advertising market was their ability to receive assistance from domestic joint venture companies in acquiring advertisers. However, even this phenomenon gradually collapsed as they attempted a transition to direct business operations (Min, 1993b).

Since the Korean-American Advertising Working Group allowed for foreign advertising companies to hold up to 49% investment stakes in October 1987, until 1990, four advertising companies (HDM Korea, Cheil Bozell,

Cord, Kumgang Planning) pursued joint ventures with foreign advertising companies through share transfers and the establishment of joint subsidiary companies.

As evidenced, top-tier domestic advertising companies were the first to establish or pursue joint subsidiary companies. This was a strategic move to secure foreign advertisers through joint ventures in response to full market opening in 1991 and enhance international competitiveness by adopting advanced advertising production techniques. The increase in joint advertising companies due to market opening exposed significant issues in the domestic advertising industry, including labor shortages and market erosion due to advertiser migration (Cho, 1991).

Furthermore, with the market opening, there was a significant increase in newly established advertising companies as societal awareness of the advertising industry improved. However, while the increase in new advertising companies was desirable from the perspective of economic freedom and openness, it led to excessive competition in attracting advertisers and talent poaching among advertising companies, deteriorating the advertising transaction order and exacerbating conflicts among advertising companies, ultimately hindering the overall development of the advertising industry. Particularly, the indiscriminate establishment of advertising companies affiliated with large corporations raised numerous issues regarding the professionalism of advertising.

The Increase in Global Advertising Productions

Another significant change in the Korean advertising market following its liberalization was the allowance for foreign-produced completed advertisements, which were previously not permitted, to be aired domestically. The first instance of a foreign-produced completed advertisement being aired in South Korea was in December 1992 with an IBM advertisement. Prior to this, the prevailing method for multinational corporations to advertise was to bring only the script from headquarters and produce the advertisement domestically (Sampson, 2014). The Broadcasting Commission did not allow the airing of foreign-produced completed advertisements, considering them as reproductions of foreign-produced materials, until then, under Article 87 of the Broadcasting Review Regulations.

The first foreign-produced completed advertisement permitted to air in South Korea was an IBM advertisement from the United States. Initially, when requesting permission for broadcast, the Broadcasting Commission rejected it, citing Article 87 of the review regulations regarding the "reproduction of foreign-produced materials." However, after much controversy and fearing trade friction with the United States if the broadcast were blocked, the Broadcasting Commission reversed its decision and ultimately allowed the airing of the IBM advertisement. Shortly after the airing of the IBM advertisement, the Australian Tourism Board also requested permission from the Broadcasting Commission to air an Australian tourism promotion TV advertisement produced in Australia and received approval.

Acceleration of the Migration of Advertising Personnel

As multinational advertising companies entered the domestic market, the movement of advertisers accelerated. Alongside this, the perception that foreign advertising companies offer superior terms and compensation spread, leading to top advertising talent starting to migrate to foreign advertising companies. The most significant reason for Korean advertisers transitioning from domestic to global advertising companies is the flexibility of working conditions and higher compensation.

Intensification of Excessive Competition in the Advertising Industry

The intensification of excessive competition in the

advertising industry began alongside the opening of the advertising market, with the major cause being the transfer of advertising agency rights of multinational corporations to multinational advertising companies in 1991. Following the partial and full opening of the advertising market (1990 - 1993), the number of advertisers who transitioned to solo or joint investment companies reached 13, while domestic advertisers reached 17. Additionally, there were 1 company that transitioned through equity participation and 27 domestic advertisers.

The Movement of Affiliated Advertisers and Non-affiliated Advertisers

Before the opening of the advertising market, industry insiders predicted that with market liberalization, there would be minimal movement among advertising volumes held by conglomerate-affiliated companies, which accounted for 70% of the total advertising volume, while there would be significant movement among non-affiliated advertising companies, which held 30% of the overall market. Indeed, an analysis of advertiser movements over the three years following market liberalization from 1990 to 1993 confirmed these predictions. While there were only four movements among affiliated advertisers during this period, there were numerous movements among non-affiliated advertisers.

| Changes in the Advertising Production Environment

Regulations prohibited the use of overseas-produced advertising materials or foreign footage in domestic advertisements. However, starting from 1989, the government allowed this practice, creating a foundation for the active utilization of the advertising industry. This policy change was aligned with the government's globalization and liberalization policies, coinciding with the qualitative improvement of domestic advertising materials and the competition with foreign products entering the domestic market. The implementation of liberalization and autonomy policies led to institutional improvements aimed at maximizing the autonomy of the industry (Korea Commercial Film Production Association, 1995; Sampson, 2014).

A significant turning point related to the opening of the advertising production market occurred in December 1992 when IBM applied for broadcast advertising review. Previously, there had been cases where multinational companies like Coca-Cola brought storyboards from headquarters and produced advertisements domestically. However, IBM's advertisement was the first to request broadcast permission for content produced directly abroad. Despite initial rejection citing regulations on "replication of foreign-produced materials" by the Broadcast Advertising Review Committee, it was challenging to classify IBM's advertisement as a replicated advertisement, leading to its eventual approval for broadcast in April 1993.

Following this, advertisements from the Australian Tourism Board also began appearing on domestic TV using a similar approach. Amidst these significant changes, the Korea CF Production Association expressed concerns to the government and advertising organizations in 1993 about the negative effects of broadcasting foreign-produced foreign products on domestic TV (Min, 1993a).

The main concerns outlined in the opinion included the strengthening of consumer tendencies towards foreign products, the impact on the sales of Korean products influenced by foreign advertisements, capital outflow, the influence on Korean advertising companies, the globalization of broadcasting, the collapse of domestic production due to poor domestic production environments, and the unfair competition between domestic and foreign productions due to the burden of manpower training, employment, and taxes.

Upon the complete opening of the TV advertising production market, the industry accepted the environmental changes without much resistance. Directly producing advertisements overseas provided an opportunity for collaboration and joint work with local advertising professionals to acquire foreign advertising techniques and directly contact foreign advertising industries, positively influencing the development of the Korean production industry.

Using local media for local advertising in foreign markets when selling domestic products led to the development of international competitiveness by adapting to local marketing situations and the senses of locals, contributing positively to the advancement of domestic advertising creativity.

However, an excessive preference for foreign-produced advertisements has been evaluated negatively, as it may hinder the development of the Korean advertising industry. Using foreign models excessively, regardless of the advantages of the product or consumer benefits, to deceive consumers into thinking that the product is preferred by foreigners, thus promoting overconsumption, is also considered a negative influence.

| The Change in Perception Regarding Marketing

After the opening of the advertising market, the most significant change in the marketing environment is the emergence of micro-marketing. Before the market opening, our country's advertising environment was characterized by mass production and sales targeting a non-specific mass audience. However, with the opening of the advertising market and the increase in income levels, industries that produce a variety of products in small quantities and adopt sales systems targeting specific customer segments have rapidly increased. While macro-marketing, targeting non-specific mass audiences, aligns with mass production by companies, micro-marketing can be considered a sales approach suitable for industries engaged in diverse product lines and small-scale production (Min, 1993a).

Table 3 **The Transformation of the Domestic Advertising Industry**

Aspect of Change	Key Changes
Foreign Investment Policies	Foreign advertising agencies allowed to establish branches in Korea post-1988, elevating the advertising industry status in the industrial classification.
Capital Structure of Agencies	Joint ventures formed with foreign agencies; increased competition led to talent poaching and market challenges for domestic agencies.
Global Advertising Productions	Foreign-produced advertisements permitted for broadcast starting in 1992, beginning with IBM ad, despite earlier restrictions.

Aspect of Change	Key Changes
Migration of Advertising Personnel	Korean advertising talent migrated to multinational agencies due to better compensation and working conditions.
Excessive Industry Competition	Competition intensified post-market liberalization, with foreign agencies gaining major advertisers.
Movement of Advertisers	Affiliated advertisers saw little movement, while non-affiliated advertisers experienced significant shifts post-liberalization.
Advertising Production Environment	Policy changes allowed foreign-produced content, enhancing collaboration and creativity but also raising concerns about domestic industry impact and consumer preferences.
Perception of Marketing	Shift from macro-marketing targeting mass audiences to micro-marketing focused on diverse, small-scale product lines.

The Positive and Negative Aspects of Opening up the Advertising Market

The opening up of the advertising market has led to increased competition, fostering innovation and creativity among companies. It has also provided consumers with a wider range of choices and access to diverse products and services. Additionally, it has created opportunities for smaller businesses to enter the market and compete on a level playing field (Cho, 1991; Korea Broadcasting Advertising Corporation, 1996).

However, the opening up of the advertising market has also resulted in clutter and saturation, making it challenging for companies to stand out amidst the noise (Sampson, 2014). It has led to an increase in advertising expenditures, as companies strive to capture consumer attention. Moreover, there are concerns about the ethical implications of certain advertising practices, such as targeting vulnerable populations or promoting harmful products (Decker, 2001; Shin, 2001)..

Table 4 **The Positive and Negative Aspects of Opening up the Advertising Market**

Aspect	Key Features
Positive Aspects	1. Increased competition fosters innovation and creativity. 2. Consumersgainaccesstoawiderrangeofproductsandservi ces. 3. Opportunitiesforsmallerbusinessestocompetefairly.
Negative Aspects	1. Market clutter and saturation make it harder for companies to stand out. 2. Increasedadvertisingexpendituresstraincompanybudge ts. 3. Ethicalconcerns,suchastargetingvulnerablepopulationsor promotingharmfulproducts.

| The Impact on Advertising Agencies

In the long term perspective, the opening of the advertising market has positively contributed to the qualitative improvement of the creative and marketing fields, as well as enhancing the treatment of advertising professionals and expanding the pool of specialized advertising talents. It has also helped establish an external competitive framework.

However, due to the limitations of the domestic advertising market size, there have been instances of dumping competition and confusion caused by personnel migration. The increase in opportunities for foreign product consumption can affect domestic industries, while the influx of Western images and lifestyle patterns may accelerate cultural confusion and cultural dependence among the Korean population (Han, 1997; Mooij, 1994).

Overall, while the opening of the advertising market presents new opportunities for growth, it also requires advertising agencies to adapt and evolve in order to remain competitive in the changing landscape.

| The Impact on Advertising Production Companies

Due to significant differences in scale, financial structure, equipment, and production techniques between domestic and foreign production companies, it was expected that the opening of the advertising market would have a greater negative impact on production companies than positive. Additionally, the qualitative competition in production is anticipated to lead to increased costs related to securing specialized equipment, rising production expenses, and heavier personnel expenses for talent acquisition. Consequently, financially weak small-scale production companies are expected to face a high risk of dissolution.

In terms of specialized personnel, fierce competition for talent scouting is expected, as even foreign production companies must heavily rely on domestic production talent. Domestic production companies are also likely to face exacerbated shortages of specialized personnel. However, it is suggested that improvements in compensation for specialized personnel, enhancement of the qualitative standards of productions, and the development of related industries could have positive impacts.

Overall, while the opening of the advertising market presents new opportunities for growth, it also requires production companies to adapt and innovate in order to remain competitive and thrive in the changing landscape.

The Impact on Direct mail, Sponsorships, and Outdoor Advertising

In the domestic industry at that time, the field of advertising was notably underdeveloped compared to other sectors. Particularly in terms of advertising techniques, production methods, and methods for measuring advertising effectiveness, there was a lack of specialization and a shortage of skilled professionals. Consequently, this field was considered one of the most vulnerable areas for the entry of global advertising companies, and without institutional protection, there was a high likelihood of domination by foreign advertising firms.

The opening of the advertising market is expected to have both positive and negative effects on direct mail, sponsorships, and outdoor advertising. On the positive side, increased competition may lead to more innovative and targeted direct mail campaigns, as well as enhanced sponsorship opportunities with a wider range of companies entering the market. Similarly, outdoor advertising may see improvements in creativity and effectiveness as advertisers strive to stand out in a more competitive landscape.

However, there may also be negative consequences, such as increased clutter and saturation in these advertising channels, making it harder for individual campaigns to capture consumer attention. Additionally, pricing pressures may arise as companies compete for limited advertising space, potentially impacting the profitability of these advertising mediums. Overall, while the opening of the advertising market presents new opportunities for growth and innovation, it also poses challenges that advertisers and advertising agencies must navigate.

| The Impact on Research Firms

For research firms, the market was already open, and several foreign companies were active in the domestic market. With the entry of foreign advertising firms, it was expected that research firms would be heavily utilized, leading to increased activity in the research field. This would enable the development of rational and effective advertising strategies based on objective research data on the influence of media, consumer preferences, market conditions, and more.

However, there were concerns that domestic companies might overly value the reputation and credibility of foreign advertising firms, potentially leading to subordination. Additionally, while the adoption of advanced research techniques and expertise from advanced companies could enhance the qualitative level of research firms and facilitate their development, there were expectations that smaller domestic research firms might face challenges due to intensified competition in terms of business operations.

| The Impact on Advertisers

The entry of multinational advertising companies into the domestic market was expected to impact all foreign advertising clients (branches, foreign investment companies, technology or business partnership companies, companies using foreign trademarks, etc.). Additionally, companies within the sphere of influence of foreign buyers were also anticipated to experience significant effects (Han, 1998).

For purely domestic brand companies, there was initial interest in foreign advertising firms due to expectations of new advertising techniques and services. In this scenario, there was a possibility that domestic brand companies might consider moving to foreign advertising firms. However, due to differences in language, culture, and the unique characteristics of the Korean market, some believed that the impact would be limited. Furthermore, there were opinions suggesting that there would be no movement in affiliate group advertising (Han, 1997).

Overall, while the opening of the advertising

market presented both opportunities and challenges for advertisers, it ultimately provided them with the potential to reach their target audience more effectively and efficiently.

| The Impact on the Economy, Society, and Culture

The impact on the economy, society, and culture varied depending on the degree of openness. The dominant opinion regarding the positive economic impact included the activation of the domestic advertising and service industries, which would contribute to job creation and enhance participation opportunities in the international advertising market. Additionally, competition from foreign products could stimulate the improvement of domestic product quality (Han, 1998).

However, concerns were raised regarding the potential negative economic, social, and cultural impacts of fully opening the advertising market. This included a potential loss of competitiveness for domestic advertising companies, external dependency, and negative effects on the balance of payments in the long term. Moreover, the exposure of domestic industries to foreign companies could create opportunities for foreign firms to develop favorable economic strategies. Advertisement of foreign products might increase purchasing power for foreign brands, promoting a preference for foreign goods and potentially dampening domestic production and sales.

In terms of social and cultural impacts, positive effects were anticipated in terms of contributing to the internationalization of national consciousness. However, negative impacts were also predicted, such as the cultural influence of advertisements not being based on local characteristics but rather part of an international strategy. This could lead to the spread of Western images, values, and ideologies, potentially undermining cultural identity and traditional values in Korea. Additionally, advertisements could influence consumption patterns and lifestyle preferences, promoting homogeneity between Western and Eastern cultures.

Table 5 **The Positive and Negative Impact on Advertising Industries**

Impact Area	Positive Impacts	Negative Impacts
Advertising Agencies	Qualitative improvement in creativity, marketing, and talent pool; external competition fostering innovation.	Dumping competition, migration confusion, and cultural dependency due to Western influences.

Impact Area	Positive Impacts	Negative Impacts
Advertising Production Companies	Improved compensation for specialized personnel and qualitative standards; development of related industries.	High risks for small-scale firms due to rising costs; talent shortages; financially weak companies face dissolution.
Direct Mail, Sponsorships, and Outdoor Advertising	Increased competition drives innovation and targeted campaigns; enhanced creativity and effectiveness.	Clutter, saturation, and pricing pressures; reduced campaign visibility and profitability.
Research Firms	Increased use of advanced research techniques; adoption of global standards; enhanced effectiveness of advertising strategies.	Subordination to foreign firms; challenges for smaller domestic research firms due to competition.
Advertisers	New techniques and services from foreign firms; potential for better audience targeting and efficiency.	Language, culture, and market uniqueness limit impact; possible movement of domestic brands to foreign firms.
Economy, Society, and Culture	Job creation, activation of the advertising industry, and improved domestic product quality; internationalization of national consciousness.	Loss of competitiveness for domestic firms; external dependency; cultural homogenization and loss of traditional values.

The Significance and Evaluation of the Opening of the Advertising Market

The opening of the advertising market was a contentious issue for both the government and the industry in our country. However, it was difficult to resist the wave of liberalization in the service industry following international trends. The key challenge was to formulate industrial policies that could protect domestic industries and enhance their competitiveness. The opening of the advertising market could have economic ramifications, such as market erosion by foreign companies and exacerbation of the talent shortage in domestic advertising firms due to the migration of skilled professionals to foreign companies (Min, 1993b).

From the perspective of advertisers' mobility, although some industry experts believed that domestic advertising industry led by conglomerate affiliates would not experience significant shifts in advertiser preferences, the reality unfolded differently. Domestic advertising companies, lacking international competitiveness compared to their external counterparts, faced a high risk of subordination to foreign advertising firms (Decker, 2001).

The impact of multinational advertising companies entering the domestic market on domestic advertising companies can primarily be seen in the movement of advertisers. It was anticipated that current foreign advertisers doing business with domestic advertising companies would switch to foreign advertising companies, and securing new foreign advertisers entering the domestic market would be extremely challenging. Additionally, the gradual erosion of the domestic market by multinational advertising companies was expected to reduce the income of domestic advertising companies (Lim, 2001).

The positive effects of the influx of multinational advertising companies were also evident. The opening of the advertising market contributed to the improvement of the domestic advertising industry by providing opportunities to learn from advanced multinational advertising companies in terms of marketing communication strategies, creative levels, research techniques, as well as rational changes in management and organizational operations. Furthermore, competition from multinational advertising companies in attracting advertisers could lead to the establishment of standards or regulations in the current disorderly trading system, fostering media activation and reevaluation of advertising-related professionals.

Overall, while there were concerns about negative impacts, the opening of the advertising market also had significant positive effects, contributing to the internationalization and globalization of the domestic advertising industry, rationalizing management and organizational operations of domestic advertising companies, and providing a basis for our advertising companies to enter foreign markets.

The Global Service of Advertising Agencies and Its Cultural Impact

The advertisements themselves are just a manifestation of social phenomena and are merely combinations. However, the phenomenon of advertising encompasses much more social and cultural significance beyond these advertisements. Advertising plays a cultural role for companies beyond mere economic activities. The entry of Western culture-based global advertising companies into foreign markets to provide advertising services has significant cultural ramifications for countries in the East Asian cultural sphere, such as South Korea.

As discussed in other parts of this book, Western and Eastern cultures have various cultural differences, including individualism versus collectivism, high-context versus low-context cultures, humanism versus materialism, uncertainty avoidance, male-centric culture versus female-centric culture, egalitarianism versus authoritarianism, and traditional family values versus modern family values. For instance, in the context of detergent advertisements, in the East Asian cultural sphere, detergents are often perceived as collective cleansing agents for all family members, whereas in the Western cultural sphere, there is a higher tendency to perceive detergents as individual cleansing agents.

Advertising is a cultural product of a society, and therefore, advertisements reflecting the cultural values of that society tend to dominate. Culture ultimately influences advertising and marketing communication phenomena significantly. Therefore, understanding advertising from a cultural perspective is crucial for the effective utilization of advertising and marketing communication tools in the global market (Min, 1993b).

The realistic and economic reasons for global advertising agencies expanding their services overseas can be summarized as follows:

Firstly, it aids in simultaneous expansion into foreign markets with multinational corporations. Global corporations have steadily expanded their business scope globally since World War II, and advertising agencies working with these corporations have also established overseas branches along with their clients' global expansions. The motivation behind multinational advertising agencies entering the global market includes advertising services, exploring new markets, and gaining access to local advertisers who have expanded abroad (Cho, 1991; Park, 1989).

Secondly, the majority of advertisers currently being serviced by advertising agencies are global advertisers. Global corporations have larger revenues in foreign markets than in domestic markets. Therefore, global advertising agencies such as Bates have even set their company motto as "Globalize or Die." Furthermore, 60% of WPP advertisers deal with international business, and 75% of McCann's advertisers are global advertisers.

Thirdly, overseas expansion is necessary to retain existing global advertisers. Advertisers are more likely to choose advertising agencies they are familiar with and have worked with previously when expanding overseas, thus maintaining their relationship with advertisers by expanding abroad themselves.

Fourthly, overseas expansion is essential for increasing profitability for global advertising agencies. According to the economies of scale, minimizing investment costs and increasing efficiency through integrated services can lead to relatively higher profit margins. By expanding overseas, advertising agencies can extend existing markets without the need for new planning for advertisers and minimize investment costs by reusing existing resources (Min, 1993a).

Fifthly, overseas expansion is necessary to diversify revenue sources for global advertising agencies. Advertising agencies can establish more stable and profitable relationships by assisting global advertisers in adapting to local markets and providing various integrated services beyond advertising.

Sixthly, overseas expansion is necessary for maintaining long-term relationships with global advertisers. In modern society, companies engage in various global activities, and maintaining long-term contracts in overseas markets can be helpful.

Seventhly, global advertising agencies contribute significantly to rapid growth. To achieve annual growth rates of over 10%, globalization is a prerequisite. The growth rates of successful global advertising agencies operating in overseas markets are higher than those of advertising agencies that have not expanded overseas.

Eighthly, overseas expansion is required to adapt to the organizational structure of globalized advertising advertisers. As advertisers become globalized, specialized titles such as "Chief Marketing Officer" and "Global

Branding Officer" are being established. Consequently, advertising agencies naturally manage global brands worldwide as counterparts to these positions.

Ninthly, overseas expansion is necessary to adapt to the evolving organizational structures of globalized advertisers. As advertisers become more globalized, specialized positions such as "Chief Marketing Officer" or "Global Branding Officer" are being established. Advertising agencies naturally appoint "Global Brand Managers" as their counterparts to manage worldwide brands.

Finally, overseas expansion is required to respond to advertisers' movements towards consolidating or integrating advertising agencies for overseas marketing. Another reason compelling advertising agencies to expand overseas is the concern that advertisers may lose advertising rights by consolidating their business into a few advertising agencies capable of handling overseas tasks. Advertisers believe that such consolidation of advertising agencies can lead to cost savings and easier control, thus perpetuating this trend. The reasons for advertisers to consolidate advertising agencies include concentrated management of global brands, reduction of advertising agency commissions, and strengthening their influence over advertising agencies as major advertisers.

Chapter 4

Methodology

Cross-cultural Studies in International Advertising Research

Unlike the emic approach, the etic approach is a research method that seeks out global concepts of attitudes and behaviors and develops pan-cultural or culture-free measures. The main purpose of this method is to compare the results of research across cultures and to seek general laws of human behavior. Therefore, using this method, cross-cultural scholars can directly compare and analyze various phenomena that have occurred between different cultures.

To explain emic and etic more easily, let's take an example comparing apples and oranges (Triandis, 1979). Apples and oranges are both fruits, and have common (etic) attributes such as weight, size, color, and selling price. On the other hand, the two fruits also have their own unique (emic) attributes, such as the taste of apples and the taste of oranges. We can objectively compare the etic properties of apples and oranges, such as weight, size, color, and selling price. For example, in comparing the two fruits, everyone agrees that apples are heavier than oranges. But we need to know the emic attribute, taste, to give a unique description of apples and oranges. A person who has never eaten an apple cannot understand an apple with only information about its etic properties such as weight, size, color, and selling price. In other words, the emic approach is essential for understanding one unique

With the introduction of the concept of global marketing, research on international advertising has been actively conducted in the United States since the 1960s. Research papers analyzing international advertising from the perspective of comparative culture are frequently published, such as of *International Journal of Advertising*, and *Journal of Advertising*. In addition, Korean advertisers are greatly aware of the importance of international advertising research at the time when foreign multinational advertising agencies are entering Korea in earnest with the complete opening of the domestic advertising market, and the research of academic journals and agencies including advertising research Recently, a lot of information on international advertising theory and practice has been introduced in company newsletters.

Since studies on international advertising so far have been mostly conducted in the United States, most studies have applied theories limited to the United States and measurement tools developed in the United States to studies of other cultures other than the United States (Han, 2021). In other words, measurement tools and theories suitable for the special cultural conditions of the United States were not modified and supplemented to be appropriate for researchers or subjects belonging to other cultures (Triandis, 1995), but only translated into other languages and used to analyze advertisements in countries other than the United States.

For example, several studies have compared cross-cultural comparisons of informative content in advertisements (Madden, Caballero, and Matsukubo, 1986; Martenson, 1987; Rice and Lu, 1988), Resnik and Stern's informational content analysis system of advertisements used in the case of analyzing the contents of advertisements in the United States (the contents of advertisements can help consumers choose wisely among various products) 14 informational categories were applied to analyze advertisements in Australia, Japan, Sweden and China.

The researchers hypothesized that the classification method of Resnik and Stern could be applied to analyze advertisements in other countries as well. However, although their information content analysis classifications are widely used and suitable for analyzing American advertising (Stern, Krugman, and Resnik, 1981), the question of whether their classifications are actually applicable in other cultures is questionable. Since there are no empirical research results yet, I think it is necessary to reconsider comparing the differences between cultures in the informational appeal of advertisements by using their coding outlines as they are to analyze foreign advertisements.

Undoubtedly, this uni-cultural research, that is, research centered on American culture, contributed to understanding international advertising and showed interesting results about the role of culture in advertising (Douglas and Craig, 1983; Green and White, 1976). However, since these studies were conducted without considering the methodological problems that arise when comparing and analyzing two or more cultures, many weaknesses are also revealed (Choudhry, 1986; Van de Vijver and Leung, 2021).

Cross-cultural research is not simply an extension of uni-cultual. When simultaneously analyzing advertisements from more than one culture, researchers must consider several methodological issues that are not considered when working within a single culture (Cheng, 2014; Lonner and Berry, 1986; Van de Vijver and Leung, 2021). In researching international advertising, it is extremely difficult to generalize the results of previous research conducted ignoring the methodological considerations of cross-cultural research, which many scholars have pointed out. The purpose of this chapter is to examine cross-cultural equivalence, emic-etic distinction, and experimenter or interviewer, which are three important methodological considerations necessary for more effective cross-cultural research and appropriate cultural comparison. It aims to look at the experimenter or interviewer effects and suggest solutions to them.

Cross-cultural Equivalence

Brislin (1983) and Triandis (1979), who have established theories and methodologies of cross-cultural research since the 1950s, found that the most ideal case for comparative analysis of two or more cultures is equivalent stimulation between cultures (equivalent stimuli), It is claimed to have equivalent manipulations, equivalent samples of subjects, and equivalent response continua. In other words, when all the cultures to be studied have equivalent or identical systems, we can accurately compare and analyze the differences between cultures. However, in reality, since people from different cultural backgrounds cannot have the same organizations, it is desirable for cross-cultural researchers to try to maintain equality between cultures in all processes of collecting, analyzing, and writing reports (Cheng, 2014; Liamputtong, 2008; Van de Vijver and Leung, 2021).

Without first considering equivalence between cultures, cross-cultural researchers make the mistake of comparing apples from one culture to oranges from another (Gudykunst and Ting-Toomey, 1988; Triandis, 1979). In other words, it is not appropriate to discuss differences between cultures based on measurements taken with questions, manipulations, or samples that are not equivalent between the two cultures (the debate over IQ tests is the best-known example). In researching international advertisements, researchers should consider various types of equivalence in order to objectively compare the differences in advertisements between countries, abandoning the prejudice of analyzing biased toward the country leading the research. Linguistic, functional, conceptual, sample, and metric equivalence are five concepts of equivalence that must be considered in researching international advertising.

Linguistic Equivalence

The equivalence of languages is closely related to the problem of translating one language into another, which is very tricky in cross-cultural studies. Direct translation is the most commonly used translation method in cross-cultural research. In this method, a bilingual translator directly translates a sentence from one language into another language in one step for use in another culture. This method is the most widely used because it is the most simple, less time-consuming, and less expensive, but many problems are revealed when a questionnaire is created using this method to compare differences between cultures (Cheng, 2014).

The most frequent problem when translating questionnaires written in one language into another language is that it is difficult to directly translate into another language while maintaining the meaning of a certain term or sentence in one culture. The following example shows how a direct translation of an advertisement written in one language into another language can have a significantly different meaning between the two cultures.

In the early 1950s, an American ink manufacturer ran an out-of-home advertisement titled "Avoid resentment (from leaks and stains)" as an advertisement for selling ink to Mexico. The ad, which warned Americans not to be embarrassed about breast cancer, seemed appropriate to Americans, but to Spanish-speaking Mexicans, the ad's "embarrassed" meant "to become pregnant." Many Mexicans believed the ad sold birth control devices. Pepsi also mistranslated their ads, which hindered their sales abroad. When the successful U.S. campaign "Come Alive With Pepsi" was translated into German, "come alive" became "come alive" in German erroneously to mean "alive out of the grave" (Ricks, Fu and Arpan, 1974; Slater, 1984). Thirdly, an example of an American airline can be given. The airline has advertised "rendezvous lounges" in its planes for the convenience of travelers. However, while having a meeting place in a small plane is a good idea, to Portuguese-speaking travelers, "rendezvous lounges" is an absurd expression. was Because "rendezvous" in Portuguese meant a place rented for love-making (Mazze, 1964; Van de Vijver and Leung, 2021).

As shown in the examples above, it is extremely difficult to translate directly into another language while retaining the meaning of one language. To compensate for this problem of translation, cross-cultural psychologists have proposed a method of double translation with decentering (Albaum, Erickson, and Strandskov, 1989;

Miracle, 1990; Triandis and Brislin, 1984). An example of the process of translating a questionnaire written in Korean into English is as follows.

As a first step, ask bilingual #1, who speaks both Korean and English well, to translate a sentence in Korean (let's call it Hangul 1) into English (let's call it English 1). In the next step, have the second bilingual translate the English translation (English 1) back into Korean (Hangul 2), and compare Hangul 1 and Hangul 2. If English does not have parallel words that can express the words or ideas that appear in the original text of Hangul, Hangul 1 and Hangul 2 will be slightly different (because when translated Hangul 1 into English 1, it is difficult to accurately convey the meaning of Hangeul). Because there is a problem with term selection, English 1 cannot be equal to Hangul 1, and Hangul 2, which is a translation of English 1 into Korean, is not the same as Hangul 1). When Hangul 1 cannot be accurately translated into English, we must transform Hangul 1 into sentences that can be more easily and accurately translated into English in order to maintain cross-cultural parity.

Information can be obtained by comparing Hangul 1 and Hangul 2 as to how to transform Hangul 1. The researcher compares Hangul 1 and Hangul 2, and if Hangul 3 is written by modifying Hangul 1, Hangeul 3 should retain the meaning of Hangul 1 and at the same time be translated equally better into English than when Hangul 1 was translated. It should be borne in mind that there must be In the next step, another bilingual #3 translates Korean 3 into English (English 2), and another bilingual #4 translates English 2 back into Korean 4. Next, when comparing Hangul 3 and Hangul 4, if they are

Figure 1 Double-translation with Decentering

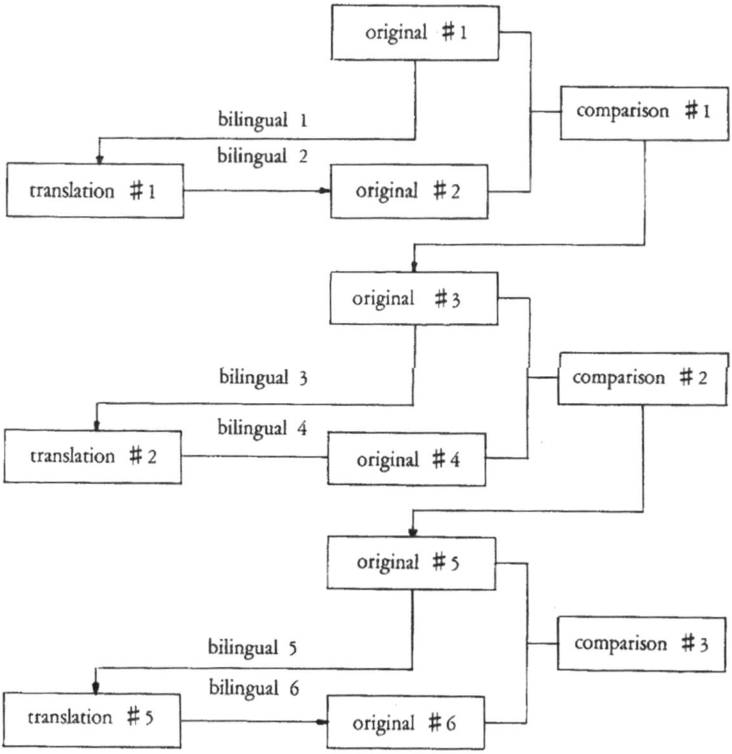

original #1
comparison #1
bilingual 1
bilingual 2
translation #1
original #2
original #3
comparison #2
bilingual 3
bilingual 4
translation #2
original #4
original #5
comparison #3
bilingual 5
bilingual 6
translation #5
original #6

identical, this means that the Korean sentence and the English sentence are equivalent (linguistic equivalence). However, if Hangul 3 and Hangul 4 are different, we have to repeat the above process until the two Hangul sentences (Hangul 5 and Hangul 6, Hangul 7 and Hangul 8, etc.) are identical (see Figure 1). .

While this method has the disadvantages of being complex, time-consuming, and costly, several scholars have argued that it is the most suitable translation technique for developing instruments for cross-cultural research (Brislin, 1980; Lonner and Berry, 1980). As an example of cross-cultural psychological research using this method, Brislin (1970) used the Marlowe-Crowne Social Desirability Scale in English to measure Guam and the northern part of the Mariana Islands in the South Pacific. In order to maintain linguistic equivalence between the two cultures, the double-translation with decentering method was used. To take one of the many scales as an example, the original scale of English (English 1), "I like to gossip at times," was transformed into "I sometimes like to talk about other people's business" through a multi-step decentering process, measured in the United States and Guam. (because the Chamorro language lacked a suitable word to express the English gossip).

In order to reduce the complexity of translating

one language into another using double-translation with decentering, Brislin (1) use simple sentences rather than complex sentences, and (2) avoid using pronouns. Five rules: (3) avoid using metaphors and colloquialisms, (4) avoid using English passive voice sentences, and (5) avoid using subjunctive and subjective emotional sentences are suggested.

The above presented the process of double-translation, which is widely used when studying two cultures, but of course, when studying more than three cultures (languages), this process becomes more complicated.

Functional Equivalence

Equivalence of function means whether the concept, idea, or action to be studied is functionally equivalent or not equivalent in all cultures related to it (Cheng, 2014; Liamputtong, 2008; Van de Vijver and Leung, 2021). Frijda and Jahoda (1966) suggested that if the same action has different functions in different cultures, it is not possible to compare differences between cultures with regard to the importance of functional equivalence in cross-cultural studies. and Jahoda amplified the proposal, arguing that if there is no equality of function between cultures, cross-cultural research is virtually impossible. Their argument well points out how important the existence or non-existence of functional equivalence between cultures is in analyzing cross-cultural studies.

However, despite the fact that many products perform different functions in different cultures, existing consumer behavior studies compare and analyze differences between cultures by applying variables or situations that are not functionally equivalent across cultures (Green and White, 1976). For example, in the United States, bicycles are primarily used for recreational purposes, whereas in China, the Netherlands and many developing countries, bicycles are used for transportation.

This not only theoretically implies that the bicycle cannot be considered as an equivalent variable in studying consumer behavior with two or more cultures as objects of analysis, but also implies important information in marketing practice. In the United States, bicycles should be classified as recreational products, whereas in other countries they should be classified as alternative means of transportation. Therefore, cross-cultural research that measures consumers' behavior toward bicycles is a comparative study of functionally different situations between cultures.

Equivalence of function between cultures is a very

important concept in cross-cultural research, but it is not a serious problem from the manager's point of view. This is because executives are only interested in the reaction of consumers in different countries to a particular product rather than being interested in the equivalence of functionality between products. For example, they are particularly interested in how different Country A and Country B consumers react to a particular bicycle advertising campaign, not the functional equivalence of bicycles.

The issue of equivalence of functions is not worthy of deep consideration from a practical point of view. However, in theoretical research, it is a very important concept in comparative analysis of cultures, and in practice, understanding whether or not functional equivalence exists between cultures for certain products, situations, concepts, ideas, and behaviors is essential for marketing activities in foreign countries. I think it will play an important role in establishing an advertising campaign (Cheng, 2014).

Conceptual Equivalence

To make cross-cultural comparisons, the meaning of the tools used in research (stimuli, concepts, behaviors, etc.) must be equivalent across cultures. Equivalence of concepts refers to whether a concept is equivalent across cultures or not. Regarding how difficult it is to maintain equivalence of concepts in cross-cultural research, Triandis and Brislin (1984) thought that we created a questionnaire with concepts that people living in other cultures could understand well. But people living in other cultures thought of the concept differently. It is pointed out that our questionnaire did not ask equal questions across cultures. If the concept that the researcher wants to analyze is perceived differently between cultures, the researcher cannot carry out comparative research on the difference between cultures accurately with the concept. This means that when researchers conduct research in other cultures, they must pay close attention to whether respondents from other cultures understand the questionnaire in the same way that they do in their own culture.

For example, the word family has different meanings in different cultures (Choudhry, 1986; Douglas and Craig, 1983). In the nuclear family-centered United States, families usually include only parents and children. However, in Italy, Greece, and most Northeast Asian cultures, including Korea, China, and Japan, which emphasize collectivism more than the United States, family means not only parents and children, but also all relatives such as grandparents, uncles, and cousins. do. "It has been empirically demonstrated that even the word respect has different meanings between American and Mexican students (Peck and Diaz-Guerrero, 1967).

As another example, even if the same concept exists across cultures, the concept may manifest itself in different forms of behavior across cultures. For example, innovativeness is a concept used both in the United States and in France. However, innovation in the United States includes not only the act of purchasing and using a new product, but also the act of conveying information or experience about a new product to friends or neighbors, whereas in France, innovation is not a socially highly regarded concept. Because of this, consumers who purchase and use new products are reluctant to convey information or experiences about the product to others. This example shows that although some concepts exist across cultures, they are expressed in different behaviors in different cultures (Green and Langeard, 1975).

As described above, factor analysis is a very useful method as a tool for understanding subtle conceptual differences that may exist between cultures to be studied. From the similarities or differences in factor structures, the researcher can find out whether or not there is equivalence of the concept to be studied between cultures, along with information on how each culture perceives the world (Hui and Triandis, 1985).

There are many differences between cultures in how they perceive the world. Therefore, consideration of the equivalence of concepts causes many methodological problems in cross-cultural research. Of course, this does not mean that one culture cannot be compared to another. The above examples merely point out that the concepts used in cross-cultural studies must be applied equally and mutually well across cultures (Van de Vijver and Leung, 2021).

Sample Equivalence

The fourth consideration in cross-cultural research is the issue of equivalence of samples used between all cultures studied. The problem of sampling is always inherent even when conducting research on one culture (uni-cultual), but in comparing and analyzing two or more cultures, the problem of sampling plays a very decisive role in interpreting the results of the entire study. It is difficult to generalize the results when the sample characteristics of one culture differ from those of other cultures (Van de Vijver and Leung, 2021).

The methods for obtaining equivalent samples from all cultures involved in the study are (1) a method of comparative study by extracting a representative sample from each culture, and (2) a method of obtaining a perfectly equivalent sample from each culture. There is a method of comparative study by obtaining comparable samples from two or more cultures (Choudhry, 1986).

It is desirable to conduct comparative studies of differences between cultures based on representative samples of each culture. However, the problem is that it is very difficult to obtain samples representative of each culture. In most developed countries, sampling frames can be easily obtained by using telephone directories or voting lists (of course, there is a problem with the representativeness of the sample even in this case), but in developing countries, sampling frames are not collected because such data are not collected. It is difficult to determine, and it is difficult to survey illiterate people who live in rural areas or have low incomes. Therefore, in order to obtain a representative sample, researchers must use different methods in developed and developing countries.

Also, in some countries, lower socioeconomic strata are not included in the population during the sampling process, so the upper class tends to be included in the sample more than the lower class. When sampling from a Western perspective, it is almost impossible to obtain a representative sample in these cultures (Van de Vijver and Leung, 2021).

As another example, Gabon's marital classification, which is a method of classifying the population according to the presence or absence of marriage, is a method widely used in Western society, and married, single, divorced, widowed, etc. are set as categories. . However, this classification method is used as a classification method of marriage in some cultures (especially in cultures where polygamy is allowed) because concubines and concubines are not set as nomads in countries that allow polygamy. can't be applied well. In some cultures, nearly 20 percent of women belong to these nomads. This example typically shows the problem of sampling that occurs when the Western population classification method is applied as it is without checking the possibility of use in other cultures just because it is widely used in the West (Mueller, 1990).

Since obtaining a representative sample from each culture is not only methodologically difficult, but also costly and time-consuming, the most commonly used sampling method in cross-cultural research is a comparable sample (at least the gender and age of samples extracted from each culture). , income level, level of education, social class, etc. must be equal). For example, in each culture, a sample of university students living in a large city is studied, or in each culture, a sample of housewives living in a small city is a method of research. However, as described above, the method using a specific subgroup of each culture is also not a perfect method to maintain equivalence between samples. Because the socio-cultural traits of university students in developed countries are different from those of under-developed countries when a study is conducted using college students as a sample, the differences between cultures in the research results are not only due to the actual differences between cultures but also due to differences in sample characteristics. The difference between the two also contributes to this.

Therefore, cross-cultural research using subgroups contributes to cross-cultural research in that it provides various differences that exist between cultures. However, there are some problems in generalizing the research results in the context of the entire culture. Choudhry (1986) argued that when using comparable samples in cross-cultural studies, researchers should try to maintain the dynamics of gender, age, educational background, occupation, and income level of subgroups. It was pointed out that if sample characteristics differ between cultures, these problems and limitations must be considered in analyzing the research results, and these problems and limitations of sampling should be reported so that readers can recognize them when writing a report.

Metric Equivalence

The fifth equivalence to be considered in cross-cultural research is the matter of measurement. In particular, the issue of equivalence of measurements is important when collecting and analyzing quantitative data. Because different cultures have different judgment styles and response styles, some cultures use extreme scales while others do not use extreme scales, even when giving substantially the same response (Van de Vijver and Leung, 2021).

As pointed out by Hui and Triandis (1989) and Triandis (1972), Northeast Asian cultures, where extreme reactions are culturally undesirable, tend to be more intermediate than end points of the scales. Evaluate something using the middle of the scales. On the other hand, in Mediterranean and North American cultures, they tend to use extreme scales because it is culturally undesirable to give halfway responses and extreme clear responses are perceived as honest.

This tendency of response method has been empirically proven in research on advertisements as well. Fields (1980) compared advertising strategies between

Westerners (US) and Japanese using a 7-point scale of "excellent" and "terrible". In measuring advertising strategy, Westerners mainly used an extreme scale of 1 (excellent) or 7 (terrible), whereas Japanese mainly used an intermediate scale from 3 to 5, and rarely used an extreme scale. Fields suggested that different responses to advertising should be evaluated and understood in their cultural context rather than directly compared across cultures.

The difference in extreme response style that differs between cultures in this form causes methodological problems in the case of social psychological research by extracting samples from two or more cultures. As an example, factor structures found by factor analysis of questionnaire responses are affected by the response method. If there is a difference in the extreme response between the two cultures when studied using the Likert scale, as in the example above, this affects the magnitude of correlation coefficients in factor analysis, so that one culture It is possible that the factors extracted from the responses of the population differ significantly from factors extracted from other cultures.

As discussed above, because the response method is different between cultures, if the results of the study are simply statistically compared with average values or analyzed by factors, there may be cases where differences between cultures cannot be accurately analyzed. can Therefore, I think that the researcher should understand the cultural background of this response method and refer to it in analyzing the data (Cheng, 2014).

Another problem with measurement is how many point scales are used (Stening and Everett, 1984). One of the study found that 5-point or 7-point scales were most commonly used in the United States, whereas 10-point or 20-point scales were used more frequently than 5-point or 7-point scales in the other cultures they studied. there was. Therefore, it is also necessary to consider the possible problems that may arise when subjects in a culture accustomed to 10-point or 20-point scales, which can classify a problem in more detail, are forced to measure on a 5-point or 7-point scale. For example, Hui and Triandis (1989), who analyzed extreme response patterns between Hispanic and non-Hispanic groups in the United States, found that the extreme response patterns between the two samples were significantly different when a 5-point scale was used, but a 10-point scale was used. When used, it was reported that the distribution of response patterns between the two groups was almost similar.

While equivalence of language, equivalence of function, equivalence of concept, and equivalence of sample can be reviewed prior to data collection, equivalence of measurement can only be reviewed after data are collected and cannot be considered in advance. Therefore, researchers should consider what number of scales is the most appropriate measurement and how the respondent's response pattern differs from culture to culture by referring to prior surveys, consultations with experts, experiences, and existing studies in all cultures involved in the study (Van de Vijver and Leung, 2021).

Table 1 Five Types of Equivalence in Cross-Cultural Research

Type of Equivalence	Key Characteristics	Examples
Linguistic Equivalence	Focuses on accurately translating meanings across languages. Challenges include retaining meaning and cultural nuances. Double translation with decentering is commonly used	Pepsi mistranslation ('Come alive with Pepsi' as 'come alive out of the grave') or airline 'rendezvous lounges' misinterpreted in Portuguese
Functional Equivalence	Ensures that concepts or actions have the same function in all cultures studied. Differences in product functions across cultures, like bicycles as recreation vs. transportation, are critical	Bicycles used recreationally in the US but as transportation in China, requiring different classifications for cross-cultural studies

Type of Equivalence	Key Characteristics	Examples
Conceptual Equivalence	Examines whether research tools or concepts hold equivalent meanings across cultures. Differences in perceptions, like 'family' or 'innovativeness,' highlight the challenge	'Family' means nuclear in the US but extended in Italy, Korea, etc. 'Innovativeness' in the US includes sharing, while in France, it does not
Sample Equivalence	Ensures samples are comparable across cultures. Challenges include varying representativeness and socio-cultural traits in different populations	Western samples often exclude lower socioeconomic groups, making generalization difficult. Example: Gabon marital status classification
Metric Equivalence	Focuses on differences in response styles and measurement scales across cultures. Extreme responses vary culturally (e.g., US vs. Japan). Scale formats (5-point vs. 10-point) affect responses	Western cultures use extreme responses (e.g., 1 or 7), while East Asian cultures prefer intermediate scales (e.g., 3 - 5). Scale formats influence data
Economy, Society, and Culture	Job creation, activation of the advertising industry, and improved domestic product quality; internationalization of national consciousness.	Loss of competitiveness for domestic firms; external dependency; cultural homogenization and loss of traditional values.

Features of Emic-Etic

Cross-cultural psychologists have long used the distinction between emic and etic approaches (Hornik, 1980; Irwin, Klein, Engle, Yarbrough, and Nerlove, 1977; Triandis and Marin, 1983). The term is derived from the approaches of phonemics and phonetics, which represent two different perspectives for studying, analyzing, and explaining intercultural phenomena in linguistics, and was originally used by the linguist Pike (1966). Phonemics refer to sounds that apply only to a single linguistic system, whereas phonetics refer to universal aspects of language. In the above two words, emics and etics, the two remaining suffixes after dropping phon, are used as terms that represent local versus universal culture in various academic fields.

Emic is an approach to best describe the attitudinal and behavioral phenomena that occur uniquely within a culture by applying concepts used in a culture.)am. The instruments of research can only be applied to one culture, and the purpose of research is to understand the uniqueness of that culture. Thus, the emics approach is the study of idiographic. As a result of research applying this approach, researchers cannot compare differences between cultures, nor can they suggest or test general laws about attitudes and behaviors.

culture, whereas the etic approach is useful for comparing different cultures.

Analyzing the debate on cross-cultural psychological research, Berry (1980) identified two approaches as comparing (1) the researcher's point of view, (2) the number of cultures studied, (3) the structure of the research, and (4) the behavior. The differences between the two methods were summarized and compared by classifying them according to criteria (see Table 1)

Table 2 **Comparison of characteristics between Emic and Etic**

Criteria	Emic Approach	Etic Approach
Researcher's Point of View	Focuses on understanding unique cultural phenomena from within the culture.	Seeks universal laws of behavior applicable across cultures.
Number of Cultures Studied	Typically studies one culture at a time.	Compares multiple cultures.
Structure of Research	Idiographic approach, tailored to a specific culture.	Nomothetic approach, aiming for generalization.
Behavior Analysis	Analyzes behaviors as unique to a single culture.	Analyzes behaviors to identify universal patterns.

* Source : Douglas, S., and Craig, C. (1983). *International Marketing Research*. Englewood Cliffs, NJ, USA : Prentice-Hall.

When emic-etic is applied separately to advertising and consumer behavior, the emic approach analyzes advertising in a specific culture by focusing on thoroughly understanding the role of advertising in a culture and the relationship between advertising and economic structure. can be used suitably. On the other hand, the etic approach can be used in research to generalize the concept of involvement in consumer behavior research. These studies examine the extent to which variables related to involvement and decision-making work equally in different cultures. The main purpose of the study of this etic approach is to generalize the concept of engagement across cultures rather than culture itself.

These two approaches represent the two extremes of cross-cultural research methodology. Emic emphasizes the uniqueness of culture, while etic focuses on the panculturalism of human behavior. Therefore, both emic and etic are essential elements for cross-cultural psychological research. The emic-etic dilemma arises because without the etic there is no comparison, and without the emic there is a problem understanding the unique properties of culture.

Triandis, Malpass, and Davidson (1971) suggested two ways to solve this dilemma. The first method is the pseudoetic or imposed etic approach, which has been criticized methodologically despite being most commonly used in cross-cultural studies so far. Criticism of the pseudoetic approach stems from the difficulty of developing an etic measurement tool that is appropriate and equally usable in all cultures studied.

This method considers the emic measurement tool (usually a measurement tool developed in Western culture, especially in the United States) as an etic measurement tool and uses it as it is in foreign countries. In other words, this method is a research method in which items that reflect the situation in the United States are translated and used abroad without verifying the reliability and validity of their use in other cultures. As an example of international advertising research, as mentioned in the introduction, researchers applied Resnik and Stern's (1977) informational content classification method developed in the United States to various cultures in order to analyze the differences between cultures in advertising. It is possible to compare and analyze differences between cultures by applying them as they are.

This approach assumes that measures developed in one culture are equally measurable in foreign cultures. This research method compares differences between cultures based on the data analyzed with these advanced measurement tools. However, this method is in fact an emic approach because language and cognitive structures differ between cultures (Davidson, Jaccard, Triandis, Morales and Diaz-Guerrero, 1976), and measured Since the results can be over-interpreted or under-interpreted for actual differences between cultures (Han and Shavitt, 1994), it is not possible to compare differences between cultures that are logically valid from research results obtained using this method (Cheng, 2014; Liamputtong, 2008; Van de Vijver and Leung, 2021).

Miracle (1990) argued that researchers should avoid the pseudoetic approach that has been used so far and use the etic concept in order to maintain the objectivity of comparison even in studying international advertising, and Triandis and Marin (1983) Using personalism and collectivism samples, it was empirically shown that the study using the pseudoetic method can more accurately detect differences between cultures than the study using the pseudoetic method.

Second, as a way to harmonize the emic and etic dilemma, Triandis, Malpass, and Davidson (1971) presented a combined emic-etic approach. Developing a 'combined emic-etic' requires a three-step process. The first is the process of finding an etic construct that is considered to be common worldwide. The second is the process of developing a method to measure this concept in the way of emic in each culture and verifying whether this method is valid. Finally, the third is the process of comparative analysis of differences between cultures with the concept of etic defined in the way of emic.

In order to develop the Etic concept into an emic content, this approach proceeds with independent experiments in each culture. Factor analysis is the most suitable statistical method to find out the etic constructs or factors that make up the Emic elements in the course of an experiment. As already explained above, it is possible to find each emic measurement tool to be used in culture A and culture B by examining the elements that make up factors by performing factor analysis in all cultures targeted for research. The cross-cultural semantic differential model developed by Osgood (1967) and the subjectvie culture model presented by Triandis (1972) are the most representative examples of studies using the 'combined emic-etic' approach (Triandis, 1979).

As described above, the 'combined emic-etic approach' is more objective than the pseudoetic approach in comparative studies of cultural differences despite the disadvantages of being complicated, costly, and time-consuming to create measurement tools (one without being biased by culture), several scholars prefer this method (Hui and Triandis, 1985; Triandis and Marin,

1983).

Unfortunately, however, in the analysis of international advertising studies so far, no case of comparative analysis of advertisements between cultures using the combined emic-etic approach has been found. Rather, almost all studies have used the pseudoetic approach. This is because researchers have either been ignorant of or indifferent to the methodological problems to be considered in cross-cultural research, because so far, international advertising research has analyzed differences in advertising between cultures from a theoretical standpoint and a practical aspect rather than a theoretical standpoint.

As examined above, the dilemma between the emic and the etic brings about a very difficult point for researchers to overcome methodologically in cross-cultural research. Therefore, future researchers should create a measurement tool centered on their own culture based on the subjective judgment of the culture to which the researcher belongs, which is a common error in comparative analysis of various cultures, avoid using it in other cultures, and avoid using it in other cultures. It should be borne in mind that the concepts of emic and etic must be taken into account in order to develop an unbiased measurement tool.

Experimenter or Interviewer Effects

When research is conducted through experiments, depending on the characteristics of the experimenter (or the interviewer in the case of a research study, hereinafter, the effect of the experimenter or interviewer in an experiment and a research study is almost similar, so the case of a survey is omitted) significantly affects how the subject responds is known to affect Therefore, where possible, experimenters should be equal in all cultures being studied. If the experimenter's race, gender, age, language, clothing, and atmosphere are similar across cultures, it helps to reduce the experimenter effect in the study. However, when working with multiple cultures, it is very difficult to keep these points equal across cultures.

Even in uni-culture research, when a subject perceives that he or she is in an experimental situation, he/she guesses an experimental hypothesis and responds intentionally to support the hypothesis or, conversely, to reject the hypothesis. Researchers must be careful in selecting experimenters and subjects because they conduct acts that obscure the research results in such a way. In addition, while some subjects faithfully follow the experimenter's instructions and explanations on the questionnaire as much as possible, some subjects tend to ignore the instructions and explanations and answer insincerely (Van de Vijver and Leung, 2021).

In the case of an insincere answer, the researcher uses an internal analysis or an item-total correlation analysis to find out whether the subject answered insincerely, so that the reliability is low. You can reduce the problem by removing the item. However, the effects of these subjects often contaminate the overall results. This tendency may increase or decrease depending on who the experimenter is. Generally speaking, it is known that such intentional behavior of the subject can be reduced when the subject is unable to discern who the experimenter is and cannot guess the hypothesis of the study.

In addition to the effect that occurs between the experimenter and the subject in mono-cultural research, it has been reported that in cross-cultural research, the subject's response appears differently depending on the experimenter's nationality (Brislin, 1973). People in certain cultures tend to answer questions in a socially desirable way rather than answering questions honestly. Therefore, if a culture that answers as it is and a culture that tends to answer in a socially desirable direction are the subjects of research, a researcher cannot compare the difference between one culture and another culture only with the numerical results shown in statistics.

Some cultures tend to give different answers when the experimenter is a native or a foreigner. For example, according to a study by Triandis (1989), when asked a question directly related to Japan, Japanese people gave more positive answers when the experimenter was a foreigner than when they were Japanese. When the experimenter was a foreigner, they tended to give more negative answers than when the experimenter was Japanese. Cross-cultural researchers must consider the interaction between content and experimenter.

Another consideration is the bias in research results caused by the difference in the attributes of subjects in the two countries in the case of research using subjects from a country where experimental research is actively progressing and subjects from a country where experimental research is rarely conducted. It's a problem. In particular, as in the United States, where experimental research is often conducted at universities, freshmen and sophomores must participate in experiments several times every semester as part of their department classes, and subjects in countries where experimental research is rarely conducted. In the case of comparative research on differences between cultures, since the attitudes, motives, sincerity, response methods, and ability to predict hypotheses are very different between the subjects of the two countries, the researcher must train the experimenters well to reduce these effects. You have to make an effort.

In cross-cultural research, what factors of the experimenter (or interviewer) affect the response of the respondent are summarized as follows.

Table 3 Experimenter's (or Interviewer's) Factors Influencing the Experiment

Category	Factors
Experimenter's Background	1. Affiliation (relationship with participants or institutions) 2. Experimenter's image (perceived traits or authority) 3. Distance between experimenter and respondents (social or professional distance) 4. Bias of the experimenter (personal or cultural influences)
Experimental Environment	1. Location (physical setting of the experiment) 2. Relevance of the subject matter 3. Sensitivity of the subject matter 4. Cultural appropriateness of the experiment 5. Social desirability (respondents providing socially acceptable answers)
Respondent's Background	1. Past experiences 2. Response style (tendency or patterns in answering)

Category	Factors
Cultural Background	1. Courtesy norm (cultural expectations of politeness in responses) 2. Reticence (degree of reservation or reluctance in answering) 3. Game-playing norm (cultural attitudes towards participation and engagement)

* Source : Pareek, U., and Rao, V. (1980). Cross-Cultural Surveys and Interviewing. In H. Triandis (Ed.), *Handbook of Cross-Cultural Research Psychology, 127-180.*

In order to minimize the experimenter problems that arise in cross-cultural research, it is desirable to train local experimenters belonging to the culture to be studied and participate in the research, if possible. By doing so, the interaction effect between the experimenter and the subject and the interaction effect between the experimenter and the contents of the questionnaire can be reduced. Another method is to use methods that prevent subjects from being aware that they are participating in an experiment (unobtrusive measures). However, while this method helps a lot in reducing the effect of the experimenter, it often raises serious ethical problems. This is because experiment participants can claim to be victims if they perceive that they are being used in an experiment. They also think negatively about the experiment, which hinders future researchers from working in the area.

Considerations of International Advertising Research Methodology through Cross-cultural Research

Advertising campaigns that are successful in one culture are not necessarily successful in other cultures. Therefore, when executing advertisements in foreign countries, marketers should understand the cultural characteristics of the society they want to advertise and reflect them in setting advertising strategies, planning, research, media selection, and production direction. As briefly mentioned at the beginning, due to the rapid increase in international advertising volume, the opening of the advertising market, and many difficulties in successfully executing advertising in other countries, theoretically and practically research on international advertising has been actively conducted recently (Cheng, 2014; Liamputtong, 2008; Van de Vijver and Leung, 2021).

Unlike other fields, research on the relationship between advertising and culture among many areas of international advertising research is relatively more theory-oriented than practice-oriented, and is published in various academic journals. Not only international advertising researchers, but also cross-cultural psychologists analyzed advertising as a form of social communication, focusing on the fact that advertising provides important information for studying culture because it reflects the cultural values and norms of the society. Comparative study of differences between cultures.

However, despite the fact that international advertising has been actively studied theoretically in terms of cross-culture, many limitations have been revealed because the analysis so far has been carried out ignoring methodological matters that must be considered in cross-cultural research (Liamputtong, 2008).

In the case of a comparative study of two or more cultures, it is not desirable to apply a measurement tool developed for one culture as it is without examining its applicability in other cultures. When researching with more than one culture, researchers must consider various issues that do not need to be considered when researching in a single culture. Nonetheless, these points were not included in the study because the existing international advertising research was conducted mainly on practical issues. Such monoculture-centered research, that is, research that imposes theories or measurement tools developed in the culture that drives the research as it is on other cultures, has helped to understand the advertising phenomenon between countries or cultures, but it has helped to develop international advertising theory. is becoming an impediment.

In this chapter, when studying international advertising from a cross-cultural perspective, the basic issues to be considered methodologically by researchers are the equivalence of language, equivalence of function, equivalence of concept, equivalence of sample, equivalence of measurement, and emic presented by various scholars. -Etic classification and experimenter or interviewer effects were examined, and solutions to them were presented. Researchers who analyze cross-cultures must correctly understand these problems and apply them to future international advertising research in order to increase the reliability and validity of their research results.

Chapter 5

Cultural Variability

Advertising is undoubtedly a reflection of the times, but at the same time, it also serves as a mirror of culture. Advertising is a social institution that vividly reflects the complex facets of a society. With the advent of the global era, multinational companies seek to capture attractive foreign markets by understanding and reflecting the society and culture of their target markets through advertising communication strategies (Martinez and Fieulaine, 2015; Taylor, 2023).

In western countries such as the United States, the United Kingdom, and France, hard-sell advertisements that persistently appeal to consumers with logic and numbers are common, reflecting the cultural characteristics of advertising. However, unlike the West, in East Asian cultures such as Korea, Japan, and China, advertisements focus more on emotions and sentiment than on reason and logic. Soft-sell advertisements that implant images are more effective than hard-sell advertisements in East Asian cultures. This contrast is a discourse that must be discussed when comparing Western and Eastern advertisements (Mooij, 2022).

Eastern and western cultures are characterized by various differences. Considering advertising as the center of culture and dynamically comparing various cultural differences helps to understand the relationship between advertising and culture. Because advertisements effectively reflect culture, advertising is a subject in our daily lives and find it interesting.

Advertisements are easily understandable to the general public because their messages are concise (Han, 2024). Recognizing cultural differences in global marketing is important. Both the academic and advertising industries will contribute to higher-level research on cultural diversity.

In this chapter, we aim to examine the various dimensions of culture that are considered the most important factors in researching the relationship between advertising and culture. While there is no universally agreed-upon standard for the various dimensions of culture, this chapter focuses on Hofstede's (2001) cultural typology criteria, which are most frequently cited in the advertising marketing field: individualism and collectivism, uncertainty avoidance, power distance, masculinity and femininity, as well as high-context and low-context cultures as defined by Hall.

Individualism and Collectivism

Many scholars agree that advertising reflects the unique culture of a given society. Understanding how the culture of each country is embedded in advertisements is crucial for multinational advertisers. This is because information about cultural differences expressed in specific types of advertising appeals not only provides insights into differences in cultural norms and values (Holbrook, 1987) but also serves as an important guideline for establishing international advertising strategies and production directions (Cavallone, 2013; Han and Shavitt, 1994; Taylor, 2023).

Research on cultural differences in advertising, based on the theory of individualism and collectivism—identified in cross-cultural psychology as a fundamental dimension of cultural variability—is essential for understanding international advertising strategies. Many researchers have conducted empirical studies on how these cultural differences manifest in advertising concepts in Western and Eastern cultures, which are distinct from each other in terms of individualism and collectivism.

For example, Mueller (1987) analyzed Japanese and American print advertisements by categorizing them into traditional appeals and modern/westernized appeals. Through this content analysis, she examined the role of culture in advertising. The study found that advertisements in each country are somewhat sensitive to their respective cultural norms, values, and characteristics. However, it also revealed that Japanese advertisements, in certain aspects, emphasize Western thinking significantly. One surprising finding was that the assumption that Japanese advertisements would use more group consensus appeals than American advertisements was not supported. Only 7% of Japanese ads emphasized group consensus, compared to 9% of American ads. To explain this unexpected result, the researcher suggested that Japanese advertisers had realized that emphasizing the growing Western individualism, rather than the traditional sense of collectivism that was gradually fading in Japan, would be more beneficial for their companies.

Hong et al. (1987) conducted a comparative analysis of three types of advertising appeals—emotional appeal, informative appeal, and comparative appeal—in American and Japanese advertisements. The authors hypothesized that, due to cultural differences, Japanese advertisements would use more emotional appeals than American advertisements, whereas American advertisements would use more informative and comparative appeals than their Japanese counterparts. While the study confirmed the general view that advertising expressions differ between the two countries, it also found an unexpected result: Japanese magazine advertisements used more informative appeals than American magazine advertisements across all product categories (both personal and non-personal products). Thus, the study did not fully support the general belief that advertisements always reflect the unique culture of a country.

Marquez (1975) analyzed the cultural content of advertisements published in Philippine daily newspapers and weekly magazines from 1970 to 1972 to determine whether they reflected the unique culture of the Philippines. Surprisingly, the study found that Philippine print advertisements reflected Western culture rather than their own indigenous culture. Marquez offered three explanations for why Philippine advertisements embodied Western thinking. First, since advertising originated in the West and has inherently Western cultural tendencies, it is natural for advertising content to convey Western culture. Second, Philippine advertisers tend to imitate American and European advertisements. Third,

Western advertisements influence Philippine advertising. Despite these findings, the author argued that, in terms of advertising effectiveness, Philippine advertisements reflecting Western culture would be less persuasive than those that incorporate the local culture, due to the ongoing interaction between culture and communication.

As seen above, previous research not only focused on the crucial issue of cultural variability but also presented intriguing findings regarding the role of culture in advertising. However, past cross-cultural advertising studies have not definitively proven the general assumption that advertisements always reflect the unique culture of their respective countries. In some ways, this inconsistency between advertising content and culture is understandable. As previous researchers (Marquez, 1975; Mueller, 1987) have argued, advertising content is influenced by various factors beyond culture, such as product characteristics, individual creative styles, the homogenization of global consumer values, and direct influences from other cultures. For this reason, it is reasonable to predict that advertising content may not always reflect the unique culture of a given country.

Furthermore, even if cultural differences in advertising content clearly exist, determining which cultural dimension to examine to accurately predict these differences is challenging. Just as previous studies have sometimes failed to identify such differences, researchers must carefully consider which cultural dimensions are most relevant for comparative analysis. However, by applying dimensions already established in cross-cultural research to advertising, it is more likely that meaningful differences in advertising content can be identified. If cross-cultural advertising research focuses on dimensions such as individualism and collectivism—well-established in cross-cultural psychology—it would be reasonable to predict that advertisements from a given cultural region will reflect that culture's distinct characteristics.

Although a variety of cultures exist worldwide, defining the concept of culture is extremely difficult (Triandis et al., 1988). One way to analyze culture is to identify dimensions of cultural variability and use them to understand how culture influences individual social behavior. Many studies have examined different dimensions of cultural variability (Gudykunst and Ting-Toomey, 1988; Hecht, Anderson & Ribeau, 1989; Hofstede, 2001; Rhee, Alexandra and Powell, 2020). While there are various methods of classifying culture, dividing it into individualistic and collectivistic cultures has proven to be one of the most useful approaches for studying culture and communication (Gudykunst and Ting-Toomey, 1988).

The classification of cultures based on individualism and collectivism is considered one of the most significant distinctions for understanding moral values, religious beliefs, cognitive structures, modernization, national structures, and cultural patterns, as well as the cultural values of social organizations and labor-related values (Triandis, Brislin and Hui, 1988; Sharma and Bumb, 2020).

In general, individualistic cultures emphasize personal identity, interests, and independence, while collectivistic cultures prioritize the social norms of the groups to which individuals belong (e.g., family, relatives, friends, school, nation, workplace, etc.). In individualistic cultures, people tend to emphasize their unique personality and strive for independence from others, placing greater importance on personal goals rather than group goals. In contrast, collectivistic cultures value cooperation among group members, emphasize strong interpersonal bonds, and often prioritize group goals over individual aspirations. Typically, individualistic cultures highlight independence, personal competition, achievement, self-satisfaction, freedom, and personal pleasure. In contrast, collectivistic cultures emphasize interdependence, harmony among group members, social status, family security, and cooperation (Hofstede, 2001; Hornikx and Groot, 2017, Kim, 2020).

Since individualism and collectivism have been widely recognized as etic (universal) concepts in cross-cultural research (Cavallone, 2013; Gudykunst, 1987; Han, 2024; Hofstede, 2001; Mooij, 2022; Triandis, 1995), studying cultural differences in advertising through these concepts holds both academic and practical significance. Triandis and his colleagues (1988) attempted an etic analysis of individualism and collectivism across diverse cultures and identified four universal factors that characterize these dimensions worldwide. Individualism is associated with two factors: independence from the in-group and self-confidence combined with hedonism. Collectivism, on the other hand, is linked to two factors: family integrity and prioritization of group consciousness along with interdependence.

The concept of individualism and collectivism is not only rooted in the theoretical framework of cross-cultural psychology but also serves as a suitable etic concept for studying advertising content and expressions across cultures. Furthermore, since the individualism-collectivism dimension has been identified as a crucial classification criterion in various research fields (Hofstede, 2001; Hornikx and Groot, 2017; Mooij, 2022), it is reasonable to predict that advertising content will reflect the attributes of individualism or collectivism in a given cultural context, assuming that advertising is a reflection of culture.

For instance, when selecting countries to study whether individualistic and collectivistic cultures are reflected in advertising, researchers widely acknowledge the data from Hofstede's (2001) study, which examined individualism and collectivism across 53 countries. According to Hofstede's findings, the United States scored 91 on the individualism scale (with 100 being the maximum), making it the most individualistic country in the world. In contrast, South Korea scored 18 on the same scale, categorizing it as a highly collectivistic society. The United States can generally be characterized as a culture that emphasizes self-autonomy and personal image, whereas South Korea is distinguished by its strong sense of collectivism. Therefore, it can be predicted that advertisements in these two countries will reflect their respective cultural orientations toward individualism or collectivism. In other words, American advertisements are likely to emphasize themes such as personal identity, individual success, and independence, whereas South Korean advertisements will highlight appeals related to group welfare, family happiness, and harmony with societal norms.

This pattern of advertising appeals across cultures aligns with the universalism-particularism concept, one of the various cultural classifications proposed by Parsons (1951; Parsons and Shils, 1951). Individualists tend to be universalistic, categorizing people or objects based on universal standards, whereas collectivists tend to be particularistic, categorizing people or objects differently depending on the situation (Gudykunst and Ting-Toomey, 1988; Shaw, 2006; Triandis, Bontempo, Villareal and Lucca, 1988). Such cultural variability in universalism and particularism can significantly influence advertising content. That is, in an individualistic culture, which is expected to have a strong universalistic tendency, advertisements tend to emphasize individualistic appeals across all product categories. In contrast, in a collectivistic culture, which is expected to exhibit a strong particularistic tendency, advertising appeals may vary depending on the characteristics of the product.

Research on the impact of individualistic and collectivistic cultures on advertising has practical implications for multinational corporations when determining whether to localize (adapt) or specialize their advertising messages for each country or to use standardized advertising messages globally.

Proponents of standardization in international advertising (Kotler and Keller, 2016; Usunier and Lee, 2013) assume that basic consumer needs, desires, and purchasing motivations are similar or identical worldwide. Therefore, they argue that a successful advertising campaign in one country can also be successful in another because consumers across different markets can be persuaded using similar or identical advertisements. According to this perspective, people worldwide are increasingly adopting similar products and lifestyles while also sharing common values. As a result, multinational corporations should focus on the common needs, desires, and purchase motivations shared by consumers across different countries rather than on cultural differences when crafting advertising messages.

Conversely, scholars advocating for localization or adaptation in international advertising (Kotler and Keller, 2016; Usunier and Lee, 2013) argue that consumers in different countries have distinct needs, desires, and purchasing motivations, as well as culturally diverse backgrounds. Therefore, they contend that it is impossible to satisfy all consumers worldwide with a single advertising message, making it necessary to tailor advertising messages to the characteristics of each country or region. This school of thought emphasizes social, cultural, and economic differences among nations. Accordingly, international advertisers must thoroughly research the unique local environments of foreign markets and carefully analyze the target audience within each country before selecting advertising messages that suit the specific characteristics of those markets.

However, before concluding the debate on standardization versus localization in international advertising, one critical issue must be considered: Do the results of advertising content analysis necessarily align with advertising effectiveness? In other words, does the most commonly used advertising appeal in a given culture also represent the most effective advertising strategy? Since content analysis alone is insufficient to draw conclusions about advertising effectiveness, there is an urgent need for cross-cultural experimental studies that manipulate individualistic and collectivistic advertising appeals to measure which type of advertisement is more effective in different cultural contexts.

Table 1 Dimensions of Individualism and Collectivism

Dimensions	Individualism	Collectivism
Cultural Characteristics	Independence, high competition, self-sufficiency, freedom, pleasure, horizontal relationships, equality, achievement, and efficiency	Interdependence, low competition, family security, cooperation, vertical relationships, equity, harmony, and modesty

Dimensions	Individualism	Collectivism
Child-Rearing Patterns	Focus on autonomy, self-reliance, and creativity. Parent-child bond weaker than spouse-spouse bond	Focus on obedience, reliability, and proper behavior. Parent-child bond stronger than spouse-spouse bond
Social Emphasis	Focus on personal progress, achievement, and development	Focus on harmony within the group and avoidance of conflict
Economic Correlation	Strong correlation with high GDP. Found in affluent societies like the U.S.A., Australia, and Britain	Associated with lower GDP. Found in poorer societies in Asia, Africa, and Latin America
Antecedents	Affluence, urbanization, social mobility, small family size, complex cultural structures, and high levels of education	Large family size, rural settings, limited mobility, and simpler cultural structures

High Uncertainty Avoidance and Low Uncertainty Avoidance

Uncertainty avoidance refers to the tendency of individuals to avoid uncertainty or fear associated with ambiguous situations or decisions by taking specific actions or strategies. This cultural value has significant implications for consumer decision-making and purchasing behavior, making it crucial in advertising communication. As understanding of cultural values is closely related to advertising communication content, advertisers seek to incorporate consumers' tendencies toward uncertainty avoidance into advertisements. Consumers strive to minimize and cope with risks arising from uncertainty and prefer systematic situations over non-systematic ones.

In advertising communication scenarios, uncertainty avoidance can manifest in various ways. The most preferable approach for consumers is to gather as much information as possible about the product before making a purchase decision. Another approach is to seek psychological safety by choosing familiar brands over new ones. Consumers tend to seek psychological stability by making choices with high certainty. This tendency toward uncertainty avoidance is reflected in the growth of industries like insurance. Lastly, consumers may choose to defer purchase decisions in high uncertainty situations (Hilton, 2022; Sharma and Bumb, 2020).

Advertising messaging strategies in cultures with high and low uncertainty avoidance should be tailored to reflect these cultural dimensions to contribute to consumer persuasion. In cultures with high uncertainty avoidance, consumer assurance is crucial. Therefore, advertising messages benefit from evidence-based explanations, detailed product copies, experiments, scientifically proven data, and credible experts. Reflecting cultural values by conveying stability and safety to consumers while avoiding uncertainty is essential.

Table 2 Characteristics of High and Low Uncertainty Avoidance

Dimensions	High Uncertainty Avoidance	Low Uncertainty Avoidance
Definition	Strong preference for minimizing uncertainty and ambiguity.	Acceptance of ambiguity and uncertainty in decision-making.
Consumer Behavior	- Seek extensive product information. - Prefer familiar brands for psychological safety. - Postpone decisions in uncertain situations.	- Willing to take risks with new products. - Open to experimentation and innovation.
Preferred Advertising Strategies	- Emphasis on assurance and certainty. - Use of evidence-based claims, detailed product explanations, and scientific data.	- Emphasis on innovation and novelty. - Simple, creative messages highlighting excitement and adventure.
Cultural Communication	Focus on conveying safety, stability, and reliability.	Highlight flexibility, openness, and adaptability.

Dimensions	High Uncertainty Avoidance	Low Uncertainty Avoidance
Industry Examples	Strong growth in insurance, healthcare, and safety-related products.	Popularity of tech gadgets, adventure tourism, and creative industries.

High Power Distance and Low Power Distance

Power distance refers to the degree of imbalance in power among various members within a society or organization, indicating the extent of societal perception of authority. How power or authority is distributed and exercised within an organization varies depending on culture.

In cultures with high power distance, the opinions and decisions of those in positions of power are highly valued, and lower-ranking members often find it challenging to express their own opinions or ideas. In contrast, in cultures with low power distance, diverse opinions from both authoritative and non-authoritative individuals are accepted, and the decision-making process tends to be more open and collaborative (Mooij, 2022).

Power distance is manifested in horizontal and vertical dimensions. Horizontal power distance refers to how power or authority is distributed among various members within a culture, regardless of their actual power status. In cultures with high horizontal power distance, there is a significant difference in power among members, leading to decision-making dominated by those with high authority. Vertical power distance refers to how clearly power differences between high and low-ranking individuals are delineated within a culture. In cultures with low vertical power distance, the distinction between high and low-ranking individuals is relatively minimal, and diverse opinions are respected. In contrast, in cultures with high vertical power distance, the opinions of the powerful group prevail, and the opinions of lower-ranking members are often disregarded (Mooij, 2022; Mooij and Hofstede, 2011).

Advertising strategies in cultures with high and low power distance differ due to the varying significance attributed to authority. Numerous studies on power distance have found that in countries with high power distance such as Korea and Japan, advertisements featuring celebrities with authority are more prevalent and effective compared to countries with low power distance like Sweden and Norway. Additionally, in East Asian cultures where respect for elders is high, advertisements often feature older celebrities as models. Advertisements frequently depict relationships based on social hierarchy such as parent-child or teacher-student relationships.

Understanding cultures with high and low power distance and reflecting them in advertising can lead to more effective advertisements by appealing to consumers' sensibilities.

Table 3 **Characteristics of High and Low Power Distance**

Dimensions	High Power Distance	Low Power Distance
Definition	Significant power imbalance within society; authority figures hold significant influence.	Minimal power imbalance; authority is distributed more equally among members.
Decision-Making	Decisions dominated by individuals in positions of power.	Collaborative and open decision-making processes involving diverse opinions.
Expression of Opinions	Lower-ranking members find it challenging to express ideas or opinions.	Diverse opinions, including those from non-authoritative individuals, are respected.
Preferred Advertising Strategies	Frequent use of authority figures, celebrities, or older individuals in advertisements; emphasis on hierarchy.	Advertisements focus on inclusivity and equality; authority figures less emphasized.

Dimensions	High Power Distance	Low Power Distance
Cultural Examples	East Asian countries like Korea and Japan, where respect for elders and hierarchy is emphasized.	Scandinavian countries like Sweden and Norway, where egalitarian values are prevalent.

Masculinity vs. Feminity

The distinction between masculinity and femininity in cultural dimensions refers to characteristics associated with gender roles. Masculinity culture refers to cultures where masculine traits are highly valued. In masculinity cultures, traits such as independence, competitiveness, goal-orientation, assertiveness, and subordination of women are highly emphasized. Consequently, in Masculinity cultures, competition among individuals is strong, and achieving results holds significant importance, with greater emphasis on independent actions and decision-making (Mooij, 2022; Mooij and Hofstede, 2011).

On the other hand, femininity culture traditionally prioritizes feminine traits over masculine traits. In Femininity cultures, values such as harmony, cooperation, gentleness, generosity, sensitivity, and empathy are highly regarded. Cooperation and harmony are generally valued over competition, and balancing work and family life is considered more important than competition and success. Decision-making involves considering diverse opinions of members.

Masculinity cultures clearly delineate gender roles, where men exhibit strong independence, assertiveness, and pursue material success, while Femininity cultures highly value feminine traits, emphasizing harmony, humility, and gentleness, with less distinct separation of gender roles.

The cultural dimensions of masculinity and femininity are also evident in advertising. In countries with a strong Masculinity culture, advertising often features competitive, comparative, and directly persuasive messages reflecting cultural dimensions. In contrast, in countries with a strong Femininity culture, advertising emphasizes harmony with society, kindness, gentleness, and finding happiness in small things.

Moreover, advertisements in masculinity-oriented cultures often promote messages focused on work and success, while those in Femininity-oriented cultures emphasize relationship-oriented and harmonious living.

While there is theoretical evidence suggesting a high relevance between Masculinity and Femininity cultures and advertising, empirical research on this topic is not as prevalent, making it challenging to find case studies for empirical analysis.

Table 4 **Characteristics of Masculinity and Femininity**

Cultural Dimension	Key Traits	Decision-Making Style	Advertising Characteristics	Gender Roles
Masculinity	Independence, competitiveness, goal-orientation, assertiveness, strong gender roles	Emphasis on independent actions and result-driven decisions	Competitive, comparative, directly persuasive messages focusing on work and success	Clear distinction between roles; men pursue independence and material success
Femininity	Harmony, cooperation, gentleness, generosity, sensitivity, empathy, balanced gender roles	Emphasis on considering diverse opinions and achieving harmony	Messages emphasizing societal harmony, kindness, gentleness, and relationship-oriented living	Less distinct separation of roles; focus on harmony and humility

High Context Culture and Low Context Culture

High context culture and low context culture are concepts used to describe communication styles based on the amount of reliance placed on contextual cues and interpretation of meaning in communication. These concepts, classified by Hall, play a crucial role in understanding and appropriately responding to communication in various fields, including advertising messages.

In high context cultures, most of the information in communication relies heavily on contextual clues such as delays, backgrounds, relationships between interlocutors, and other environmental factors, rather than primarily on verbal communication. Therefore, communication should consider non-verbal behaviors, social atmospheres, and the relationship between communicators, in addition to language. There can be differences between expressed meaning and intended meaning, with much emphasis placed on non-verbal elements and situational context. Communication in high context cultures depends on context, highlighting the importance of understanding the context. Many countries, including Korea, Japan, China, and several Middle Eastern countries, are classified as high context cultures. Advertising communication in these countries utilizes situational elements, considering human relationships and surrounding circumstances. Advertising messages reflect situational contexts and symbolic associations rather than focusing solely on information

(Mooij, 2022; Mooij and Hofstede, 2011).

In low context cultures, communication primarily relies on linguistic elements for clear and direct transmission. People in these cultures do not heavily depend on context or situations, as language itself expresses all meanings. Explicit language and direct expression are emphasized, leading to direct and clear communication. Many Western countries such as the United States, Germany, Sweden, and Australia are classified as low context cultures. Advertising communication in these countries emphasizes scientific, logical, and data-based direct appeals. In low context cultures, situational context is largely ignored, and information-focused, explicit, and direct persuasive messages are more commonly utilized than in high context cultures.

The differences in situational cultures between these cultural regions show that low context cultures such as the United States, Germany, Sweden, and Australia tend to favor information-oriented, rational appeals more than high context cultures such as Korea, Japan, China, and the Middle East. Conversely, advertising in high context cultures utilizes situational cues more frequently, employing soft-sell advertising techniques compared to low context cultures.

Table 5 **Characteristics of High and Low Context Cultures**

Aspect	High Context Culture	Low Context Culture
Communication Style	Indirect and relies on context	Direct and explicit
Reliance on Context	Heavily reliant on situational and environmental cues	Primarily reliant on linguistic elements
Use of Non-Verbal Cues	Emphasizes non-verbal elements and situational context	Minimal emphasis on non-verbal cues
Advertising Approach	Soft-sell techniques; symbolic and relational appeals	Hard-sell techniques; rational and data-driven appeals
Examples of Countries	Korea, Japan, China, Middle Eastern countries	United States, Germany, Sweden, Australia

The Major Research on the Impact of Cultural Variability on Advertising

While it is possible to study the relationship between advertising and cultural variability by separately examining these variables, the dynamism of advertising and the diversity of consumers impose some limitations on generalizing research findings.

In the field of advertising marketing, understanding cultural dimensions such as individualism and collectivism, uncertainty avoidance, power distance, masculinity and femininity as defined by Hofstede, and high-context and low-context cultures as defined by Hall, is crucial. Numerous studies in advertising, marketing, and social psychology, primarily centered around the United States, have actively investigated the relationship between these cultural dimensions and persuasive messaging (Desmarais, 2017; Glenn, Witmeyer an d Stevenson, 1977; Han, 2024).

In particular, journals like the *Journal of Advertising* and *International Journal of Advertising* have recently featured special issues on global advertising, summarizing existing research on the cultural dimensions of advertising and emphasizing the significance of research in this area. In this section, we aim to explore this phenomenon and introduce the most recent research.

The Impact of Cultural Changes on Advertisement (Han, Choi and Yu, 2016)

This study investigates the evolution of cultural values in Korean society over the past 30 years and its impact on advertising. During this transitional period, Korea has shifted from a traditional, collectivistic society to one influenced by Western individualism and materialism. Through a longitudinal content analysis of 320 Korean magazine advertisements, the research highlights how cultural modernization has transformed advertising messages to reflect changing societal norms and economic development.

Advertising is inherently culture-bound, reflecting and reinforcing dominant cultural values. Previous studies, such as Han and Shavitt's comparison of US and Korean magazine ads, reveal distinct cultural orientations. Korean ads traditionally emphasized collectivism and group harmony, while US ads favored individualism and personal achievement.

Similarly, Zhang and Gelb found that participants in collectivistic cultures, like China, responded more positively to group-oriented appeals, while those in individualistic cultures, like the US, preferred ego-oriented messages. This study builds on such research by exploring Korea's cultural shift and its reflection in advertising.

The study aims to analyze how Korean magazine advertisements have transitioned from traditional to modern cultural values, focusing on three cultural dimensions. Individualistic societies prioritize personal goals, while collectivistic cultures emphasize group well-being. Materialistic values center on possessions and personal wealth, whereas humanistic values focus on spirituality and social connections. Future-oriented cultures value planning and innovation, while past-oriented cultures emphasize traditions and heritage.

Korean magazine advertisements have used collectivistic claims less frequently and individualistic claims more frequently since the 1980s.

Humanism claims have declined in favor of materialism claims over the same period. Past orientation claims have decreased, with future orientation claims becoming more prevalent.

The study analyzed 320 advertisements from a leading Korean news magazine, sampled every ten years from the 1980s to the 2010s. March and September issues were chosen to ensure reliable comparisons across years. Ads were coded based on their cultural dimensions, with guidelines developed from prior research in persuasive communication.

The analysis revealed a significant increase in individualistic claims and a corresponding decline in collectivistic claims. In the 1980s, collectivistic appeals were equally prominent as individualistic appeals, but by the 2010s, individualistic appeals dominated Korean advertisements.

Materialistic claims showed a significant rise over

the studied period, while humanistic claims declined. Ads increasingly highlighted personal possessions and wealth rather than spiritual or social values.

Future-oriented appeals, emphasizing progress and innovation, became more prevalent, whereas past-oriented appeals, focusing on tradition and heritage, declined significantly.

The findings underscore the transformation of Korean cultural values from traditional to modern as reflected in advertising. Economic development, urbanization, education, and exposure to Western influences have driven this shift. Individualistic and materialistic values, once secondary in Korean society, now dominate advertising narratives, aligning with Korea's transition to a high-tech, consumer-driven economy.

Traditional values such as collectivism and humanism, while still present, have diminished in prominence. Similarly, the emphasis on future-oriented appeals reflects Korea's focus on progress and innovation, departing from its historical reverence for tradition.

This study highlights the dynamic relationship between cultural evolution and advertising. For marketers, understanding these shifts is essential for crafting effective messages that resonate with evolving consumer values. While traditional appeals may still hold relevance for specific demographics, modern appeals aligned with individualism and materialism are likely to be more persuasive in contemporary Korea.

Korean advertisements have mirrored the nation's cultural transformation over the past three decades, transitioning from collectivistic and traditional values to individualistic and modern orientations. This evolution underscores the role of advertising as both a reflection of and an influence on societal change, providing valuable insights for cross-cultural advertising research and practice (Han, 2021, 2024).

Chapter 6

Coordinating and Controlling Cross-Cultural Advertising

Standardization vs. Differentiation Strategy

In accordance with the recent trend of corporate marketing activities being globalized, advertisements are also becoming internationalized. As a result, every year more and more companies around the world advertise to sell goods and services outside their home countries (Buzeta, Keyzer, Dens and Pelsmacker, 2024).

Advertising Age data, which announces the advertising expenses of major advertisers and advertising agencies around the world every year by dividing them into domestic and foreign categories shows the international advertising activities of major advertising agencies and advertisers. When total advertising expenditure is divided into domestic and foreign categories, most of Korean big companies that spend the most on advertising in the world advertise more abroad than in Korea. Comparing with past data, it can be seen that the share of overseas advertising expenditures by major global companies is increasing every year.

Major global advertising agencies are also actively advancing overseas. McCannEricsson has entered more than 100 countries, including 29 countries in the Americas, 22 countries in Europe, 16 countries in Asia/Pacific, and 19 countries in Africa/Middle East, leading the way among advertising agencies in terms of overseas expansion. Saatchi & Saatchi and Gray Advertising had the second largest overseas expansion with advertising activities in a total of 66 countries, including 21 countries in the Americas and 23 countries in Europe, respectively. Among global agencies, 5 agencies entered 60 countries and 7 agencies entered more than 50 countries. Dentsu and Hakuhodo, both based in Japan, have entered more than 50 countries and are actively promoting overseas advertising. These data show that the world's major corporations and major advertising agencies are increasingly advertising in the world's diverse cultures rather than advertising in their home countries (Ad age, 2021).

Dunn and Barban pointed out five factors that contributed to the rapid growth of international advertising. First, as the number of multinational companies increased, international advertising grew rapidly. Second, with the advent of world-class brands, international advertisements were actively carried out.

Third, international advertising became necessary due to the expansion of world trade. Fourth, the improvement of living standards of people around the world also contributed to the growth of international advertising. Fifth, with the development of communication and transportation, international exchanges have been actively carried out, and advertisements between countries have increased (Brinol, Rucker and Petty, 2015).

Academic research on international advertising has also been steadily progressing since the 1960s, and recently, attention has been focused on advertising scholars to the extent that it is covered as a special issue in major advertising-related journals. In particular, most of the research papers were related to the debate about standardization and localization or specialization strategies among various areas of international advertising research. However, international advertising researchers and practitioners have yet to come to a clear conclusion about standardization and differentiation strategies, which are the most critical issues in international advertising research (Maheswaran and Shavitt, 2014).

In conducting an advertising campaign worldwide, which strategy is more desirable: standardizing all advertising messages equally or differentiating them by region? Advertising researchers have raised conflicting claims about this (Okazaki and Taylor, 2006). The school of thought that standardizing advertising messages globally is effective assumes that everyone in the world has basically the same needs, desires, and motivations. Therefore, it is possible to persuade anywhere in the world with similar or identical advertising messages. According to this school's argument, essential similarities between countries or cultures are important, and it is effective to use messages that can be used universally in producing and executing advertisements.

On the other hand, scholars who support differentiation or localization of international advertising claim that consumers are different according to countries and cultures, and therefore, each country or culture must develop an advertising campaign tailored to its characteristics. To summarize the argument of this school, although it is true that human nature is similar all over the world, the laws related to advertising differ from country to country (sometimes, in order to advertise in a foreign country, the content of the advertisement must be modified), and from country to country Advertising is the most difficult element to standardize among various marketing elements because of the great differences in the characteristics of advertising media and cultural differences. Therefore, this school recommends that a differentiated strategy of international advertising, which takes into account the differences among consumers living in different cultures and countries, produces different advertising messages (Kanso and Nelson, 2002).

Standardization strategy and differentiation strategy for international advertising are completely opposite arguments, but both schools of thought seem persuasive (Han, 1997). A few years ago in *Advertising Age*, a debate between Harvard University professor Theodore Levitt (advocating standardization strategy) and Northwesten University professor Philip Kotler (advocating differentiation strategy), both schools of thought are widely recognized. In addition, the results of existing studies have received similar empirical support to the extent that it is impossible to answer which method is more effective between the standardization strategy and the differentiation strategy of international advertising.

However, we have no choice but to raise a question as to why the results are contradictory to each other depending on the researcher and the research subject. One of the reasons for the conflicting results can be pointed out that, like most existing studies on international advertising, research in this field did not consider the various methodological problems that can arise when studying more than one culture or country

(Cavallone, 2013; Manrai, 2018; Okazaki and Taylor, 2006).

Uni-cultural research, that is, American culture-centered research, has contributed to some extent in understanding international advertising (most research papers on standardization strategy and differentiation strategy It was to find out which strategy was more effective), and it can be said that it was an important research weakness that led to conflicting results depending on the researcher and the research subject in the study of the standardization and differentiation strategy of international advertising (Cheon, Cho and Sutherland, 2007; Han, 2024). In addition, it can be said that the lack of research based on theories that can systematically reveal differences in advertising between cultures (because the studies so far have been mainly conducted from a practical standpoint) was a major cause of the conflicting results (Cavallone, 2013; Kanso and Nelson, 2002).

Therefore, future research in an effort to find a clue to resolve the debate between standardization strategy and differentiation strategy in international advertising should be based on theory according to methodological considerations that must be considered when studying two or more cultures.

Standardization Strategy

This school of thought (Professor Levitt of Harvard University is a representative scholar of this school) argues that the world is becoming a common marketplace where everyone wants the same products and lifestyles, no matter where they live. Therefore, multinational corporations must ignore the unique differences between countries or cultures and focus their efforts instead on satisfying universal needs on a global scale. Regarding this, Lynch said, "Everyone in the world has the same tastes and desires. Love, hatred, fear, desire, jealousy, joy, patriotism, obscenity, the pursuit of material comfort, mystery, and the role of food in life, people in the world are alike in every respect," it was announced, so advertising should be standardized accordingly (Kanso and Nelson, 2002).

Therefore, scholars who support standardization of international advertising believe that advertisements that are recognized as good advertisements in one country may be good advertisements in all other countries (Okazaki and Taylor, 2006). The point of view is that you can sell a product anywhere in the world with the same advertisement. Even scholars and practitioners who defended this view emphasized that international advertising is just one example of an extreme market segmentation strategy, and that it is no different from slightly changing the message according to a domestic market segmentation strategy (Cavallone, 2013; Kanso and Nelson, 2002).

The standardization strategy of international advertising was first proposed by Elinder and Fatt in the 1960s. Elinder pointed out that advertising around the world is becoming more or less the same due to the influence of European style advertising. In addition, since the similarity of consumption habits of people all over the world is more important than the differences between countries or cultures, it is argued that companies can efficiently succeed in international advertising with a standardized approach (Cheon, Cho and Sutherland, 2007; Han, 2021). People living in every country from Argentina to Zanzibar share the same hopes and desires (the pursuit of beauty, freedom from poverty, health, etc.) despite differences in culture and language. Therefore, it was argued that a standardized international advertisement is desirable in any market in the world.

Miracle (1990) is also an early advocate for a standardization strategy in international advertising. Miracle said, "Advertising has a basic mission of effectively conveying and persuading information both domestically and abroad. The requirements for effective communication are complex, but not dependent on time, place or form of communication. Therefore, it is desirable to use the same method globally in the creation of advertising messages and in the selection of media." Miracle's claim can be found in many companies' advertising activities today. When advertising abroad, many companies still make decisions in their home country (head office) regarding media selection, cost control and use of messages.

The reason for using the standardization strategy has been suggested by several researchers. Buzzell cited cost reduction, delivery of a unified image, ease of the advertising planning process, and widespread use of good ideas. Kaynak and Mitchell also suggested six reasons for the growing use of standardized international advertising: (1) political borders no longer limit psychological and emotional attitudes; (2) Planning and testing can be carried out more effectively, and therefore international advertising can be executed more objectively; (3) The speed of product innovation and the simultaneous development of new products worldwide make it necessary to create identical advertising messages worldwide; (4) an advertising message that is successful in one country is very likely to be successful in other countries; (5) costs can be effectively controlled; And finally (6) global advertising can be effective with forthcoming international television broadcasts.

Meanwhile, Meffert and Althans investigated and presented the reasons for using standardization strategies in international advertising. The survey results show that the most important reason (more than 50%) for companies to use a standardization strategy is cost reduction. 38% of companies cited unification of corporate image through the same advertisement as the reason. 31% of responding companies cited controlling and coordinating advertising campaigns as a reason. 9% of companies answered that it helps to form a good image (the sum of all responses exceeded 100% because duplicate answers were allowed).

As seen in the survey results of Mephet and Alden, the most important reason for standardizing advertising in foreign markets is cost reduction. Cost reduction is possible through economy of scale through standardized advertisement execution and copy concept. In addition, because the same advertisement is produced in many countries, the production cost can be clearly reduced compared to producing different advertisements for each country. The second important reason for a standardization strategy is to keep a corporate image the same anywhere in the world. By presenting the same trademarks, brand names and logos in many different markets, advertisers can maintain the same corporate image, and by running different advertisements in different countrics, they can avoid confusion for people traveling to different countries. As many multinational companies produce products in several countries and sell them under the same brand in many countries, the same image of products is becoming more and more important (Kanso and Nelson, 2002)..

For example, in order to ensure that it is highly regarded worldwide, AT Cross ball point pen company has corporate creative and financial control over its corporate image advertising. In addition, the headquarters planned and executed corporate advertisements in magazines sold worldwide, such as Vision, Far Eastern Economic Review and Time magazine. In Europe and Asia, the company's advertising agency purchased media, but all advertising messages were essentially the same. Delta Air Lines also used standardized international advertising. By centrally controlling its international advertising strategy, Delta ensured that all advertisements run abroad conveyed the right message about Delta in terms of quality and quantity. "We pay a lot of attention to how our company name is presented in advertising," said Jim Porter, Delta Worldwide Advertising Director. What Delta means to Americans should be the same as what Delta means to Europeans."

However, the standardization strategy of international advertising is not supported by all scholars and practitioners. Harris points out four main arguments for or on the merits of a standardization strategy: (1) one and the same advertising message can increase brand image and sales in markets around the world, and (2) the characteristics that all markets around the world are increasingly similar. (3) if the standardization strategy is not used internationally, the management technique of the company is less used, (4) cost can be reduced by achieving economies of scale by using the standardization strategy (Cheon, Cho and Sutherland, 2007; Kotler and keller, 2016; Kanso and Nelson, 2002).

Table 1 **Obstacles of Standardization on 4 P's**

Standardization Obstacles	Product	Price	Distribution	Promotion
Economic Factors	Diverse income levels	Diverse income levels	Differences in distribution structures	Usability of media
Cultural Factors	Consumer preferences and habits	Price negotiation habits	Purchasing patterns	Differences in language and attitudes

Standardization Obstacles	Product	Price	Distribution	Promotion
Competitive Factors	Nature of existing products	Competitors' raw materials and prices	Competitors' dominance in distribution channels	Competitors' budget and advertising methods
Legal Factors	Product regulations	Price regulations	Distribution regulations	Regulations on advertising and media

* Source : Terpstra, V. (1980). *International Dimensions of Marketing*. Boston, MA, USA : Kent Publishing Co.

Localization Strategy

In contrast to the standardization strategy of international advertising, which completely transfers the advertising message between cultures, the school of differentiation or localization argues that advertising messages should be implemented differently in different cultures and countries. This school argues that although people in different cultures may have similar basic needs, cultural differences create different needs in consumers. Therefore, in order to effectively cope with the cultural differences that exist in various countries, different advertising messages suitable for the characteristics of the advertising area must be produced.

This school of thought was advocated by Lenormand, who pointed out that finding common ground between cultures in order to communicate worldwide was extremely difficult. "Problems arise from differences in mental makeup, religious beliefs, habits, standards of living, laws, advertising media, agency structure and natural resources," Lenormand argued. With all these obstacles, it is unreasonable to standardize international advertising campaigns.

scholars who advocated a differentiated strategy of advertising argued that it is desirable to create different advertising messages for each culture because consumers are different depending on culture. The use of standardized international advertising is undesirable because demographic, cultural and social factors vary widely from country to country. Green, Cunningham and Cunningham, who studied consumers in four countries, the United States, France, Brazil, and India, announced that there is a marked difference between consumers in the United States and those in other countries. The authors therefore conclude that there is little possibility of a standardization strategy for international advertising. Dunn and Lorimar, who wrote an introductory text on international advertising and marketing, also noted that international marketers need to understand what can happen when advertising in foreign markets, as there are many factors that can prevent a strategy of advertising with the same message globally. It has been announced that various problems that exist should be learned through experience and preliminary investigation.

The point of this school is that you cannot advertise in different cultures of the world with the same or similar advertising messages. Therefore, always keep in mind which culture or country you are advertising in order to convey the benefits of the advertised product to your target audience. Also, among the marketing 4Ps, products and services can be standardized globally, but advertising cannot. The reason is that communication is different for each culture due to differences in culture (differences in environment, differences in values and lifestyles, differences in traditions, differences in music, etc.). Since the purpose of advertising is to convey information and persuade potential customers in order to have a preference for and want to buy the advertised product after viewing it, great advertising cannot be made without understanding the culture.

The role of culture in advertising is very important. Hall writes, "It is impossible to avoid culture, no matter how hard humans try, because it penetrates the roots of the human nervous system and determines how humans perceive the world. Human beings cannot act or interact in any way except through the medium of culture", emphasizing the closeness between culture and communication.

One of the concepts widely used in studying the relationship between culture and communication is the distinction between low-context culture and high-context culture, and this distinction suggests that a differentiated strategy for international advertising is desirable (Wells, Burnett and Moriarty, 1985). In a high-context culture, the meaning of a message cannot be understood ignoring the surrounding environment (context), but in a low-context culture, the meaning of a message is independent of the surrounding environment and can be understood completely independently. Therefore, the difference in communication between these cultures is that an advertising message to persuade people in a low-context culture cannot succeed in a high-context culture, and conversely, a persuasive message from a high-context culture cannot succeed in a low-context culture. hint
In addition, Day-After Recall, which is frequently used as a method of measuring advertising effectiveness, is appropriate in low-context culture, but Wells pointed out that it is not an appropriate method in high-context

culture (Mooij, 2022).

The problem of language, especially translation, that arises when an advertisement made in one country is executed in another country as it is, also shows that standardization strategies are practically difficult. A typical example is the failure of Pepsi-Cola, which translated "come alive with Pepsi" in the United States as "come out of the grave with Pepsi" in Germany. Also, "Body by Fisher" was advertised as "Corpse by Fisher". An American ink company has also failed by mistranslating advertisements in Mexico. An outdoor advertisement titled 'Avoid embarrassment (from leaks and stains)' was put up. The meaning of this advertisement was that there would be no problem with using this ink because it would never leak, so it was an appropriate advertisement for Americans. However, to Spanish-speaking Mexicans, 'embarrassed' in this advertisement meant 'to be pregnant'. Mexicans who did not know English mistook this outdoor advertisement for an advertisement for contraceptives, not an ink advertisement. Errors that occur in the process of translating advertisements from one language into another are examples of various difficulties in standardizing international advertisements (Han and Shavitt, 1994).

Differences in cultural factors related to tradition, custom, and religion also suggest that a differentiated strategy is preferable to a standardized strategy in international advertising. For one thing, different cultures have different concepts of language. The term innovativeness includes not only the act of purchasing and using a new product in the United States, but also the act of passing on information or experience about a new product to friends and neighbors, but innovation in France is socially highly regarded. Because it is a concept that does not work, consumers who purchase and use a new product do not try to convey the attributes, information or experience of the product to the people around them. This example suggests that it is necessary to check what the meaning of words used in advertisements has in foreign countries, and that standardization strategies for international advertisements are not easy.

The school of differentiation strategy of international advertising puts special emphasis on differences between cultures. Therefore, in order to execute a successful international advertising campaign, it is necessary to understand the differences between cultures and to create advertising messages that reflect these differences.

Compromise Ctrategy

There are scholars who argue that it is more realistic to use a compromise between the two strategies depending on the situation, rather than using an extreme (or absolute) distinction between the standardization strategy and the differentiation strategy of international advertising (Han, Choi and Yu, 2016). They emphasize that the localization strategy and the differentiation strategy should be well balanced according to the situation, carefully considering the advantages and disadvantages of the standardization strategy and the additional costs of the differentiation strategy. This intermediate strategy has the advantage of being able to make use of both the strengths of the standardization strategy (economy of scale, formation of the same image, etc.) and the strengths of the differentiation strategy (development of messages tailored to the characteristics of the advertising area).

Indeed, the findings of previous research suggest that an increasing number of multinational companies are adopting either a standardization strategy or a differentiation strategy. Rather than using only one strategy, it was shown that a combination of the two strategies was used. According to the results of the study published in 1976, 70% of companies used a standardization strategy, 20% used a differentiation strategy, and only 10% compromised between the two strategies. However, the study published in 1986 found that, unlike in 1976, firms used differentiation strategies (45%) more than standardization strategies (20%) and compromised strategies (35%). According to the results of the most recent study found that more than half of companies (56%) are using a compromise strategy.

In contrast, only 8% of companies use a standardization strategy, compared to 36% using a differentiation strategy. Comparing the degree of use of standardization, localization, and compromise strategies by year, the number of companies using standardization strategies has decreased by 62% in the last 12 years, from 70% in 1976 to 20% in 1986 and 8% in 1988. The number of companies using the localization strategy increased from 20% in 1976 to 45% in 1986, but decreased again to 36% in 1988, two years later. On the other hand, the number of firms using compromise strategies increased by about 5.5 times over the past 12 years, from 10% in 1976 to 35% in 1986 and 56% in 1988. These results show that in recent years, multinational companies have gradually reduced the frequency of using the standardization strategy and the differentiation strategy in conducting international advertising, and compared the strengths and weaknesses of

Figure 1 **Use of Standardization, Differentiation and Compromise Strategies (%)**

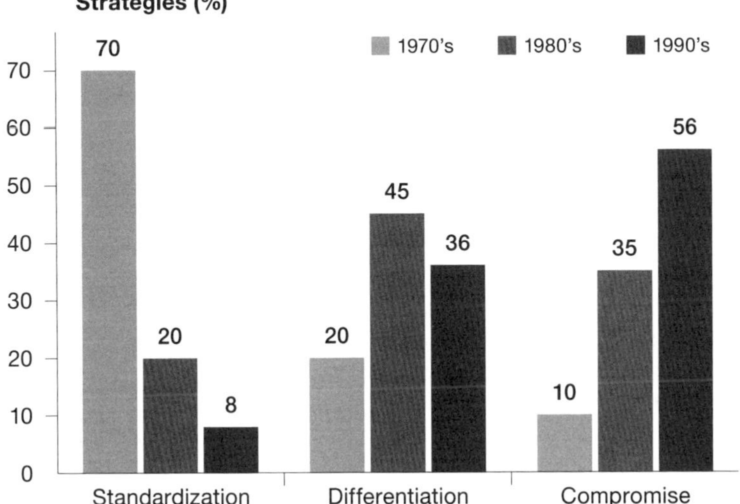

the two extreme strategies to select a compromise strategy that suits the characteristics of the company (Han, 2024).

On the other hand, the use of a standardization strategy and a differentiation strategy should be considered according to the following 11 conditions, suggesting that the standardization strategy and differentiation strategy should be used in combination appropriately depending on the situation: (1) home country and host country markets with similar economic conditions are more likely to use a standardization strategy (on the other hand, markets with different economic conditions are more likely to use a differentiation strategy). (2)

standardization strategies are more effective when products are marketed to all consumers worldwide (rather than targeted to specific regions). (3) standardization strategy is advantageous when consumer behavior and lifestyle are similar. (4) standardization strategy is possible if the function of the product is equivalent in different cultures. (5) standardization strategy is desirable when the competitive situation of a company is similar in various markets. (6) standardization strategy can be used when the marketing problem to be solved by a company is similar in various markets. (7) for industrial goods and high technology products, it is appropriate to use a standardization strategy. (8) the more similar the conditions of the social production base are, the more advantageous the standardization strategy is. (9) standardization strategy is more effective when the company's decision maker considers the whole world as a common market. (10) in major decision-making on standardization issues, the standardization strategy is more effective as long as a strategic consensus can be reached between the parent company and its own company.
(11) it is desirable to pursue a standardization strategy in companies where policy establishment and resource distribution are centralized.

Table 2 Comparison of Characteristics of International Advertising Strategies

Strategy	Definition	Advantages	Disadvantages	Examples
Standardization	Focuses on satisfying universal needs by standardizing advertising messages across different markets	Cost reduction, unified corporate image, ease of planning, economies of scale	May overlook cultural differences, less effective in markets with diverse consumer behaviors	Global campaigns with consistent messaging, e.g., Delta Airlines' global ads
Localization	Adapts advertising messages to the specific cultural and market characteristics of each region or country	Effectiveness in addressing cultural differences, tailored messaging, stronger connection with local consumers	Higher costs, more complex planning and execution, potential for inconsistent brand image	Localized campaigns addressing specific cultural norms, e.g., region-specific Pepsi ads
Compromise	Combines elements of both standardization and localization to balance cost efficiency with cultural adaptation	Leverages cost advantages of standardization while maintaining cultural relevance through localization	Can be challenging to balance, may still involve higher costs than pure standardization	Use of a combination strategy depending on market conditions, e.g., many multinational corporations' flexible campaigns

Problems of Standardization Strategy and Localization Strategy and Direction for Future Research

Problem

Although the debate about standardization strategy and discrimination and strategy in international advertising has continued for the past 30 years, no clear conclusion has yet been reached. Since the research so far has been mainly descriptive research for advertising practice rather than theoretical analysis, it may be a natural result that these researchers disagree. Therefore, I think it is important to present the problems of the existing research and what needs to be improved for future research (Han, 2021).

Problems related to standardization strategy and differentiation strategy and suggestions for future research can be presented at the same time. In the following, this chapter briefly reviews what the problems are and then makes suggestions for future research. The problems include four things.

First, the definitions of standardization strategy and differentiation strategy were used differently depending on the researcher. Some researchers classify the standardization strategy and the differentiation strategy according to whether international advertising decisions are made in the home country or the local country, while others classify the two strategies according to how much the head office influences the local branch. In addition, some scholars classify standardization and differentiation strategies according to matters to be considered when establishing international advertising strategies, and some scholars analyze the contents of advertisements and analyze the degree of standardization and differentiation strategies. Some researchers have even distinguished between standardization strategies and differentiation strategies according to whether the model (spokesperson) was changed when producing advertisements abroad. This confusion will be eliminated only when the definition of standardization strategy and differentiation strategy is preceded, and research is conducted accordingly.

Second, the standardization and differentiation strategies of international advertisements can vary greatly depending on various factors such as cultural factors, product types, agency philosophies, government regulations, existence of advertising media, and product life cycle. However, studies so far have been conducted without considering these factors at all. In other words, although identifying the moderating factors between standardization strategy and differentiation strategy is very useful for multinational advertisers and marketers in setting the strategy or production direction of international advertising, existing studies have excluded these factors and only Overall, the standardization strategy and differentiation strategy were analyzed.

For example, the use of a standardization strategy and a differentiation strategy may differ depending on the type of product. Han and Shavitt's research results found that the degree of advertisement use and effect differed between individualistic and collectivistic cultures depending on personal items (chewing gum, sneakers, etc.) and collective items (detergent, iron, etc.). In the case of personal products, individualistic advertising appeals were widely used and more effective in all cultures, regardless of individualism or collectivism. However, in the case of collective goods, collectivistic appeals were used more often than individualistic appeals in collectivistic cultures and were more effective in persuading people, whereas individualistic appeals were more used and more persuasive in individualistic cultures. These results show that the use and effectiveness of standardization strategies and differentiation strategies differ greatly depending on the type of product. In other words, it implies that the standardization strategy is effective for personal products, but that advertising messages should be differentiated according to the characteristics of culture for collective products.

A study by Weinberger and Spotts, which analyzed the contents of an American advertisement and a British advertisement by classifying them into an FCB grid, also showed that the advertising appeal method differs greatly depending on the type of product. In the case of high-involvement-thinking products, the rates of usage of the US and UK advertisements were similar at 23.9% and 25%, respectively. It turned out to be used a lot. In particular, in the case of high involvement-emotional products (clothing, cosmetics, perfume, sunglasses, etc.), US advertisements did not use Yuumo at all. This study shows that standardization strategies are somewhat feasible for high-involvement-incident products using Yuumo appeals, but differentiation strategies are more desirable for other product groups

Third, it is difficult to generalize the research results because existing studies are too biased toward developed countries such as the United States and Japan in the selection of study countries. In order to generalize the research results, it is not desirable to consider too practical positions when selecting a country to be studied. In particular, it is foolish to try to apply the results of a survey conducted only to extremely limited countries, such as the United States and Japan, to advertisements in other countries as well. Despite the difficulties of the study, it will be possible to generalize the research results only when a survey in this field is conducted targeting several countries in Asia, the Middle East, Africa, South America, and Europe. How the selection of research target countries is desirable will be explored in the proposals for future research.

Fourth, understanding the homogeneity and differences between different cultures is also very important in this field of research. It is very important to understand the local culture in order to successfully execute advertising in a country with a completely different culture. Therefore, understanding the characteristics of consumers living in different cultures and using them when establishing an advertising strategy can help companies decide whether to use a standardized strategy or a differentiated strategy when advertising abroad. To this end, international advertising researchers must look at what methodological issues to consider when conducting research on two or more cultures.

First is the distinction between etic and emic. The emic approach is a culture-specific study that uses concepts that can only be applied in a particular culture to study attitudes and behaviors that occur uniquely within that culture. The ethic approach, on the other hand, is a research method that seeks out global attitudes and behaviors and develops a pan-cultural or culture-free measure. Therefore, the emic approach is a study of individual cultures, and with this approach, the researcher cannot compare the differences between cultures and cannot suggest universal general laws. However, the ethic approach can compare differences between cultures and seek general laws of human conduct. Although the distinction between emics and ethics must be made in international advertising research, studies so far have applied emics or pseudoetics, so it has not been a correct way to compare differences between cultures. The results of the investigation using the pseudoetic method also help to understand the differences between cultures to some extent. However, when interpreting the study results, it is necessary to interpret them carefully, taking into account the limitations of pseudoetics. A pseudo-etic approach can widen and, in some cases, narrow the real differences between cultures. Therefore, combined emic-etic rather than pseudo-etic is a better method for studying differences between cultures, and it is more desirable to use a combined emic-etic in international advertising research. . In addition to emic and ethic issues, other issues to be considered when studying two or more cultures simultaneously include equivalence of language, equivalence of function, equivalence of concept, equivalence of sample, and equivalence of measurement. Details of this will not be discussed in this article due to space constraints.

As examined above, studies on the standardization strategy and differentiation strategy of international advertisements contain several problems. Although research in this field has been continued for a long time, no clear conclusion has been drawn due to these problems. Next, focusing on the four problems presented above, we will find out what needs to be considered in future research for the development of research on the standardization strategy and differentiation strategy of international advertising.

Table 2 **Problems and Suggestions for Future Research**

Problems	Explanation	Suggestions for Future Research
Inconsistent definitions of standardization and differentiation strategies	Definitions vary by researcher, leading to confusion in research and inconsistent findings.	Establish consistent definitions of standardization and differentiation strategies for clarity.

Problems	Explanation	Suggestions for Future Research
Lack of consideration for moderating factors in strategy selection	Factors like cultural differences, product types, government regulations, and media availability are often ignored.	Incorporate moderating factors such as product type, cultural differences, and media availability into analysis.
Bias toward developed countries in study focus	Existing studies focus excessively on countries like the U.S. and Japan, limiting the generalizability of results.	Expand research scope to include diverse countries across Asia, Africa, South America, and the Middle East.
Limited understanding of homogeneity and differences between cultures	Studies often fail to balance emic (culture-specific) and etic (universal) approaches, leading to methodological issues.	Adopt a combined emic-etic approach and ensure linguistic, functional, conceptual, sampling, and measurement equivalence.

Future Study of Standardization and Localization Strategy

In the case of cross-cultural research targeting two or more cultures or countries, the researcher must consider additional issues in addition to the issues to be considered when conducting research within one culture. Nevertheless, studies so far have mostly applied measurement tools applied in the United States (the culture leading the research) to other cultures as well. Although these single culture-centered studies have contributed to some extent in understanding the advertising phenomenon between countries or cultures, it is thought that there are still many areas to be improved. The following will improve the problems of the research on the standardization strategy and differentiation strategy described above, and make some suggestions for future research for the development of research in this field (Maheswarna and Shavitt, 2014; Hilton, 2022).

First, multiple method studies should be conducted to increase the validity of the research results (Han, 1990). As mentioned before, it is difficult to interpret the results of studies in more than one culture or country as they are. Therefore, multi-method studies are needed to overcome the inherent disadvantages of each methodology. For example, in the case of research on standardization and differentiation strategies of international advertising, content analysis and experimental research are conducted at the same time, and the results of the two methods are compared and supplemented. Content analysis analyzes social phenomena as they are (high external validity), but cannot deduce causal relationships between variables (low internal validity). On the other hand, experimental research has high internal validity because variables are manipulated and external variables are controlled, but external validity is low because the manipulation of variables is artificial and the subject can sense the experimental situation, so it cannot be studied in a natural environment. Therefore, by using both methods that are complementary in terms of internal validity and external validity, problems that may arise when studying two or more cultures can be minimized. In addition, if the results of the two method studies are the same, the possibility of generalization of the study results will increase, and if conflicting results are obtained, it will provide an opportunity for additional research to find out why different results are obtained depending on the research method.

Second, studies so far have mainly analyzed the contents of advertisements executed in various countries or investigated the use status of standardization strategies and differentiation strategies by asking questions to practitioners using a questionnaire method. Therefore, it is insufficient to identify which strategy is more effective between the standardization strategy and the differentiation strategy. It is assumed that this tendency is because content analysis or questionnaire surveys are less controversial than effect studies, are more convenient to study, and are cheaper in terms of cost. However, if the ultimate goal of advertising is sales, it is expected that effect research should be conducted despite the difficulties of research.

Third, a time series study should be conducted in the future rather than a fragmentary study of a certain period. As examined in Chapter 2, the current state of research, the degree of standardization, differentiation, and use of compromise strategies in international advertising has changed greatly from the 1970s to the 1980s. Time-series studies will not only show trends in these changes, but also reveal the underlying causes of why they occur.

Fourth, in international advertising research, the research target country should be expanded. Research so far has been conducted only on very limited countries, mainly the United States and Japan, making it difficult to generalize the research. As pointed out in the problems of research in this field, it is desirable to examine the strengths and weaknesses of standardization strategies and differentiation strategies through studies in various countries around the world. However, in reality, it is impossible to conduct research on all countries of several continents, such as Asia, America, Europe, and Africa, due to cost, time, and limitations of researchers. Therefore, at least a more scientific method should be applied in selecting the research target country compared to the previous methods (Abuhashesh et al., 2021).

Fifth, it is desirable that the country of origin of the researcher diversify along with the expansion of the research target country. In the field of cross-cultural research, a considerable number of research papers published in academic journals have 5 to 10 researchers. In particular, in some studies, as many researchers participate as the number of countries to be studied, each researcher studies his or her own country, and in the end, it is often seen that all researchers discuss in common. It is thought that such a study is also necessary in international advertising research. In the case of advertisers and advertising agencies, it is believed that such a study is possible because they are active in many countries.

Sixth, studies so far mainly investigated whether a standardization strategy or a differentiation strategy is effective when US companies advertise overseas. This has happened because until now, most countries except the United States have not shown much interest in international advertising. In the era of globalization and openness, countries other than the United States are now more often advertised overseas. Therefore, rather than applying the contents of research centered on the United States to other countries as it is, it is necessary to pioneer this field through research in its own way.

Seventh, in the future, research should be conducted to find out the factors mediating the standardization strategy and the differentiation strategy. Studies so far have focused on which strategy is more desirable when viewed as a whole, without considering the circumstances or characteristics of the product. However, as pointed out in the problem, the standardization strategy and the differentiation strategy were found to be affected by the situation or product. Therefore, beyond the stage of researching whether it is an absolute standardization strategy or an absolute differentiation strategy, it should be planned to find out various possible variables that affect it (Maheswaran and Shavitt, 2014). Only these studies will be of practical help to practitioners in advertising to set up advertising strategies abroad.

Eighth, it is necessary to expand the international advertising research area. So far, only the practical status of standardization and differentiation has been studied through the empirical method. International advertising laws, media conditions, advertising conditions, government policy, creative style, advertising agency management, agency commission system, relationship between advertisers and agencies, and agency organizations should also be taken into consideration.

Finally, it may be a good way to develop and

investigate a model to find out the standardization and differentiation of international advertising. The developed model not only enables other researchers to see at a glance how research has been conducted, but also enables repetition of research, one element of scientific research.

Table 3 **Summary of Future Study of Standardization and Localization strategy**

Future Research Focus	Key Issues
Multiple Method Studies	Combine methods like content analysis and experimental research to address validity issues, ensuring complementary internal and external validity
Effectiveness Studies	Focus on effectiveness studies to measure which strategy (standardization vs. differentiation) achieves better sales outcomes
Time-Series Studies	Conduct longitudinal studies to identify trends and underlying causes of changes in strategy use over time
Expansion of Research Target Countries	Expand research to cover diverse countries beyond the US and Japan, ensuring generalizable results
Diversification of Researchers' Origin	Include researchers from diverse countries to provide a more comprehensive perspective in cross-cultural advertising studies

Future Research Focus	Key Issues
Beyond US-Centric Studies	Shift focus from US-centric studies to research methods applicable across diverse nations in a globalized era
Identifying Mediating Factors	Investigate situational and product-specific variables mediating standardization and differentiation strategies
Expanding Research Areas	Incorporate aspects like advertising laws, media conditions, government policy, creative styles, and agency management
Developing Models	Develop models to standardize research methods and enable reproducibility and broader applicability of results

Conclusion

Along with the internationalization of the advertising industry, research on international advertising has been actively conducted since the 1960s. Among various areas of international advertising research, the debate on standardization strategy and differentiation strategy is the most published and researched. Scholars advocating a standardization strategy argue that differences between countries are only differences in degree and not fundamentally. In other words, since consumers around the world have basically similar wants and needs, the same advertisement can satisfy them worldwide.

On the other hand, scholars who insist on a differentiation strategy argue that consumers living in different cultures have different needs and desires, so differentiated advertisements tailored to each culture should be considered in consideration of cultural differences that exist between different cultures. Although the majority of studies have argued about these two opposing schools, recent scholars have suggested that it is preferable to compromise between the two strategies depending on the situation rather than to make an extreme distinction between the two schools. The intermediate strategy is the view that a better advertisement can be made by taking the advantages of both strategies.

However, research in this area has not yet yielded clear conclusions. This chapter summarizes the research so far on standardization, differentiation strategy, and compromise strategy, which are the most important areas of international advertising research, and presents research problems and suggestions for future research. As for the problems of the study, confusion in the definition of standardization strategy and differentiation strategy, lack of research according to the situation, problem of country selection and methodological problems were examined. And, as suggestions for future research, multi-method research, implementation of effect research, time series research, expansion of research target countries, discharge of researchers with diverse cultural backgrounds, research in countries other than the United States, intervention factors, expansion of research areas and model development.

Chapter 7

Empirical Studies of Cross-cultural Advertising

Advertising and Culture (Comparative Cultural Perspective)

Han, S., and Shavitt, S. (1994). Persuasion and Culture: Advertising Appeals in Individualistic and Collectivistic Societies. *Journal of Experimental Social Psychology*, 30(4), 326-350.

This study explores the influence of cultural dimensions, specifically individualism and collectivism, on advertising appeals in different countries. Grounded in Hofstede's cultural framework and Triandis' work on cultural variability, the research aims to examine how these cultural orientations manifest in persuasive communication and determine their effectiveness in individualistic versus collectivistic societies. The research is motivated by the growing recognition of culture's role in shaping consumer behavior and advertising strategies.

The authors draw on seminal works in cultural

psychology, including Hofstede's (2001) and Triandis' (1995) studies, which highlight individualism and collectivism as core cultural dimensions. Individualistic cultures prioritize personal goals, autonomy, and independence, while collectivistic cultures emphasize group harmony, familial ties, and collective well-being. Prior research has identified cultural differences in communication styles, but there is limited empirical evidence on how these differences translate into advertising appeals. The study aims to address this gap by examining cross-cultural advertising in the United States and Korea.

The study posits two primary hypotheses: First, advertisements in individualistic cultures (e.g., the United States) will predominantly feature appeals to individual benefits, personal success, and independence. Second, advertisements in collectivistic cultures (e.g., Korea) will emphasize group benefits, harmony, and family ties more frequently.

The research comprises two studies. Study 1 (Content analysis of magazine advertisements from the United States and Korea. The researchers examined the frequency and type of advertising appeals in a representative sample of ads) and Study 2 (Experimental analysis assessing the persuasiveness of culturally congruent versus incongruent appeals. Participants from the United States and Korea were exposed to tailored advertising messages, and their responses were measured).

U.S. advertisements significantly favored appeals to individual benefits, personal achievements, and autonomy, consistent with an individualistic orientation. In contrast, Korean advertisements more frequently emphasized ingroup benefits, social harmony, and familial bonds, reflecting a collectivistic culture. Participants' evaluations of advertisements were more favorable when the appeals aligned with their cultural orientation. U.S. participants rated ads with individualistic appeals higher, while Korean participants showed stronger preferences for collectivistic appeals.

The findings underscore the profound impact of cultural values on advertising strategies and consumer receptiveness. The study highlights the importance of cultural congruence in persuasive communication, providing valuable insights for global marketers. By aligning advertising appeals with cultural orientations, brands can enhance message effectiveness and consumer engagement. This research contributes to the broader understanding of cross-cultural communication and underscores the need for culturally sensitive advertising in international markets.

Shavitt, S., Ashok K., Shang, J., and Torelli, C. (2006). The Horizontal/Vertical Distinction in Cross-Cultural Consumer Research. *Journal of Consumer Psychology*, 16(4), 325–356.

This paper introduces the horizontal/vertical distinction in cultural orientations as a significant refinement to the widely studied individualism-collectivism (INDCOL) framework. Horizontal orientations value equality, while vertical orientations emphasize hierarchy. The study investigates how these dimensions provide new insights into consumer behavior and advertising, complementing and extending the traditional INDCOL framework.
The primary purpose is to explore the implications of horizontal and vertical cultural distinctions for personal values, consumer persuasion, self-presentation, and methodological approaches.

The authors build on foundational cross-cultural theories, such as Hofstede's cultural dimensions and Triandis' INDCOL framework, highlighting the limitations of the broad individualism-collectivism distinction.
They integrate insights from studies on power distance, self-construals, and cultural values to emphasize the distinctiveness of horizontal and vertical orientations. Prior research reveals that horizontal societies (e.g., Denmark, Sweden) prioritize equality and modesty, while vertical

societies (e.g., the United States, Korea) focus on status, competition, and hierarchy. These orientations influence self-construals, consumer preferences, and advertising effectiveness.

The study aims to address the following questions. How do horizontal and vertical cultural orientations predict consumer values and behaviors?

What distinct patterns of self-presentation and advertising responses emerge across horizontal and vertical societies? How does the horizontal/vertical distinction enhance the understanding of INDCOL effects in cross-cultural consumer research?

This research is primarily conceptual, supported by empirical findings from prior studies and new analyses. Key methodologies include three methods. Content analysis of advertisements across cultures to assess the prevalence of hierarchy and status themes. Surveys measuring horizontal and vertical cultural orientations and their relationship with consumer behaviors and values. Experimental designs testing the persuasiveness of culturally congruent advertising appeals.

The results of the study showed the following. Horizontal individualism (HI) is associated with values of uniqueness, self-reliance, and equality, while vertical individualism (VI) emphasizes status, achievement, and power. Horizontal collectivism (HC) fosters sociability and benevolence, whereas vertical collectivism (VC) stresses hierarchy and deference to authority. Advertising appeals focusing on hierarchy and status are more effective in vertical cultures, while egalitarian and community-oriented appeals resonate in horizontal cultures. Cultural orientation influences self-presentation styles, with HI linked to self-deceptive enhancement and HC to impression management.

The horizontal/vertical distinction provides a nuanced understanding of cross-cultural consumer behavior, offering predictive value beyond the traditional INDCOL framework. It highlights the importance of considering hierarchy and equality as distinct cultural dimensions in advertising and consumer research. The study advocates for future research to develop methodological tools for measuring these orientations and to examine their implications across diverse cultural and consumer contexts. This work contributes to the refinement of cultural theories and practical applications in global marketing strategies.

Geng, C., Xiaoyan, Y., Wang, H., and Liu, H. (2012). Culturally Incongruent Messages in International Advertising. *International Journal of Advertising*, 31(2), 355–376.

This study examines the effects of culturally incongruent messages in international advertising on consumer responses. It seeks to understand how cultural values (terminal vs. instrumental) and the ethnic background of advertising models (local vs. foreign) moderate the effectiveness of such messages. By leveraging Social Judgement Theory (SJT), the authors aim to analyze the role of message congruency in shaping consumer attitudes, counter-arguments, brand perception, and buying intentions. This research addresses the strategic importance of culturally sensitive advertising in global markets.

The study integrates insights from Hofstede's cultural dimensions and prior cross-cultural advertising research. It highlights the prevalence of standardized international advertising and the challenges posed by cultural incongruencies. Previous findings show that congruent messages generally yield positive consumer responses, while incongruent messages can provoke cultural conflict. However, emerging evidence suggests that incongruent messages might succeed under specific conditions, such as the use of foreign models or appeals based on less central cultural values.

The paper posits the following hypotheses. Responses to incongruent ads using terminal values are less positive than those using instrumental values (H1). Incongruent ads with local models elicit more negative responses than those with foreign models (H2). Counter-arguments are greater for incongruent ads using terminal values compared to instrumental values (H3). Counter-arguments are greater for incongruent ads with local models compared to foreign models (H4). Counter-arguments mediate the interaction effects of message congruency and contextual variables (H5). Message congruency and contextual variables significantly affect brand attitude and buying intention (H6).

A 2×2×2 experimental design was used to manipulate message congruency, cultural values, and model backgrounds in print advertisements for a fictional digital camera. The study included 320 undergraduate students in China as participants. Dependent variables included attitude towards the advertisement (Aad), counter-arguments (CA), attitude towards the brand (Ab), and buying intention (BI). Manipulation checks ensured the effectiveness of the experimental design.

Ads with congruent appeals yielded more positive Aad, Ab, and BI than incongruent appeals. Terminal values in incongruent messages provoked significantly more counter-arguments than instrumental values, supporting H1 and H3.

Foreign models reduced negative responses to incongruent messages, confirming H2 and H4. Counter-arguments mediated the effects of message congruency and contextual variables on Aad, validating H5.

While message congruency and contextual variables significantly affected Aad, their impact on Ab and BI was limited. H6 was partially supported.

The findings highlight the nuanced dynamics of culturally incongruent advertising. Instrumental values and foreign models mitigate the adverse effects of cultural incongruencies, providing actionable insights for marketers targeting diverse cultural audiences. The study underscores the importance of framing and positioning strategies, such as foreign consumer cultural positioning (FCCP), to enhance ad effectiveness in global markets. These findings contribute to the broader understanding of cultural value interactions and their implications for international advertising strategies.

Advertising and Culture (Individualistic Culture and Collectivist Culture)

Hornikx, J., and de Groot, E. (2017). Cultural Values Adapted to Individualism–Collectivism in Advertising in Western Europe: An Experimental and Meta-analytical Approach. *International Communication*, 79(3), 298–316.

This study investigates the impact of cultural value adaptation in advertising on persuasion and consumer liking within Western European contexts. Specifically, it evaluates whether culturally adapted advertisements based on individualism-collectivism (INDCOL) are more persuasive and better received than unadapted advertisements. The research is motivated by previous findings that showed the effectiveness of cultural adaptation in North America and Asia but found inconsistent results in Western Europe. The authors aim to clarify these inconsistencies through six experiments and a subsequent meta-analysis.

The study builds upon the theoretical foundation of Hofstede's cultural dimensions and prior cross-cultural advertising research. It highlights the importance of value congruity—the alignment of advertising appeals with culturally significant values—in enhancing consumer responses. Research has consistently shown that culturally congruent messages are more persuasive in individualistic (e.g., U.S.) and collectivistic (e.g., China) cultures. However, European studies often reveal weaker or non-significant effects, suggesting that Western European consumers might be less sensitive to value adaptation due to cultural dynamics or value hierarchies.

The study addresses two primary research questions. Is a culturally adapted, individualistic value appeal more persuasive than a collectivistic appeal for Western European consumers (RQ1)? Is a culturally adapted, individualistic value appeal better liked than a collectivistic appeal for Western European consumers (RQ2)?

The study employs six experiments conducted in Belgium, the Netherlands, and the United Kingdom, targeting 574 participants. Each experiment uses a between-subjects design, with participants exposed to either an individualistic or collectivistic advertisement for various products (e.g., laptops, mobile phones). Dependent variables include persuasion (attitudes toward the product and purchase intentions) and ad liking. The experiments are complemented by a meta-analysis combining the results of these experiments with prior studies on INDCOL value adaptation.

The experiments show no consistent evidence that

individualistic appeals are more persuasive or better liked than collectivistic appeals in Western Europe. For instance, in some cases, collectivistic appeals performed equally well or better. The meta-analysis confirms these findings, indicating no significant effect of cultural adaptation on persuasion ($r = -.034$) or ad liking ($r = -.004$) for Western European consumers. Additional analyses suggest that Western European consumers' insensitivity to cultural adaptation may be influenced by factors such as value congruity, European integration, and a shift toward collective-oriented behaviors.

The findings challenge the generalizability of cultural adaptation effects in advertising, particularly in Western Europe. The authors argue that globalization and European integration may have reduced the salience of national cultural values, making consumers less responsive to culturally adapted messages. This research provides important implications for international advertisers, suggesting that adaptation strategies should consider regional nuances and evolving cultural dynamics in Europe. Future research should explore the interplay between cultural values, practices, and consumer behavior to further refine cross-cultural advertising strategies.

Hsu, S., and Barker, G. (2013). Individualism and Collectivism in Chinese and American Television Advertising. *International Communication*, 75(8), 695–714.

This study aims to understand how individualism and collectivism values are portrayed in ads targeting different generational groups in China and the United States. The research addresses how China's rapid economic growth and social changes, particularly since the 1979 open-door policy, have influenced the cultural values reflected in advertisements. It explores generational shifts in value orientations within China and contrasts them with the relatively stable cultural values in the U.S.

The study draws on Hofstede's cultural dimensions, emphasizing the individualism-collectivism dichotomy, and integrates related theories, including Triandis' horizontal and vertical distinctions. While American culture is traditionally characterized by strong individualistic values, Chinese culture has been rooted in collectivism. However, economic modernization in China has introduced individualistic elements, particularly among younger generations. Advertising, as a cultural product, reflects these shifts and serves as a lens for understanding evolving societal values. Previous studies suggest that cultural congruency in advertising enhances persuasiveness and consumer connection.

The study examines the following hypotheses. Individualistic values and modern themes are more prominent in television ads targeting younger Chinese audiences than collectivistic values and traditional themes (H1).

Collectivistic values and traditional themes are more prominent in ads targeting older Chinese audiences than in ads targeting younger audiences (H2). Compared to Chinese ads, American ads targeting both younger and older audiences exhibit stronger individualistic values and weaker collectivistic values and traditional themes (H3). There are no significant differences in cultural values between American ads targeting younger versus older audiences (RQ1).

The study employs a content analysis of 566 television ads from China and the U.S., sampled based on generational viewing preferences. Ads are coded for individualism, collectivism, modernity, and tradition using a 0-2 scale. The coding schema, adapted from Zhang and Shavitt (2003), captures the degree to which ads emphasize these values through imagery, taglines, and narratives. Data analysis involves t-tests and ANOVAs to compare value prominence across generational and cultural groups.

Ads targeting younger Chinese audiences scored

higher on individualism than those targeting older audiences, partially supporting H1. Collectivistic values were more prominent in ads targeting older Chinese audiences, partially supporting H2. American ads exhibited higher individualism and modernity and lower collectivism and tradition scores compared to Chinese ads, supporting H3. No significant differences were found in cultural values between younger and older American audiences, supporting RQ1.

Generational differences in Chinese ads reflect a cultural shift toward individualism among younger generations, influenced by economic modernization and global exposure.

The findings reveal a generational cultural shift in China, with younger audiences embracing individualistic values alongside traditional collectivistic ideals. This bicultural integration contrasts with the stable individualistic values observed in American ads. The study underscores the importance of considering generational and cultural dynamics in advertising strategies. It also highlights the need for future research to explore the interplay between economic development, cultural change, and consumer behavior in other transitional societies,

Han, S. (2016). Advertisements that Reflect Culture, Advertisements that Create Culture, Korean Journal of Advertising. 27(2), 29-54.

This study investigates the relationship between advertising and culture, focusing on how advertisements reflect and create cultural values. Unlike prior cross-cultural comparative research, this study adopts a longitudinal approach within a single cultural context to explore how advertising content in South Korea has evolved over the past 50 years (1970s to 2010s). The purpose is to understand the cultural shifts reflected in advertisements and their interplay with societal transformations driven by globalization, technological advancements, and economic growth.

The study builds upon existing theories regarding the cultural functions of advertising, emphasizing the dual role of ads as economic drivers and cultural tools. Prior research has identified four main trends. The influence of national cultural values on advertising effectiveness in foreign markets.

Comparative analyses of advertising content and effectiveness between Eastern and Western cultures. Investigations into cultural values embedded in international advertisements. Debates on whether advertisements primarily reflect existing cultural values or create new ones. Key theoretical frameworks include Hofstede's cultural dimensions (e.g., individualism vs. collectivism) and theories of social judgment and cognitive congruence in consumer response.

The study seeks to address four primary research questions. How have individualistic and collectivistic values in South Korean advertisements changed over the past 50 years? What shifts have occurred in egalitarian versus authoritarian values in South Korean ads during this period? How have traditional versus modern family values been portrayed in South Korean advertisements? What changes have occurred in the representation of materialistic versus humanistic values?

The study employs content analysis of magazine advertisements, analyzing 1,633 ads from 1973 to 2013. The sample includes two prominent South Korean magazines, selected for their broad readership and consistent publication. Ads were coded for four cultural dimensions: individualism - collectivism, egalitarianism – authoritarianism, modern – traditional family values, and materialism - humanism. Coding reliability was ensured through cross-validation, and longitudinal trends were analyzed using chi-square tests and descriptive statistics.

Individualism-Collectivism: Ads emphasizing

individualism have increased significantly since the 1980s, surpassing those highlighting collectivism. By the 2000s, individualistic messages accounted for approximately 70% of ads. Egalitarianism-Authoritarianism: Egalitarian values have gradually gained prominence in South Korean advertisements, reflecting societal shifts influenced by democratization and globalization.

Modern-Traditional Family Values: Modern family values, such as equality and generational harmony, have increasingly replaced traditional hierarchical family representations. Ads depicting progressive gender roles and shared decision-making have become more common. Materialism-Humanism: Materialistic values, characterized by messages promoting consumption and ownership, have risen, while humanistic values emphasizing ethics and spirituality have declined. This trend aligns with South Korea's economic development and consumer culture.

The findings illustrate that South Korean advertisements have both reflected and contributed to the country's cultural evolution. The increasing dominance of individualism, egalitarianism, and materialism indicates a convergence with Western cultural values, driven by economic globalization and technological advancements. The study underscores the importance of analyzing cultural shifts through longitudinal research and highlights the dual role of advertising as both a mirror and a catalyst of cultural change. Future research should explore the interplay of traditional and modern values in emerging digital advertising platforms.

Okazaki, S., Barbara M., and Diehl, S. (2013). A Multi-Country Examination Of Hard-Sell and Soft-Sell Advertising Comparing Global Consumer Positioning In Holistic- and Analytic-Thinking Cultures. *Journal of Advertising*, 53(3). 258-272.

This study explores the effectiveness of soft-sell and hard-sell advertising appeals in holistic- and analytic-thinking cultures. The authors investigate whether soft-sell appeals, characterized by implicit and image-based content, elicit more favorable consumer responses across diverse markets compared to hard-sell appeals, which are direct and information-focused. The research is grounded in the Global Consumer Culture Positioning (GCCP) framework and examines its applicability in creating effective global advertising strategies. The study's primary purpose is to assess how cultural cognitive styles influence perceptions of advertising appeals and to provide actionable insights for global branding efforts.

The study builds on the GCCP framework and

integrates concepts of holistic and analytic thinking from cultural psychology. Holistic thinkers (e.g., East Asians) focus on context and relationships, whereas analytic thinkers (e.g., Westerners) emphasize object attributes and detachment from context. Previous research suggests that soft-sell appeals align better with holistic thinking due to their abstract and indirect nature, while hard-sell appeals are more congruent with analytic thinking. The authors highlight a gap in understanding how these cultural orientations influence consumer perceptions of global advertising appeals.

The study tests four hypotheses. Soft-sell advertisements are perceived more favorably in both analytic- and holistic-thinking cultures compared to hard-sell advertisements (H1). Soft-sell advertisements are perceived as more credible in both analytic- and holistic-thinking cultures compared to hard-sell advertisements (H2). Soft-sell advertisements are perceived as less irritating in both analytic- and holistic-thinking cultures compared to hard-sell advertisements (H3). Soft-sell advertisements drive higher purchase intention in both analytic- and holistic-thinking cultures compared to hard-sell advertisements (H4).

The study adopts a multi-country survey framework, targeting consumers in five countries: Japan, France,

Italy (holistic cultures), and Germany, the United States (analytic cultures). Stimuli included professionally created advertisements for a fictitious wristwatch brand, using soft-sell and hard-sell appeals. Key dependent variables were attitude toward the advertisement, advertising credibility, advertising irritation, and purchase intention. A between-subject design was employed, and data were analyzed using t-tests and interaction effects.

Attitude Toward Advertisement: Soft-sell ads were rated more favorably in holistic cultures (e.g., Japan, France) compared to hard-sell ads. However, differences in analytic cultures were less pronounced, partially supporting H1. Advertising Credibility: Credibility differences between soft- and hard-sell ads were insignificant in most countries, except Italy, where soft-sell ads were perceived as more credible. H2 was not fully supported.

Advertising Irritation: Soft-sell ads were consistently rated as less irritating across all countries, with stronger effects in holistic cultures. H3 was supported. Purchase Intention: Soft-sell ads led to higher purchase intentions only in the U.S. Differences in other countries were not statistically significant, leading to partial support for H4.

The findings demonstrate that soft-sell advertising appeals are generally more effective in holistic-thinking cultures, reducing irritation and generating favorable attitudes. While soft-sell appeals are less consistently superior in analytic-thinking cultures, they still offer advantages over hard-sell approaches in building a uniform global brand image. The study emphasizes the importance of considering cultural cognitive styles in developing advertising strategies and supports GCCP as a practical framework for global marketing. Future research should explore additional product categories and cultural contexts to enhance the generalizability of these findings.

Cross-cultural Research Methodology

Salzberger, T., and Sinkovics, R. (2006). Reconsidering the Problem of Data Equivalence in International Marketing Research. International Marketing Review, 23(4), 390-417.

This paper examines the challenges of achieving data equivalence in international marketing research, with a focus on comparing the utility of the multigroup confirmatory factor analysis (MG-CFA) approach and the Rasch measurement theory (RMT). The study emphasizes the importance of data equivalence for cross-cultural studies, which underpins the reliability of international comparisons. It aims to determine whether RMT offers advantages over MG-CFA in ensuring measurement equivalence and to explore its applicability in real-world settings.

The authors review key concepts in data equivalence, including measurement invariance, cross-cultural validity, and dimensional consistency. They highlight MG-CFA as the dominant method within classical test theory (CTT) and contrast it with RMT, an underutilized framework in marketing research. RMT's foundations in item response theory (IRT) are presented as potentially superior for ensuring specific objectivity and addressing differential item functioning (DIF). The authors also discuss the importance of translation accuracy and scale reliability in cross-cultural research.

The study explores the following expectations rather than formal hypotheses. More items will fit the MG-CFA model compared to the Rasch model due to RMT's stricter criteria (E1). Items lacking scalar invariance in MG-CFA will exhibit DIF in the Rasch model (E2). Some items excluded under MG-CFA will fit the Rasch model in specific groups, leading to larger scales in RMT (E3).

The study uses data on technophobia collected from 927 respondents across the UK, Mexico, and Austria. Both MG-CFA and RMT approaches are applied to evaluate data equivalence. MG-CFA is conducted using LISREL software to assess configural, metric, and scalar invariance. RMT analysis is performed with the partial credit model, focusing on item fit statistics and DIF analysis. Results are compared based on fit statistics, item retention, and cross-group equivalence.

MG-CFA Analysis: Six items were retained from an initial 30-item scale, with full metric invariance established but partial scalar invariance achieved. Differences in latent means were observed, with Austria showing lower technophobia than the UK and Mexico.

Rasch Analysis: A 13-item scale was developed, including items that exhibited DIF or were excluded in MG-CFA. Only four items were invariant across all groups, while others fit specific groups.

Comparative Insights: Contrary to E1, the Rasch model retained more items than MG-CFA. Support for E2 was observed, as DIF in the Rasch model corresponded to scalar non-invariance in MG-CFA. E3 was also supported, with the Rasch model accommodating group-specific items.

The study highlights RMT's advantages in addressing data equivalence, particularly its ability to handle DIF and retain culturally specific items. While MG-CFA remains a robust method within CTT, RMT offers a more nuanced approach to measurement in cross-cultural contexts. The findings advocate for broader adoption of RMT in marketing research to enhance cross-cultural validity. Future research should investigate RMT's application in other domains and examine its integration with traditional methodologies.

Poortinga, Y. (1989). Equivalence of Cross-Cultural Date: An Overview of Basic Issues. *International Journal of Psychology*, 24(6), 737-756.

This paper addresses fundamental issues related to the equivalence of cross-cultural data in psychological research. The study emphasizes the importance of establishing comparable measurement scales across cultures to ensure the validity of cross-cultural comparisons. Poortinga argues that the absence of scale equivalence can lead to erroneous conclusions and highlights the necessity of rigorous methodological frameworks to validate cross-cultural studies.

The paper builds on the logic of cross-cultural comparisons, focusing on measurement equivalence as a cornerstone of valid inferences. It references prior work in cross-cultural psychology, psychometrics, and statistical validation methods to establish a theoretical foundation.

Key topics include levels of measurement (nominal, ordinal, interval, and ratio) and their implications for cultural research. The study draws on a broad range of sources to contextualize the challenges of ensuring scale identity across diverse populations.

The central research question examines how cross-cultural equivalence can be defined and empirically validated. Specific hypotheses include as follows. Equivalence at different measurement levels (e.g., structural, functional) is necessary for valid cross-cultural comparisons. Statistical analyses can identify and correct for non-equivalence in psychometric data. The interpretability of cultural differences depends on the extent to which equivalence is achieved.

The paper presents a conceptual framework rather than empirical data. Poortinga classifies inferences about cross-cultural differences and discusses the logical and empirical feasibility of these inferences. Statistical techniques, including factor analysis and item response theory, are discussed as tools for assessing psychometric equivalence. The study also outlines steps for validating measurement instruments across cultures.

A classification system for cross-cultural inferences, categorized by the type and level of measurement equivalence. Criteria for assessing equivalence, including metric, scalar, and functional equivalence. Practical recommendations for designing studies that ensure valid comparisons across cultures. The paper highlights the potential pitfalls of ignoring equivalence, such as cultural bias and misinterpretation of results.

Poortinga's work underscores the critical role of measurement equivalence in cross-cultural psychology. The study provides a comprehensive overview of theoretical and methodological challenges, offering guidelines for researchers to enhance the validity of their work. By emphasizing the need for rigorous statistical and conceptual frameworks, the paper contributes to the advancement of cross-cultural research methodologies.

International Advertising Strategy (Standardization Strategy vs. Localization Strategy)

Cheon, H., Cho, C., and Sutherland, J. (2007). A Meta-Analysis of Studies on the Determinants of Standardization and Localization of International Marketing and Advertising Strategies. *Journal of International Consumer Marketing*, 19(4), 109-147.

This meta-analysis investigates the determinants of

standardization versus localization in international marketing and advertising strategies. The study aims to provide clarity on the ongoing debate by analyzing 152 studies published between 1960 and 2004, which include 1,268 statistical models. Key goals include identifying patterns and factors that influence standardization and localization and assessing their impact on marketing mix elements, advertising, and regional differences. The study's findings aim to guide multinational corporations (MNCs) in designing effective global marketing strategies.

The authors synthesize research on international marketing strategies, focusing on standardization, which seeks uniformity across markets, and localization, which tailors approaches to individual markets. Key concepts include the marketing mix (4Ps), target markets, and environmental factors. Past studies often lacked consistent methodologies or comprehensive analyses. This research addresses these gaps by systematically reviewing and quantitatively synthesizing prior findings using meta-analytic techniques.

The study examines several research questions. How do the marketing mix (product, price, place, promotion) and organizational factors affect the degree of standardization or localization? What roles do environmental factors, target markets, and market positions play in influencing strategy choice? How do advertising-related factors, such as ad appeals, media choices, and consumer perceptions, contribute to strategy effectiveness? Are there significant regional differences (e.g., North America vs. Asia, North America vs. Europe) in strategy effectiveness?

The study employs a quantitative meta-analysis methodology, aggregating data from 152 articles in top-tier journals. The analysis focuses on nine marketing and advertising moderators: product, price, promotion, distribution, target market, market position, environmental factors, organizational factors, and advertising appeals. Effect sizes are calculated to compare the impact of standardization versus localization. Statistical techniques include heterogeneity tests, confidence intervals, and fail-safe N calculations to ensure robustness.

Marketing Mix and Organizational Factors: Standardization is generally more effective for product, price, promotion, and distribution strategies, with minimal support for localization. Organizational factors, such as centralized decision-making, also favor standardization. Target Market and Environmental Factors: Localization shows moderate effectiveness for target markets and environmental factors due to cultural and economic variability. However, the impact is context-dependent.

Advertising Appeals: Informational (hard-sell) appeals slightly favor localization in high-context cultures, while affective (soft-sell) appeals strongly support localization, emphasizing cultural congruence in ad messaging.

Regional Differences: Standardization is more effective in North America and Europe, whereas localization is preferred in Asia due to distinct cultural and consumer behavior patterns.

The findings highlight the nuanced interplay between standardization and localization, suggesting that a contingency approach may often be the most effective strategy. Marketing mix elements and organizational factors favor standardization, while advertising appeals and target markets benefit from localization. The study underscores the importance of adapting strategies to regional and cultural contexts to maximize effectiveness. Future research should explore emerging markets and integrate digital advertising trends to extend the findings.

Kanso, A., and Nelson, R. (2002). Advertising Localization Overshadows Standardization. *Journal of Advertising Research*, January/February, 79-89.

This study examines the debate between localization and

standardization in international advertising strategies, focusing on the effectiveness of localized campaigns in diverse cultural contexts. The authors argue that localization, which tailors advertisements to specific cultural and market conditions, often yields superior results compared to standardized global campaigns. The primary purpose is to challenge the prevailing emphasis on standardization in global marketing and provide evidence supporting the value of culturally sensitive advertising.

The study builds on theoretical foundations from international marketing and cross-cultural communication research. It reviews key concepts such as advertising appeals, cultural congruence, and consumer perception. Previous research often highlights the cost-efficiency and consistency of standardization, while localization is associated with higher engagement and cultural relevance. However, empirical evidence supporting localization's superiority remains limited. The authors also explore the role of media channels and regional preferences in shaping advertising effectiveness.

The study seeks to answer the following questions. How does localization compare to standardization in terms of consumer response and brand perception? What factors influence the effectiveness of localized versus standardized advertising campaigns? Are there specific product categories or market conditions where localization is more advantageous?

The authors conduct a qualitative meta-analysis of case studies and prior research on international advertising campaigns. They analyze successful and unsuccessful examples of standardized and localized strategies across various industries and markets. Additionally, they review industry reports, consumer surveys, and cultural studies to identify patterns in advertising effectiveness. The study includes an assessment of campaigns in regions such as Asia, Europe, and North America.

Localization Effectiveness: Localized advertising consistently outperformed standardized campaigns in culturally diverse markets, particularly in Asia and the Middle East. Cultural congruence and relevance were critical factors driving consumer engagement.

Standardization Challenges: Standardized campaigns often faced resistance due to cultural misalignment, leading to misinterpretation and reduced impact.

Product Categories: Localization was especially effective for culturally sensitive products (e.g., food, clothing) and services requiring a strong emotional connection.

Regional Insights: In Western markets, standardized campaigns were moderately effective for utilitarian products but less so for hedonic or luxury items, where emotional resonance was crucial.

The findings underscore the importance of localization in international advertising, particularly for markets with distinct cultural identities. While standardization offers cost benefits and brand consistency, its limitations in addressing cultural nuances can hinder effectiveness. The authors advocate for a hybrid approach, combining standardized elements (e.g., brand identity) with localized content to optimize engagement. This study provides actionable insights for multinational corporations seeking to balance global reach with cultural sensitivity in their advertising strategies. Future research should explore the integration of digital media and emerging technologies in enhancing localization efforts.

Future Research Direction in Global and Cross-cultural Advertising Researsh

Maheswaran, D., and Shavitt, S. (2000). Issues and New Directions in Global Consumer Psychology. *Journal of Consumer Psychology*, 9(2), 59-66.

This study addresses the emerging field of global consumer

psychology, focusing on the interaction between culture and consumer behavior. Despite the growing recognition of culture's pivotal role, cross-cultural consumer research remains underdeveloped. The authors aim to identify key conceptual and methodological issues in the field, such as the emic versus etic research approaches and the challenge of achieving measurement equivalence. The paper highlights the need for expanded research on cultural constructs, geographical regions, and mediating processes to advance theoretical and practical insights into consumer psychology.

The authors review the foundational frameworks of cross-cultural consumer behavior, emphasizing the dichotomy between individualism and collectivism as a dominant construct. They discuss the relevance of other dimensions, such as power distance, uncertainty avoidance, masculinity versus femininity, and horizontal versus vertical cultural orientations. Prior research often relies on theoretical frameworks developed in the U.S., leading to a lack of validation in other cultural contexts. The paper advocates for integrating indigenous perspectives to enrich global consumer psychology.

The study explores several critical questions. How can emic and etic research approaches be integrated to improve cross-cultural consumer research? What methodologies ensure measurement equivalence across cultures? How can the study of cultural constructs be expanded beyond individualism and collectivism? What are the mediating processes that drive cultural differences in consumer behavior?

The paper adopts a conceptual and theoretical approach rather than empirical methods. It synthesizes existing literature and identifies gaps in cross-cultural consumer research. Key recommendations include the followings. Using Berry's (1989) integrated model of emic and etic approaches to develop universal frameworks. Applying advanced statistical techniques, such as item response theory, to address measurement equivalence. Expanding cultural dimensions studied in consumer psychology and exploring their implications for marketing and advertising.

Investigating mediating variables, such as self-construals and cognitive processing styles, to understand cultural influences on consumer behavior.

The paper provides a comprehensive framework for advancing global consumer psychology. Emic and etic approaches are not mutually exclusive; their integration can yield robust cultural insights. Measurement equivalence requires attention to conceptual, construct, item, and scalar equivalence to ensure valid cross-cultural comparisons. Horizontal and vertical dimensions of individualism-collectivism, along with other cultural constructs, deserve more research focus. Mediating variables, such as self-construal and cognitive processing, can illuminate the underlying mechanisms of cultural differences in consumer responses.

The study underscores the importance of blending theoretical rigor with methodological innovation to advance global consumer psychology. It calls for a broader geographical focus, incorporating underrepresented regions like Latin America and Africa, and highlights the need for collaboration with indigenous scholars to capture culture-specific insights. Future research should aim to generalize theoretical frameworks across cultures while acknowledging cultural uniqueness, paving the way for more effective global marketing strategies.

Chapter 8

Cross-cultural Advertising Blunders

Why Cultures Matter in Cross-cultural Settings?

In cross-cultural advertising, understanding the cultural context of the target market is crucial for successful communication (Wells, Burnett and Moriarty, 1995). Advertising is not just about promoting products or services; it is about creating a connection with the audience by aligning with their cultural values, beliefs, and emotions (Mooij, 1994). When brands operate globally, they encounter a wide variety of cultural settings where customs, traditions, and social norms differ significantly (Brinol, Rucker and Petty, 2015). A lack of sensitivity to these cultural differences can lead to significant advertising blunders that may damage brand reputation and cause financial loss.

Cultures provide the framework through which audiences interpret messages (Gudykunst and Ting-Toomey, 1988; Mooij, 2022). In cross-cultural settings, these interpretations can vary dramatically. For example, humor, symbolism, color meanings, and even language can carry very different connotations depending on the cultural background. In one culture, a symbol might be seen as positive and uplifting, while in another, it may be considered offensive or inappropriate. For instance, the color white is often associated with purity and weddings in Western cultures, while in some Asian cultures, it is associated with mourning and funerals. Humor also varies significantly—what is considered funny in one culture may be seen as rude or confusing in another. As a result, companies must carefully navigate these cultural waters to ensure that their advertising resonates positively and avoids unintended negative impacts (Mooij, 1994).

Another important consideration is the role of non-verbal cues, such as gestures, facial expressions, and body language. Non-verbal communication can differ significantly between cultures. For example, a thumbs-up gesture, which is generally seen as a positive sign in many Western countries, can be offensive in certain Middle Eastern countries. The use of imagery and symbolism must also be approached with cultural awareness, as these elements carry different meanings across various cultural contexts. Understanding these nuances is essential for brands to avoid potential pitfalls and effectively communicate their intended messages.

In addition, the pace of societal changes and generational differences within cultures can further complicate advertising efforts (Han and Shavitt, 1994). Younger generations may adopt global trends and values that differ from those of older generations, even within the same cultural context. For example, while older consumers in Japan may prefer advertisements that emphasize tradition and harmony, younger audiences might respond more positively to modern, innovative, and individualistic messages. Advertisers must stay attuned to these intra-cultural differences to create campaigns that resonate across different segments of the population (Glenn, Witmeyer and Stevenson, 1977).

To successfully navigate cross-cultural advertising, companies should invest in local market research, collaborate with cultural experts, and involve local talent in the creative process. By doing so, they can gain a deeper understanding of the cultural nuances that shape consumer behavior, allowing them to tailor their messages appropriately and avoid missteps that could harm their brand image (Ford, Mueller and Mueller, 2023).

Understanding Culture and Advertising to Success in Cross-cultural Advertising

The relationship between culture and advertising is intricate. Culture shapes individuals' worldviews, behavior, and preferences, which in turn influence how they perceive advertising messages (Mooij, 2022). In cross-cultural advertising, understanding and respecting these cultural elements is crucial to developing effective campaigns that communicate intended messages clearly and accurately (Ford, Mueller and Mueller, 2023; Han and Shavitt, 1994).

Hofstede's cultural dimensions theory provides an insightful framework for understanding cultural differences (Hofstede, 2001). It highlights factors such as individualism vs. collectivism, power distance, masculinity vs. femininity, uncertainty avoidance, and long-term vs. short-term orientation - all of which play a role in shaping consumer perceptions and reactions to advertising. For example, in individualistic cultures, advertisements often emphasize personal achievement, independence, and self-expression, while in collectivist cultures, ads may focus more on family, community, and group harmony. This distinction affects not only the content but also the tone and appeal of advertising messages. Advertisers must understand these cultural dimensions to craft messages that resonate with the values and expectations of their audience (Han and Shavitt, 1994).

Another critical aspect of cross-cultural advertising is language. The literal translation of slogans or promotional text can lead to misinterpretations if the cultural context is not taken into account. For example, idioms and colloquial phrases that work well in one language may lose their intended meaning or even become offensive when directly translated. Furthermore, imagery, symbols, and color choices all have cultural significance that can vary widely across different regions. For instance, the color red is often associated with good fortune and celebration in China, while it can symbolize danger or warning in some Western countries. What may be considered an auspicious color in one country could symbolize mourning in another. Thus, cultural awareness is key to ensuring the success of advertising campaigns in diverse cultural settings.

The role of humor in advertising is another area where cultural differences play a significant role. Humor is often culturally specific, relying on shared references, social norms, and linguistic nuances. A humorous ad that performs well in one market might fall flat or even offend in another. For example, British humor, which often includes sarcasm and irony, may not be easily understood or appreciated in cultures that value direct and straightforward communication. Therefore, advertisers must be cautious when using humor in cross-cultural campaigns, ensuring that it aligns with the local audience's sense of humor and cultural sensitivities (Zafran and Masud, 2023).

Additionally, cultural attitudes towards authority and social hierarchy can influence how advertising messages are received. In high power distance cultures, where hierarchical structures are respected, advertisements that feature authoritative figures or endorsements from respected leaders may be more effective. In contrast, in low power distance cultures, consumers may prefer messages that emphasize equality and challenge authority. Understanding these cultural attitudes allows advertisers to tailor their campaigns in a way that resonates with the target audience's values and social dynamics.

The concept of masculinity vs. femininity, as described by Hofstede, also affects advertising strategies. In cultures with a high masculinity index, such as Japan and Italy, advertisements may focus on themes of success, competitiveness, and strength. Conversely, in cultures with a higher femininity index, such as Sweden and the Netherlands, ads may emphasize care, quality of life, and social welfare. These cultural values impact not only the product positioning but also the emotional appeals used in advertising. By aligning the message with the cultural context, advertisers can create campaigns that effectively appeal to the target audience's priorities and preferences.

Long-term vs. short-term orientation is another cultural dimension that affects advertising. In long-term oriented cultures, such as China and South Korea, advertisements that emphasize perseverance, future rewards, and long-lasting benefits tend to be more effective. On the other hand, in short-term oriented cultures, such as the United States, ads that highlight immediate gratification, quick results, and short-term pleasures are more likely to resonate. Understanding these temporal preferences helps advertisers position their products in a way that aligns with the cultural mindset of the audience.

Uncertainty avoidance, another of Hofstede's dimensions, refers to the degree to which people in a culture feel comfortable with ambiguity and uncertainty. In high uncertainty avoidance cultures, such as Greece and Portugal, consumers may prefer advertisements that provide clear information, guarantees, and assurances about the product. In contrast, in low uncertainty avoidance cultures, such as Singapore and Denmark, consumers may be more open to creative, abstract, or humorous advertisements that leave room for interpretation. Tailoring the level of detail and type of messaging to match the audience's tolerance for uncertainty can significantly enhance the effectiveness of advertising campaigns.

To successfully navigate these cultural differences, companies must go beyond merely translating language; they need to translate meaning. This involves adapting not only the words but also the visuals, context, and underlying messages to fit the cultural expectations of the target audience. For example, while a direct call to action might work well in a culture that values assertiveness, a more subtle approach might be necessary in a culture that values indirect communication (Buzeta, Keyzer, Dens, and Pelsmacker, 2024; Kanson and Nelson, 2002).

Cultural adaptation also extends to digital advertising, where user behavior and platform preferences can vary widely between regions. In some countries, social media platforms like Facebook and Instagram dominate, while in others, local platforms such as WeChat in China or LINE in Japan are more popular. Understanding these preferences allows advertisers to select the most effective channels for reaching their audience and ensures that the content is optimized for the platform's cultural context.

Another essential aspect of cross-cultural advertising is the concept of collectivism versus individualism in consumer behavior. In collectivist cultures, consumers are more likely to be influenced by group opinions and social norms. As such, advertisements that incorporate testimonials from family members or community leaders, or that show products being used in social settings, are more likely to be effective. In contrast, in individualistic cultures, advertisements that emphasize personal benefits, uniqueness, and self-expression are often more persuasive. This distinction affects not only the messaging but also the types of influencers or brand ambassadors that are chosen to represent the product (Han, 2024).

Finally, the concept of "glocalization" has become increasingly important in cross-cultural advertising. Glocalization refers to the adaptation of global brand messages to fit local cultural nuances while maintaining a consistent overall brand identity. Successful glocalization involves balancing the need for a cohesive global brand image with the need for local relevance. Brands like McDonald's and Coca-Cola have successfully implemented glocalization by adapting their product offerings, advertising messages, and even store designs to align with local tastes and preferences while retaining their core brand identity.

In summary, the relationship between culture and advertising is complex and multifaceted (Mooij, 1994). Advertisers must be attuned to cultural differences in values, language, humor, symbolism, social hierarchy, and consumer behavior to create campaigns that resonate with diverse audiences. By leveraging frameworks like Hofstede's cultural dimensions, investing in local market research, and adopting a glocalized approach, brands can navigate the challenges of cross-cultural advertising and build meaningful connections with consumers around the world.

Table 1 Culture and Advertising

Cultural Aspect	Key Features	Examples
Individualism vs. Collectivism	Individualistic cultures emphasize personal achievement and self-expression; collectivist cultures emphasize family and community harmony	Advertisements in the US (individualistic) vs. Japan (collectivist)
Language	Literal translations can lead to misinterpretations; idioms and symbols vary by culture	Color red: auspicious in China, danger in Western cultures

Cultural Aspect	Key Features	Examples
Humor	Humor is culturally specific and may not translate effectively across regions	British sarcasm may not work in straightforward cultures like the US
Attitudes Towards Authority	High power distance cultures value hierarchical endorsements; low power distance cultures prefer equality in messaging	Celebrity endorsements in Korea vs. egalitarian messaging in Scandinavia
Masculinity vs. Femininity	Masculinity cultures focus on success and competition; femininity cultures emphasize care and social welfare	Japan's competitive ads vs. Sweden's emphasis on harmony
Long-term vs. Short-term Orientation	Long-term cultures value perseverance and future rewards; short-term cultures emphasize immediate gratification	South Korea's ads promoting long-term benefits vs. US ads on quick results
Uncertainty Avoidance	High uncertainty avoidance cultures prefer clear and detailed information; low uncertainty avoidance cultures tolerate ambiguity and creativity	Insurance ads in Greece vs. abstract creative ads in Denmark
Digital Platform Preferences	Platform preferences vary regionally; global platforms like Facebook vs. local platforms like WeChat	WeChat ads in China vs. Instagram ads in the US

Cultural Aspect	Key Features	Examples
Collectivism vs. Individualism in Consumer Behavior	Collectivist cultures respond to social endorsements; individualist cultures value personal benefits and uniqueness	Family-centric testimonials in China vs. self-expression-focused ads in the US
Glocalization	Balancing global brand consistency with local cultural relevance (e.g., McDonald's regional adaptations)	Coca-Cola adapting flavors for local markets while keeping the global brand identity

Cases of Mistake

Pepsi in China (Source: Kotler and Keller, 2016)

In an attempt to attract Chinese consumers, Pepsi launched an advertising campaign with the slogan "Pepsi Brings You Back to Life." Unfortunately, the translation into Chinese was problematic. The phrase was interpreted as "Pepsi brings your ancestors back from the grave," which was not only culturally offensive but also insensitive to deeply held beliefs about ancestry and respect for the deceased in Chinese culture. In China, reverence for one's ancestors is a deeply ingrained tradition, and any implication of disrespect can lead to strong negative reactions. This slogan, therefore, touched on a highly sensitive cultural aspect, resulting in a backlash from the public and a tarnished brand image.

The misinterpretation occurred due to a lack of understanding of the nuances in Chinese language and culture. The phrase "back to life" can be understood metaphorically in Western cultures, but in Chinese, the direct translation had unintended and literal connotations. This case exemplifies the importance of cultural awareness and the risks involved when attempting a direct translation without considering local beliefs and traditions.

Pepsi's failure in this campaign serves as a stark reminder of the necessity of cultural localization in advertising. Companies must ensure that their messages are accurately and appropriately adapted to the cultural context of the target audience. This involves more than just language translation—it requires a deep understanding of cultural values, beliefs, and sensitivities. Had Pepsi invested in local cultural consultants and conducted thorough market testing, they could have avoided this costly mistake.

Moreover, the incident highlights the broader challenge faced by multinational companies when expanding into new cultural territories. Successful

https://baijiahao.baidu.com/s?id=1769824143940695341&wfr=spider&for=pc).
* Source : Kotler, P., and Keller, K. L. (2016). Marketing Management. Pearson.

global advertising requires a delicate balance between maintaining a consistent brand identity and adapting messages to fit local cultural norms. Pepsi eventually revised their marketing strategy in China, incorporating more culturally resonant themes and engaging local talent to help craft messages that appealed to Chinese consumers.

Ford Pinto in Brazil (Source: Ricks, 2009)

Ford's attempt to market the Pinto in Brazil is a classic example of how linguistic oversight can lead to unintended consequences. The model name "Pinto" in Brazilian Portuguese is slang for male genitals, which resulted in ridicule and embarrassment for the brand. This unfortunate naming led to poor sales, as consumers could not take the vehicle seriously, and it ultimately forced Ford to rename the vehicle in the Brazilian market.

The blunder demonstrates the critical importance of conducting thorough linguistic checks and cultural assessments before launching products in new international markets. A seemingly harmless word in one language can carry highly inappropriate or comical connotations in another, leading to a negative brand perception. In Brazil, the inappropriate meaning of "Pinto" undermined Ford's efforts to market the car as a reliable and respectable vehicle, instead turning it into the subject of jokes and derision.

This case also underscores the broader risks associated with global branding. Names, symbols, and phrases that are effective in one cultural context may carry drastically different meanings elsewhere. Ford's mistake could have been avoided with more extensive market research and consultation with local experts who understood the cultural and linguistic landscape of Brazil. By failing to do so, Ford not only faced financial losses but also suffered damage to its reputation.

In response to the backlash, Ford had to make significant adjustments, including rebranding the vehicle with a different name that would not evoke negative associations. This costly rebranding effort serves as a cautionary tale for other companies looking to expand internationally. The Pinto incident highlights the value of localizing not only advertising messages but also product names to ensure they are culturally appropriate and resonate positively with the target audience.

The Ford Pinto case has since been widely studied in business schools and marketing courses as an example of the pitfalls of inadequate cultural due diligence. It serves

* Source : Ricks, D. A. (2009). Blunders in International Business. Wiley.

as a reminder that successful international marketing requires more than just translating language—it requires an understanding of cultural nuances, sensitivities, and consumer perceptions. Brands must be proactive in conducting thorough checks and seeking local input to avoid similar missteps in the future.

KFC in China (Source: Usunier and Lee, 2013)

KFC's well-known slogan "Finger-lickin' good" became a classic example of how mistranslation can significantly impact a brand's reputation in an international market. When the slogan was translated into Chinese, it became "Eat your fingers off," which naturally caused confusion and discomfort among Chinese consumers. The mistranslation did not convey the intended positive, indulgent connotation of enjoying food but instead evoked an alarming and unappetizing image, which was far from the message KFC wanted to deliver.

The cultural misstep illustrated how crucial it is for international brands to adapt their marketing messages accurately and in a culturally appropriate way. In China, where language is often nuanced and meanings can shift dramatically depending on phrasing, failing to capture the correct tone can lead to misunderstandings that undermine a brand's image. This case serves as a reminder that cultural sensitivity in advertising is not only about translating words but also about understanding the cultural and emotional context in which those words are received.

KFC eventually rectified the mistake by working with local marketing experts who helped them craft slogans that resonated more effectively with Chinese consumers. They emphasized the joy and community aspect of dining, which aligns well with Chinese cultural values surrounding food as a social experience. The recovery effort also involved extensive consumer engagement campaigns that included locally popular promotions and culturally relevant menu items, such as congee, to appeal to the tastes of Chinese consumers.

The lessons from KFC's experience in China highlight the importance of localization beyond simple language translation. Effective localization involves adapting the marketing message to align with cultural expectations, linguistic norms, and consumer preferences. By collaborating with local experts and conducting in-depth market research, brands can avoid costly blunders and build positive relationships with consumers in new markets.

The incident also underscores the broader

https://www.businessinsider.com/global-marketing-failures-kfc.
* Source : Usunier, J. C., and Lee, J. A. (2013). Marketing Across Cultures. Pearson.

challenges that multinational companies face when expanding into culturally diverse regions. Understanding the target audience's cultural context can mean the difference between a successful campaign and a failed one. KFC's eventual success in China, after adjusting their strategy, demonstrates that while mistakes can be damaging, they can also be opportunities for learning and improvement.

Gerber in Africa (Source: Mooij, 2019)

Gerber's entry into the African market is a notable example of how a failure to adapt packaging to local cultural norms can lead to significant misunderstandings. When Gerber used the same baby food packaging in Africa as it did in the United States, featuring a cute baby on the label, it created confusion among local consumers. In many African countries, it is common practice for product labels to depict the actual contents of the package, particularly in regions with lower literacy rates where pictorial labels help convey information about the product. As a result, many consumers assumed that the jars contained baby meat, leading to confusion, discomfort, and even outrage.

This blunder highlights the importance of understanding and respecting local customs and consumer expectations when entering new markets. In this case, Gerber overlooked a crucial aspect of consumer behavior in the African market: the use of visual cues to identify the product. For many consumers, especially those who rely on imagery due to limited literacy, the baby image on the label implied that the jar's contents were somehow related to the picture—an alarming implication that damaged Gerber's brand image.

The incident underscores the broader lesson that successful cross-cultural marketing involves more than simply transferring products from one market to another without modification. Companies must invest in market research and understand the cultural and social norms of their target audience. By failing to do so, Gerber not only faced financial losses but also risked long-term damage to its reputation in the region.

In response to the backlash, Gerber had to re-evaluate its packaging strategy for the African market. The company learned that effective communication requires tailoring every aspect of the product, including its visual presentation, to meet the needs and expectations of local consumers. This adaptation is not just about language translation but also about cultural translation—ensuring that every detail aligns with how consumers perceive and understand products.

Gerber's experience in Africa serves as a powerful reminder for other multinational companies: cultural norms and consumer habits must be at the forefront of any market entry strategy. Properly researching and understanding these aspects can prevent costly missteps and help build trust and acceptance among new customers. Brands must work with local experts, conduct focus groups, and test product designs to ensure that they

GERBER IN AFRICA

When Gerber started selling baby food in Africa, they used US packaging with the smiling baby on the label.

In Africa, companies routinely put pictures on labels of what's inside, since many people can't read.

https://image1.slideserve.com/2676964/gerber-in-africa-l.jpg
* Source : Mooij, M. (2019). Global Marketing and Advertising: Understanding Cultural Paradoxes. Sage Publications.

are suitable for the target market.

Parker Pens in Mexico (Source: Usunier and Lee, 2013)

Parker Pen's marketing campaign in Mexico was intended to assure customers that their pens would not leak, using the phrase, "It won't leak in your pocket and embarrass you." Unfortunately, the word "embarrass" was mistranslated to the Spanish word "embarazar," which actually means "to impregnate." As a result, the translated message inadvertently conveyed, "It won't leak in your pocket and make you pregnant." This mistranslation led to confusion and made the advertisement a subject of ridicule, which ultimately hurt Parker Pen's image in the Mexican market.

This blunder underscores the importance of accurately translating and localizing marketing messages, particularly in cross-cultural advertising. Direct translations often fail to capture the intended meaning, especially when idiomatic or nuanced expressions are involved. In this case, Parker Pen's oversight in translation illustrated the risks of relying solely on literal word-for-word translations without considering cultural and linguistic subtleties.

The incident also highlights how seemingly small errors in communication can have significant repercussions for a brand. In a market like Mexico, where language carries cultural weight, it is crucial for companies to understand how their messages will be received by the target audience. Mistranslations can lead to unintended humor, embarrassment, or even offense, all of which can damage a brand's credibility and consumer trust. Parker Pen's marketing team failed to adequately account for local linguistic differences, resulting in a message that was not only incorrect but also absurd to the target audience.

To recover from this mistake, Parker Pen had to adjust its marketing strategy, including consulting with local linguists and marketing experts to ensure their future campaigns resonated better with the local audience. The experience taught Parker Pen a valuable lesson about the need for comprehensive market research and local involvement in crafting marketing messages. It also prompted the company to implement stricter quality control measures for translations and to seek more cultural input when developing campaigns for international markets.

This example is often cited in marketing and business courses as a classic case of why cultural localization matters. Successful international advertising is not simply about translating words; it is about translating meaning and ensuring that the message resonates culturally and contextually. Had Parker Pen conducted more thorough testing and consulted native speakers before launching the campaign, they could have avoided this costly and embarrassing mistake.

Parker Pen in Mexico

- When Parker Pen marketed a ballpoint pen in Mexico, its ads were supposed to have read, "It won't leak in your pocket and embarrass you."
- Instead, the company thought that the word "embarazar" (to impregnate) meant to embarrass, so the ad read: "It won't leak in your pocket and make you pregnant

https://image2.slideserve.com/5362508/parker-pen-in-mexico-l.jpg
* Source : Usunier, J. C., and Lee, J. A. (2013). Marketing across cultures, Pearson.

Hyundai in Japan (Source; Hollensen, 2017)

When Hyundai launched in Japan, their advertising campaign faced significant challenges that ultimately led to poor market performance. Hyundai's ads focused heavily on affordability and budget-friendly pricing, a strategy that had been effective in other international markets where cost savings were a major consumer motivator. However, this approach failed to resonate with Japanese consumers, who often associate price with quality, particularly when it comes to significant purchases like automobiles. In Japan, the emphasis on low cost led to the perception that

Hyundai vehicles were of inferior quality, which deterred consumers who prioritize reliability, craftsmanship, and long-term value in their car purchases.

This misalignment between Hyundai's messaging and Japanese consumer expectations was a critical oversight. Japanese car buyers tend to value the prestige and high-quality craftsmanship associated with more expensive brands, and they often interpret lower prices as a sign of reduced quality. Hyundai's campaign failed to account for this cultural perception, which resulted in a disconnect between what the company offered and what the target market desired. The failure to emphasize quality, durability, and advanced features—attributes that Japanese consumers hold in high regard—meant that Hyundai's brand positioning was fundamentally at odds with local market expectations.

Moreover, the competitive landscape in Japan's automotive market is characterized by a high standard of quality, with domestic brands like Toyota, Honda, and Nissan dominating due to their well-established reputations for reliability and innovation. Hyundai's attempt to enter this market without adequately differentiating its vehicles on quality left it struggling to gain traction. Japanese consumers were skeptical of a brand that primarily highlighted low cost, especially when local manufacturers were offering vehicles that were perceived as superior in quality, albeit at higher prices.

In response to the lackluster performance, Hyundai eventually had to rethink its strategy in Japan. The company shifted its focus from competing on price to improving the perceived quality of its vehicles. This included investing in better materials, enhancing the overall design, and emphasizing the features that could match or exceed those of Japanese competitors. Hyundai also began incorporating more localized marketing tactics, such as using Japanese cultural references and endorsements from trusted local figures to build credibility and appeal to Japanese sensibilities.

The Hyundai case in Japan serves as a valuable lesson for other companies looking to expand into culturally distinct markets. It underscores the importance of understanding not only the economic but also the psychological factors that influence consumer behavior. Price sensitivity does not operate in a vacuum—cultural values around quality, prestige, and consumer trust play a significant role in shaping purchase decisions. Brands must thoroughly research and adapt to these local consumer perceptions to effectively position themselves in new markets.

Chevrolet Nova in Latin America (Source: Ricks, 2009)

Chevrolet's launch of the Nova car in Latin America is a well-known example of how language can dramatically impact a brand's success in a foreign market. The car's name, "Nova," unfortunately sounded like "No va" in Spanish, which translates to "it doesn't go." This unintended meaning led many consumers to believe that the car might be unreliable or not functional, which is particularly damaging for a product like an automobile, where reliability is crucial. The unfortunate implication that the car would not run created an immediate barrier to acceptance among Spanish-speaking consumers, leading to disappointing sales results.

This case illustrates the importance of thorough linguistic and cultural checks before launching a product in a new market. A seemingly harmless product name in one language can carry negative connotations in another, resulting in unintended brand associations and, ultimately, failure in the market. The name "Nova" might have been appealing in the United States, evoking a sense of energy and excitement, but in Latin America, it was counterproductive and even detrimental to Chevrolet's efforts to market the vehicle.

The cultural misstep also highlights how critical

it is for brands to engage local experts when planning product launches. If Chevrolet had conducted more comprehensive market research and consulted with local linguists, they could have identified the problematic nature of the car's name and chosen a more appropriate one for the region. This type of oversight can lead to costly rebranding efforts and lost opportunities, as was the case for Chevrolet. After recognizing the negative impact of the name, Chevrolet had to rename the vehicle for the Latin American market, a process that involved additional expenses and time.

Beyond the linguistic issues, this case also underscores the broader lesson that consumer perception is deeply influenced by cultural context. In Latin America, where word-of-mouth and community reputation can significantly affect consumer behavior, the negative connotation of "Nova" spread quickly, further damaging the brand's reputation. It took considerable effort for Chevrolet to recover from this setback, including rebranding and launching a new marketing campaign that more effectively resonated with local consumers.

Chevrolet's experience with the Nova is now frequently cited in business and marketing courses as a cautionary tale about the importance of cultural sensitivity in international marketing. It serves as a reminder that successful product names, slogans, and branding strategies must be tailored to fit the cultural and linguistic nuances of the target market. A direct translation or a failure to understand local interpretations can lead to unintended consequences that may undermine even the best products.

Ultimately, Chevrolet's Nova debacle demonstrates the necessity of cultural due diligence in international marketing. Brands must go beyond simple translations and truly immerse themselves in the cultural fabric of the market they are trying to enter. By understanding local language, values, and consumer psychology, companies can prevent costly mistakes and create a positive brand image that resonates with their target audience.

https://assets.hemmings.com/blog/wp-content/uploads/2017/04/1975ChevroletNova_01_1000.jpg
* Source : Ricks, D. A. (2009). Blunders in International Business. Wiley.

Cases of Success

Coca-Cola in China (Source: Kotler and Keller, 2016)

Coca-Cola's entry into the Chinese market is a textbook example of successful brand localization. Instead of opting for a direct translation of the name "Coca-Cola," which could have led to nonsensical or even negative connotations, Coca-Cola's team conducted extensive research to find a suitable equivalent that both sounded similar and conveyed a positive meaning. They chose the name "Kekou Kele" (可口可乐), which roughly translates to "tasty and happy." This careful adaptation ensured that the brand retained its identity while also conveying an appealing message that resonated well with Chinese consumers.

The importance of this localization effort cannot be understated. The Chinese market presented unique linguistic challenges, as direct translations of Western brand names often fail to capture the intended emotional resonance. By choosing "Kekou Kele," Coca-Cola not only avoided a potential mistranslation disaster but also managed to evoke positive emotions associated with enjoyment and pleasure. This strategy effectively bridged the cultural gap and helped Coca-Cola establish a strong foothold in China.

Coca-Cola's localization efforts extended beyond just the brand name. The company also adapted its marketing campaigns to align with Chinese cultural values. They emphasized the themes of happiness, togetherness, and shared experiences, which are significant in Chinese society, particularly during festivals and family gatherings. Coca-Cola's focus on these values helped build an emotional connection with Chinese consumers, making the brand part of their cultural moments.

The success of Coca-Cola in China also underscores the broader importance of cultural sensitivity in global marketing. Brands must not only adapt their names but also ensure that their advertising messages, product offerings, and even packaging resonate with local consumers. For Coca-Cola, understanding the cultural context and the emotional triggers that influence consumer behavior was key to their success. This level of adaptation demonstrates how global brands can maintain consistency while also being locally relevant.

The "Kekou Kele" case has since become a benchmark in international marketing courses, often cited as an exemplary case of effective localization. It highlights how multinational companies can avoid the pitfalls of cultural miscommunication and instead use cultural

https://pics0.baidu.com/feed/42166d224f4a20a42fadfe0832f1a02d700ed085.jpeg?token=cdb64fb077030b8a87a59d2b310e2783

* Source : Kotler, P., and Keller, K. L. (2016). Marketing Management. New York, USA : Pearson.

adaptation to their advantage. Coca-Cola's approach in China shows that investing in local market research, working with local experts, and respecting cultural nuances are crucial steps in ensuring the success of a brand in a new market.

Nike in Japan (Source: Mooij, 2019)

Nike's entry into the Japanese market is a prime example of successful cultural adaptation in advertising. Traditionally, Nike's Western campaigns emphasize individual achievement, self-reliance, and personal victory—concepts that align well with the more individualistic cultures of North America and Europe. However, when entering the Japanese market, Nike recognized that these themes would not resonate as effectively in Japan, where collectivism, group harmony, and community values play a significant role in shaping social behavior and consumer preferences.

To align with these cultural values, Nike shifted its advertising focus in Japan from individual glory to teamwork and collective effort. Their campaigns highlighted the importance of group spirit, collaboration, and shared success, often showcasing athletes working together to overcome challenges. This approach resonated deeply with Japanese consumers, who value social cohesion and collective accomplishments. By portraying sports not just as an avenue for individual greatness but also as a way to foster unity and team spirit, Nike successfully tapped into a core aspect of Japanese culture.

Nike's adaptation extended beyond just advertising messages; they also localized their events and sponsorships to appeal to Japanese sensibilities. Nike organized community-based events, such as running clubs and training sessions, which encouraged participation and fostered a sense of belonging. These events helped build a strong community around the brand, reinforcing Nike's image as a promoter of health, fitness, and teamwork rather than solely focusing on individual excellence.

Furthermore, Nike leveraged endorsements from popular Japanese athletes who embodied the values of perseverance, dedication, and humility—traits highly regarded in Japanese culture. By choosing athletes who were admired not only for their skills but also for their contributions to their teams and communities, Nike was able to build a deeper emotional connection with Japanese consumers. This strategic use of local endorsements helped enhance Nike's credibility and relatability in the market.

Nike's success in Japan demonstrates the critical importance of cultural sensitivity and adaptation in international marketing. Rather than imposing a one-size-fits-all strategy, Nike took the time to understand the unique cultural dynamics of the Japanese market and adjusted its messaging accordingly. This cultural alignment helped Nike differentiate itself from competitors and establish a strong, respected brand presence in Japan.

The Nike case is now frequently cited in business and marketing courses as an example of how multinational companies can successfully navigate cultural differences to create impactful campaigns. It underscores the idea that successful branding is not about rigidly adhering to a global message but about finding ways to connect that

https://th.bing.com/th/id/R.02aad42c95d8bc308f4fd25676bfe0a8?rik=u1m7aGjXtypUZw&riu=http%3a%2f%2fmedia2.intoday.in%2findiatoday%2fimages%2fstories%2fnike-japan-story%2c-facebook_647_090116041708.jpg&ehk=SAhzAuO%2fCXR4EScFPCeYplHTQqNOf7KhFAwsBIP0HXs%3d&risl=&pid=ImgRaw&r=0

* Source : Mooij, M. (2019). Global Marketing and Advertising: Understanding Cultural Paradoxes. New York, USA : Sage Publications.

message to the local cultural context. By emphasizing teamwork and community, Nike not only avoided potential cultural missteps but also managed to foster a sense of shared identity among Japanese consumers, ultimately contributing to the brand's long-term success in the region.

McDonald's in India (Source: Hollensen, 2017)

McDonald's adaptation to the Indian market serves

as a significant example of how multinational brands can successfully localize their offerings to align with cultural values and dietary preferences. In India, where a considerable portion of the population adheres to vegetarianism due to religious beliefs—particularly among Hindus and Jains—and where cows are regarded as sacred, McDonald's faced unique challenges in menu development. The introduction of the McAloo Tikki burger, a potato patty burger infused with Indian spices, was a direct response to local tastes and cultural sensitivities. This product became highly popular and remains a staple item in McDonald's Indian menu.

In addition to launching vegetarian products, McDonald's ensured that its cooking processes met the strict requirements of its diverse customer base. Separate preparation areas and utensils were used for vegetarian and non-vegetarian items, reducing the risk of cross-contamination—a major concern for many Indian consumers. This operational adjustment demonstrated McDonald's respect for local customs and helped build trust among its customers.

McDonald's also recognized the significance of regional diversity within India. They introduced items such as the Maharaja Mac (a chicken-based alternative to the classic Big Mac) and products that catered to regional tastes, such as spicy wraps and variations of local dishes. By tailoring its offerings to different regions, McDonald's not only appealed to the broader Indian market but also built a reputation for being culturally aware and adaptable.

Beyond the menu, McDonald's advertising in India was localized to reflect family-centric values. Advertisements often highlighted themes of togetherness, sharing, and familial joy, resonating well with the collectivist nature of Indian society. The brand positioned itself as a welcoming place for families to gather, making it a popular destination for family outings and celebrations. The portrayal of McDonald's as a space where family bonds are strengthened helped foster a positive image that went

https://mcdonaldsblog.in/wp-content/uploads/2021/06/McAloo-tikki.jpg
* Source : Hollensen, S. (2017). Global Marketing. New York, USA : Pearson.

beyond its identity as a fast-food chain.

The success of McDonald's in India illustrates how deep cultural understanding and the willingness to adapt operational and marketing strategies can lead to significant gains in a challenging market. By investing in local research, respecting dietary customs, and celebrating Indian culture, McDonald's was able to position itself as a trusted and beloved brand in a market that was initially wary of Western fast food.

LG in South Korea (Source: Kim and Kim, 2020)

LG Electronics' strategy in South Korea is an excellent example of how understanding and aligning with local cultural values can enhance brand loyalty and market success. In South Korea, family values, harmony, and collective well-being are highly prioritized. LG recognized these cultural elements and tailored its advertising campaigns to emphasize how its products contributed to improving family life, comfort, and convenience.

LG's marketing campaigns frequently featured multi-generational families using LG appliances, such as refrigerators, air conditioners, and washing machines, in everyday scenarios. The advertisements showcased how LG products could bring families together—whether it was through providing fresh, healthy food stored in LG refrigerators or ensuring a comfortable home environment with advanced air conditioning systems. By focusing on these family-oriented narratives, LG successfully positioned its products as indispensable tools that contribute to a harmonious household.

In addition to advertising, LG made strategic product innovations that catered specifically to Korean consumer needs. For instance, their washing machines included features designed to protect delicate fabrics, aligning with South Korea's cultural emphasis on maintaining neat and high-quality clothing. This kind of product differentiation, based on an in-depth understanding of local consumer habits, helped LG stand out in a competitive market.

LG also used local celebrities and influencers in its marketing efforts to build trust and relatability. By leveraging endorsements from respected figures who were known for their family values and wholesome public images, LG strengthened its emotional connection with consumers. These campaigns not only highlighted product benefits but also aligned LG's brand image with the values most cherished by South Korean families.

LG's ability to integrate cultural values into both product development and advertising messaging helped it maintain a strong brand image and customer loyalty in

https://search.pstatic.net/common/?src=http%3A%2F%2Fblogfiles.naver.net%2F20120320_8%2Fkuailepangxi_1332229585767hbG79_JPEG%2Fwqdqweds.jpg&type=sc960_832
* Source : Kim, Y., and Kim, J. (2020). Korean Advertising and Consumer Culture. Routledge.

South Korea. The company's success in its home market underscores the importance of aligning brand messaging with cultural expectations and adapting products to meet specific consumer needs.

Implications for Global Advertising

Cross-cultural advertising successes and blunders alike offer valuable lessons for brands looking to expand internationally. Understanding cultural nuances, adapting language, and respecting local traditions are crucial in ensuring that advertising campaigns succeed in connecting with target audiences, rather than inadvertently offending them or missing the mark entirely. By studying both the successes and mistakes of past campaigns, advertisers can develop informed strategies that effectively bridge cultural differences and foster meaningful connections with diverse audiences (Kotler and Keller, 2016).

Successful cross-cultural advertising is ultimately about empathy, research, and a willingness to adapt—qualities that enable brands to navigate the complexities of new markets. Empathy helps advertisers put themselves in the shoes of their target audience, ensuring that messaging is respectful and resonates emotionally. Thorough market research provides the insights needed to understand cultural values, behaviors, and preferences, while adaptation ensures that global brands remain relevant at the local level (Ricks, 2009).

Brands like McDonald's, LG, Coca-Cola, and Nike have demonstrated that investing in cultural understanding and localized strategies can lead to sustained success and strong brand loyalty. By respecting cultural differences and integrating those insights into product offerings and marketing, brands can create campaigns that not only avoid missteps but also build lasting relationships with consumers across the globe. In the increasingly globalized market of today, cultural awareness is not just an advantage—it is a necessity for brands seeking to thrive in diverse and competitive environments.

A key takeaway from these case studies is that brands must prioritize understanding the unique needs and values of their target markets. This means moving beyond superficial cultural markers and delving into the deeper emotional and social contexts that shape consumer behavior. For example, in collectivist societies, emphasizing community, harmony, and shared experiences can make a significant difference in how an advertising campaign is received. By contrast, in more individualistic cultures, campaigns that focus on personal achievement, independence, and self-expression tend to be more effective (Ford, Mueller and Mueller, 2023; Han, 2024).

Additionally, the role of local partnerships and collaborations cannot be underestimated. Many successful cross-cultural campaigns have involved partnering with local celebrities, influencers, or cultural experts who have an intrinsic understanding of the target market. Such partnerships help brands navigate cultural nuances that may not be immediately apparent to outsiders and can lend authenticity to the campaign. For instance, Nike's collaboration with Japanese athletes and local influencers helped the brand resonate with younger Japanese consumers, who saw these figures as aspirational role models.

Furthermore, product adaptation is an essential element of successful cross-cultural advertising (Han, 2024). As seen in the case of McDonald's in India and LG in South Korea, modifying product offerings to meet local tastes and preferences is crucial. This might involve altering ingredients, as McDonald's did to accommodate vegetarian consumers, or adding features that cater to specific cultural practices, as LG did with its washing machines in South Korea. Such adaptations show a brand's commitment to meeting the specific needs of its consumers, which in turn fosters brand loyalty and trust.

Digital platforms and social media also play a critical role in cross-cultural advertising. Brands must consider the local digital landscape and preferences when planning campaigns. In some markets, global platforms like Facebook and Instagram dominate, while in others, local platforms like WeChat in China or LINE in Japan are more popular. Understanding which platforms are most widely used and trusted by the target audience allows brands to effectively reach consumers and tailor their content to the platform's unique culture. This kind of digital localization is key to ensuring that messages are delivered in a culturally relevant and impactful manner.

Another important aspect of successful cross-cultural advertising is the willingness to learn from failures and adapt strategies accordingly. Brands that are willing to acknowledge their mistakes, learn from them, and make necessary adjustments are often the ones that find long-term success in new markets. For example, KFC's initial mistranslation of its slogan in China could have led to long-lasting damage, but the company's swift response and subsequent adaptation of their messaging helped them recover and thrive in the Chinese market. This ability to pivot and respond to local feedback is a crucial element of resilience in international marketing.

In conclusion, cross-cultural advertising requires a careful balance of global consistency and local relevance (Mooij, 2019). Brands that take the time to understand the cultural intricacies of their target markets, adapt their products and messages accordingly, and leverage local insights are the ones that ultimately succeed. The examples of McDonald's, LG, Coca-Cola, and Nike illustrate the importance of empathy, research, and adaptability in building strong, lasting relationships with consumers across diverse cultural contexts. In today's interconnected world, cultural awareness is not just a strategic advantage

- it is an essential component of any brand's success in the global marketplace (Ricks, 2009).

Chapter 9

Theoretical Challenges and Future Directions in Global Consumer Psychology : Insights and Perspectives

Recent research in cross-cultural advertising

Cross-cultural advertising has witnessed significant developments over the past decade, with researchers focusing on how cultural values, norms, and behaviors influence consumer responses in an increasingly globalized market (Byun, et al., 2024). Recent studies have underscored the importance of tailoring advertising messages to align with cultural contexts, demonstrating that culturally adapted campaigns outperform standardized approaches in effectiveness (Taylor, 2023). This trend highlights the enduring relevance of cultural adaptation strategies in modern advertising.

One emerging area in cross-cultural advertising is the study of strategic authenticity in social media marketing. Zhu and Wang (2024) examined how financial influencers (finfluencers) from diverse cultural backgrounds construct authenticity through strategic transparency, immediacy, ordinariness, and passion. Their findings reveal that authenticity strategies are not only culturally contingent but also instrumental in fostering trust and engagement among audiences in different cultural contexts. This underscores the critical role of cultural nuances in shaping influencer marketing effectiveness.

Another noteworthy advancement is the growing application of bibliometric analyses to understand the trajectory of cross-cultural advertising research. Ford, Mueller, and Mueller (2023) provided a comprehensive review of 40 years of studies, identifying shifts in theoretical frameworks and methodological approaches. Their work revealed a steady move toward integrating digital and technological dimensions into cross-cultural advertising, reflecting the profound impact of globalization and digitalization.

Social media has emerged as a transformative platform for cross-cultural advertising. Buzeta, De Keyzer, Dens and De Pelsmacker (2024) explored the interplay between branded content, social media motivations, and cultural differences. Their cross-cultural study demonstrated that the effectiveness of branded content is significantly influenced by users' motivations for engaging with social media, such as entertainment or social interaction, which vary across cultural settings. These findings highlight the importance of aligning branded content strategies with culturally specific user motivations to enhance brand outcomes.

In addition to social media, artificial intelligence (AI) has increasingly been integrated into cross-cultural advertising practices. Shen (2022) discussed the role of AI in training cross-cultural communication talent, emphasizing how AI technologies can bridge cultural gaps in global advertising. Similarly, Al-Sharafi et al. (2023) examined how Generation Z's use of AI products varies across cultures, with significant implications for designing AI-driven advertising campaigns that resonate with culturally diverse audiences.

Recent research in cross-cultural advertising reflects a dynamic field that continues to evolve with technological advancements and shifting cultural landscapes (Taylor, 2023). By addressing the complexities of cultural adaptation, leveraging the potential of social media, and integrating AI technologies (Ford, Mueller and Mueller, 2023), scholars and practitioners can navigate the challenges and opportunities in this ever-changing domain.

Cross-Cultural Advertising Research: Cultural Similarity and Difference

Research into cultural similarities and differences has been a major focus in cross-cultural advertising (Han, 2024; Mooij, 2022). Cultural dimensions, such as those identified by Hofstede (2002)—individualism vs. collectivism, power distance, uncertainty avoidance, masculinity vs. femininity, and long-term vs. short-term orientation—serve as the foundation for understanding how consumers in different cultural settings react to advertising messages. These dimensions help advertisers identify whether a message will resonate or clash with the values of a particular cultural group.

Hofstede's (2002) cultural dimensions have been instrumental in shaping cross-cultural advertising strategies. Individualism vs. collectivism, for instance, plays a critical role in determining the type of appeals that will resonate most with an audience. In individualistic cultures, such as the United States and Western Europe, advertising messages that emphasize personal achievement, independence, and self-expression are often well received. These messages align with the cultural values of autonomy and personal success. On the other hand, in collectivist cultures, such as those found in many Asian,

African, and Latin American countries, advertisements that highlight group harmony, family values, and community are far more effective. Collectivist cultures place a greater emphasis on social relationships and interdependence, making messages that promote collective well-being more persuasive.

Power distance is another critical cultural dimension that influences how authority figures are portrayed in advertisements. In high power distance cultures, such as those in many parts of Asia and Latin America, featuring authoritative figures—such as community leaders, experts, or even celebrities—can enhance the credibility of an advertisement. These cultures tend to respect and value hierarchical relationships, and messages delivered by authority figures are often perceived as more trustworthy. Conversely, in low power distance cultures, such as in Scandinavian countries, audiences may view authority-driven messages with suspicion (Mooij, 2022). In these contexts, advertisements that emphasize equality, collaboration, and self-empowerment tend to be more successful, as they align with the cultural value of minimizing status differences.

A key study that exemplifies the role of power distance in cross-cultural advertising is Hofstede (2001). Hofstede's work is foundational in understanding cultural differences, including power distance, and has been widely cited in advertising and marketing research. In his analysis, Hofstede explains how power distance affects consumer behavior and the effectiveness of authority-based appeals in advertising. He found that in high power distance cultures, consumers are more likely to respond positively to advertisements featuring endorsements from respected figures, as these endorsements align with cultural expectations of deference to authority. Conversely, in low power distance cultures, messages that emphasize egalitarianism and challenge traditional authority structures are more appealing. This work has been instrumental in guiding marketers on how to tailor their advertising strategies based on the power dynamics of their target audience.

Another influential study by Mooij and Hofstede (2010), published in the International Journal of Advertising, further explores the impact of power distance on advertising effectiveness. The authors examined advertising campaigns in high and low power distance countries and found significant differences in consumer responses. In high power distance cultures, advertisements that used authoritative language and featured hierarchical imagery were perceived as more credible and persuasive. In contrast, in low power distance cultures, such approaches were often seen as overly controlling or paternalistic. The study concluded that understanding the power distance orientation of a culture is crucial for developing effective advertising strategies that resonate with local audiences.

These foundational studies highlight the importance of aligning advertising messages with the cultural values related to power distance. By understanding whether a culture values hierarchy and authority or prefers equality and collaboration, advertisers can craft messages that are culturally resonant and more likely to succeed in the target market.

Individualism vs. collectivism is a foundational cultural dimension that significantly affects advertising strategies. In individualistic cultures, such as the United States, Canada, and Western European countries, advertising appeals that focus on personal achievement, independence, and self-expression tend to be more effective. These cultures place a high value on autonomy and individual success, making messages that celebrate personal milestones or emphasize unique attributes resonate well. For instance, advertisements that portray a single individual achieving a goal—whether in sports, career, or lifestyle—are often well-received in individualistic societies (Han, 2024).

Conversely, in collectivist cultures, such as those found in many Asian, African, and Latin American countries, the emphasis shifts from the individual to the group. Advertising appeals that highlight group harmony, family values, and community support are far more persuasive in these cultures. Collectivist societies value social relationships, interdependence, and group cohesion, and messages that promote collective well-being or depict family togetherness tend to resonate strongly. For example, Coca-Cola's campaigns in collectivist cultures often emphasize sharing and community, portraying the brand as a facilitator of social connections and familial bonding (Mai, Ketron and Yang, 2020).

Within the framework of individualism and collectivism, it is also important to consider the concepts of vertical and horizontal orientations - referred to as vertical individualism, horizontal individualism, vertical collectivism, and horizontal collectivism (Maheswaran and Shavitt, 2014). Vertical individualism characterizes cultures that emphasize individual achievement but also accept inequality among individuals. In such cultures, people are motivated by competition and the desire to stand out, even if it means accepting hierarchical differences. The United States is an example of a culture with strong vertical individualism, where advertising often appeals to the desire for personal success and being the best in one's field. Messages that celebrate standing out from the crowd or achieving a higher status are effective in such settings.

Horizontal individualism, on the other hand, is characterized by the emphasis on individuality while maintaining a sense of equality among people. In countries like Sweden and Denmark, horizontal individualism is prevalent, and advertising appeals that emphasize uniqueness without promoting competition are often well-received. Advertisements that highlight self-expression, personal freedom, and the enjoyment of life without hierarchical connotations resonate well in these cultures.

Vertical collectivism refers to cultures that value the group but also accept hierarchical structures within that group. In countries such as China and India, vertical collectivism is common, where individuals are expected to prioritize group goals over personal ones, while also respecting authority and social hierarchy. In these cultures, advertisements that feature respected authority figures endorsing a product or messages that emphasize loyalty to family or community are highly effective. For example, ads that showcase a family elder recommending a product or a community leader promoting a brand can build credibility and trust.

Horizontal collectivism, by contrast, emphasizes

group harmony and equality among group members. In cultures like those of the Kibbutzim in Israel, there is a strong emphasis on collective well-being without significant hierarchical differences. Advertisements in such cultures are most effective when they focus on themes of equality, mutual support, and community welfare. Messages that promote products as tools for enhancing group activities or fostering equal benefits for all members tend to resonate well.

Understanding the nuances of individualism and collectivism, along with their vertical and horizontal orientations, is crucial for advertisers aiming to create culturally resonant messages. The effectiveness of an advertising campaign often hinges on how well it aligns with the underlying cultural values of the target audience, whether those values emphasize personal success, group harmony, equality, or respect for authority. By tailoring messages to fit these cultural dimensions, brands can ensure that their advertisements are both persuasive and culturally appropriate.

One of the most influential studies on individualism and collectivism in cross-cultural advertising is Triandis (1995). Triandis provides a comprehensive analysis of how these cultural orientations shape consumer attitudes and behaviors, offering profound implications for advertising strategies. In individualistic cultures, such as those in the United States and Western Europe, personal goals, autonomy, and self-expression are highly valued. Consequently, advertising messages that emphasize personal benefits and achievements tend to resonate strongly. Conversely, in collectivist cultures, such as those in Asia, Africa, and Latin America, the emphasis shifts to group harmony, family values, and community. Advertisements in these contexts are more effective when they highlight social relationships and collective well-being.

Triandis also introduced the concepts of horizontal and vertical orientations within individualism and collectivism, providing a nuanced understanding of how societal structures influence consumer preferences. Vertical individualism emphasizes personal success while accepting social hierarchies, making competitive, status-oriented messages more effective. Horizontal individualism, as seen in Scandinavian countries, focuses on self-expression without hierarchy, favoring advertisements that celebrate uniqueness without competition. Similarly, vertical collectivism prioritizes group goals with hierarchical respect, while horizontal collectivism values equality within group cohesion. These insights have significantly guided advertisers in crafting culturally congruent and resonant messages.

Markus and Kitayama (1991), in their seminal work Culture and the Self: Implications for Cognition, Emotion, and Motivation, explored the psychological underpinnings of cultural orientations. They posited that independent self-construals in individualistic cultures lead to preferences for advertisements emphasizing personal uniqueness and autonomy. By contrast, interdependent self-construals in collectivist cultures align with messages that underscore relationships, social roles, and group membership. These findings are foundational in understanding consumer behavior, highlighting how cultural self-construal influences perceptions of authenticity and emotional resonance in advertising.

These studies collectively emphasize the importance of aligning advertising messages with cultural values (Han and Shavitt, 1994; Mooij, 2019). A nuanced approach—considering both vertical and horizontal dimensions—enables advertisers to create emotionally engaging campaigns tailored to specific cultural contexts, ultimately fostering stronger consumer-brand relationships.

Uncertainty avoidance, a critical cultural dimension identified by Hofstede, significantly shapes consumer responses to advertising. Cultures with high uncertainty avoidance, such as Greece, Portugal, and Japan, prefer clear, straightforward messages that minimize ambiguity.

Advertisements in these contexts often emphasize product reliability, safety, and guarantees, catering to consumers' aversion to risk. In contrast, low uncertainty avoidance cultures, such as Denmark and the United Kingdom, are more open to creative, abstract, and novelty-driven messaging.

Hofstede and Hofstede (2004) in Cultures and Organizations: Software of the Mind offer a detailed exploration of how uncertainty avoidance influences marketing strategies. High uncertainty avoidance cultures prioritize detailed information, while low uncertainty avoidance cultures favor innovative and adventurous appeals. Similarly, Steenkamp and Baumgartner (1998) found that high uncertainty avoidance cultures respond positively to fact-based, risk-reducing advertisements, whereas low uncertainty avoidance cultures are more receptive to humor and creative metaphors.

Understanding a culture's tolerance for uncertainty enables advertisers to design campaigns that resonate with their audience's psychological comfort zones, enhancing both engagement and effectiveness.

The dimension of long-term vs. short-term orientation, as explored by Bond and Hofstede (1989), provides further insights into cultural advertising strategies. Long-term oriented cultures, such as those in China and South Korea, value perseverance, future rewards, and sustainability. Advertisements emphasizing product durability, long-term benefits, and stability align well with these cultural values. In contrast, short-term oriented cultures, such as the United States, prioritize immediate gratification and quick results, favoring promotional messages and instant benefits.

Mooij and Hofstede (2010) further examined this dynamic, demonstrating that long-term oriented cultures prefer messages centered on reliability and future rewards, whereas short-term oriented cultures respond better to messages emphasizing immediacy and spontaneity. These insights underscore the need to align advertising content with cultural temporal preferences to ensure resonance and effectiveness.

While understanding cultural differences is crucial, identifying shared values that transcend cultures allows for globally consistent advertising strategies. Universal themes, such as love, family, and happiness, enable brands to create emotionally engaging campaigns with widespread appeal. Coca-Cola's "Share a Coke" campaign exemplifies this approach by leveraging the universal desire for personalization and social connection. By combining cultural specificity with universal themes, brands can maintain a cohesive global identity while engaging local audiences meaningfully.

Mooij (2019), in Global Marketing and Advertising: Understanding Cultural Paradoxes, highlights the importance of cultural adaptability. She argues that a deep understanding of cultural values, rather than relying solely on superficial markers, fosters authentic connections with consumers. This nuanced approach ensures that advertising campaigns resonate on both local and global levels, building trust and loyalty across diverse markets.

Another study by Mele, Kerkhof and Cantoni (2021), published in the Journal of Travel & Tourism Marketing, analyzed cultural tourism promotion on Instagram through a cross-cultural lens. Their findings underscored the importance of adapting social media content to align with cultural values and preferences. For example, in cultures with high uncertainty avoidance, content that emphasizes safety and reliability is more effective, while in low uncertainty avoidance cultures, creative and novel messaging is more engaging. This study provides valuable insights for leveraging cultural dimensions in digital advertising strategies.

Cross-Cultural Advertising Research: Cultural Dynamics and Changes

Cultural dynamics and changes have emerged as a critical focus in cross-cultural advertising research. Cultures are not static; they evolve over time due to various factors, including globalization, migration, technological advancements, and generational shifts (Han and Shavitt, 2016). These changes present unique opportunities and challenges for advertisers. For instance, younger generations in traditionally collectivist societies often adopt more individualistic values, influenced by global trends and exposure to Western media. Understanding these cultural shifts is essential for advertisers to remain relevant and effectively target shifting demographics (Han, 2024; Walsh, Shiu and Hassan, 2014).

Globalization has further intensified the interplay between cultural identity and consumer behavior. This phenomenon has led to the blending of cultural elements, creating hybrid identities that incorporate both local and global influences. Such cultural hybridization necessitates a delicate balance in advertising—brands must respect local traditions while embracing global trends. To craft effective campaigns, advertisers need to understand these cultural dynamics and their impact on modern consumer identities.

One notable example of cultural hybridization in advertising is McDonald's adaptation of its menu in India. By introducing a range of vegetarian options and removing beef products to honor cultural and religious beliefs, McDonald's demonstrated its sensitivity to local norms. The inclusion of the McAloo Tikki Burger, featuring locally inspired flavors, is a prime example of aligning global branding with local cultural preferences. This strategy significantly contributed to McDonald's success in the Indian market, as detailed by Vignali (2001) in McDonald's: 'Think Global, Act Local' - The Marketing Mix, published in the British Food Journal. This case underscores the importance of adapting global brands to local markets to enhance consumer acceptance and build brand loyalty.

Similarly, Coca-Cola's Share a Coke campaign exemplifies how global branding can effectively integrate local cultural nuances. By printing popular names and culturally relevant phrases on its bottles, Coca-Cola created a personalized consumer experience that resonated with diverse audiences. For instance, in Australia, the campaign featured local slang and nicknames, while in China, the bottles highlighted family and friendship themes, reflecting collectivist values. This innovative approach combined universal personalization with cultural specificity, as highlighted by Kostiw (2014) and Walsh et al. (2014).

Robertson (1995), in his foundational work Glocalization: Time-Space and Homogeneity-Heterogeneity (published in Global Modernities), introduced the concept of "glocalization" to describe the blending of global and local cultural elements. Robertson argues that consumers increasingly adopt hybrid identities that merge local traditions with global influences. For advertisers, recognizing this duality is crucial to crafting messages that resonate with both aspects of consumer identity. The full text is accessible via Google Books.

Appadurai (1996) explored the concept of "cultural flows" in Modernity at Large: Cultural Dimensions of Globalization. Appadurai's work emphasizes how the global movement of cultural elements, facilitated by media, technology, and migration, shapes consumer identities. These "imagined worlds" reflect hybrid cultural identities, requiring advertisers to design campaigns that align with consumers' multifaceted cultural experiences. The study is accessible at Google Books.

Technological advancements, particularly the rise of social media, have significantly accelerated cultural changes. Platforms such as Instagram, TikTok, and

YouTube enable the rapid dissemination of cultural trends, fostering the emergence of global subcultures that transcend national boundaries. For advertisers, understanding these subcultures is key to engaging with niche audiences.

Shaw (2006), in Convergence Culture: Where Old and New Media Collide, examines how digital media facilitate cultural convergence. He argues that social media platforms create spaces where global and local cultural elements intersect, leading to new hybrid cultural forms. Advertisers can leverage these platforms to reach niche audiences by crafting culturally relevant and engaging content. Jenkins' insights highlight the strategic importance of understanding digital subcultures in modern advertising. The full study is available at Calcutta University's Global Media Journal.

The studies discussed emphasize the need for advertisers to adapt to the evolving cultural landscape (Han, 2024). By acknowledging the complexities of cultural hybridization, globalization, and technological influences, brands can develop campaigns that resonate deeply with modern consumers. Successful cross-cultural advertising requires an understanding of both local traditions and global influences, allowing brands to build meaningful, long-lasting connections with their audiences.

Cross-Cultural Advertising Research in the Digital Age

The digital age has fundamentally reshaped the field of cross-cultural advertising, presenting unprecedented opportunities and challenges for brands seeking to connect with culturally diverse audiences. The rise of digital platforms, social media, and artificial intelligence (AI) has provided powerful tools for personalization, consumer engagement, and global outreach. However, these advancements also necessitate a nuanced understanding of cultural differences to navigate the complexities of a highly interconnected world.

One of the most significant contributions of the digital age is the ability to leverage data-driven insights for personalized advertising. Digital platforms such as Facebook, Instagram, and TikTok offer sophisticated targeting capabilities, enabling brands to tailor their messages to specific cultural groups. Personalization allows advertisers to create culturally relevant content that resonates with individual consumers, fostering stronger brand connections.

For example, Netflix's localized marketing campaigns illustrate the effectiveness of data-driven personalization. By analyzing cultural preferences, Netflix has successfully adapted its promotional content to various markets, creating a sense of familiarity and relatability for viewers worldwide. This strategic approach highlights the importance of using consumer data to inform culturally sensitive advertising, strengthening brand loyalty on a global scale.

The digital age has also amplified the role of user-generated content (UGC) in shaping cross-cultural advertising narratives. UGC empowers consumers to co-create brand stories, reflecting their unique cultural values and perspectives. Brands such as Coca-Cola and Starbucks have effectively leveraged UGC by encouraging customers to share their experiences on social media platforms. This participatory approach enhances authenticity and allows brands to adapt organically to diverse cultural norms and values (Kaplan and Haenlein, 2010).

Okazaki and Taylor (2013) explored the transformative impact of social media on international advertising in their study Social Media and International Advertising: Theoretical Challenges and Future Directions, published in International Marketing Review. They emphasized how social media enables brands to engage directly with culturally diverse audiences, fostering interactive and personalized communication. However, they also cautioned against potential pitfalls, such as cultural misinterpretation and insensitivity, which can arise in the fast-paced digital environment. The study is accessible at Emerald Insight.

Kaplan and Haenlein (2010), in their seminal work Users of the World, Unite! The Challenges and Opportunities of Social Media, discussed how social media facilitates the rapid dissemination of cultural trends while offering brands opportunities to engage with consumers on a personal level. They highlighted the importance of cultural awareness in crafting effective social media campaigns and avoiding cultural missteps. This study underscores the dual potential of social media as a tool for both cross-cultural connection and potential conflict. The full study is available at ScienceDirect.

Artificial intelligence (AI) has emerged as a transformative tool in cross-cultural advertising, enabling brands to analyze consumer data and develop culturally adaptive content (Gao, Wang, Xie, Hu, and Hu, 2023; Rodgers and Nguyen, 2022). AI technologies such as natural language processing (NLP) and machine learning allow advertisers to identify cultural trends, preferences, and behaviors with unparalleled precision. By leveraging AI, brands can create highly relevant and impactful campaigns tailored to the cultural context of their target audience (Xu and Li, 2021).

Gao et al. (2023) provided a comprehensive review of AI advancements in advertising, discussing its applications in targeting, personalization, content creation, and ad optimization. They highlighted ethical considerations, including data privacy and algorithmic transparency, as critical factors in ensuring responsible AI use in cross-cultural advertising. These insights underscore the need for a balanced approach that combines technological innovation with cultural sensitivity and ethical accountability (Xu and Li, 2021).

While the digital era offers innovative tools for cross-cultural advertising, it also brings ethical challenges. Issues such as privacy concerns, data misuse, and the potential reinforcement of cultural stereotypes require careful attention. Advertisers must adopt ethical practices that prioritize consumer trust and cultural respect to ensure the long-term success of their campaigns.

Rodgers and Nguyen (2022), in their study on ethical AI applications in advertising, highlighted the benefits of ethical algorithmic decision-making in fostering consumer trust and satisfaction. Their findings suggest that integrating ethical considerations into AI-driven advertising strategies not only enhances campaign effectiveness but also strengthens brand reputation.

The digital age has revolutionized cross-cultural advertising, providing brands with tools to connect with diverse audiences in meaningful ways. By leveraging data-driven personalization, user-generated content, and AI technologies, advertisers can create culturally resonant campaigns that engage modern consumers (Gao, Wang, Xie, Hu, and Hu, 2023; Rodgers and Nguyen, 2022).

However, this new landscape also demands a commitment to ethical practices and cultural sensitivity (Gao, Wang, Xie, Hu, and Hu, 2023). As digital platforms continue to evolve, advertisers must navigate these complexities with a strategic and responsible approach to ensure both cultural relevance and global impact.

Table 1 Summary of Cross-Cultural Advertising Research in the Digital Age

Key Aspect	Description	Key References
Personalization & Data-Driven Insights	Digital platforms enable brands to tailor messages to cultural groups using data-driven insights. Example: Netflix's localized campaigns	Kaplan & Haenlein (2010), Netflix case study
User-Generated Content (UGC)	Consumers co-create brand narratives, enhancing authenticity. Example: Coca-Cola and Starbucks leveraging UGC.	Kaplan & Haenlein (2010), Coca-Cola & Starbucks case studies

Key Aspect	Description	Key References
Social Media Impact	Social media enables direct engagement with diverse audiences but risks cultural misinterpretation. Example: Okazaki & Taylor (2013).	Okazaki & Taylor (2013), Kaplan & Haenlein (2010)
Artificial Intelligence (AI) in Advertising	AI allows precise cultural trend analysis and adaptive content creation but raises ethical concerns. Example: Gao et al. (2023).	Gao et al. (2023), Xu & Li (2021), Rodgers & Nguyen (2022)
Ethical Challenges in Digital Advertising	Issues like data privacy, cultural stereotyping, and ethical AI use demand responsible advertising strategies. Example: Rodgers & Nguyen (2022).	Rodgers & Nguyen (2022), Gao et al. (2023)

New Trends in Cross-Cultural Advertising Research

A prominent trend in recent cross-cultural advertising research is the increasing focus on emotional appeals and storytelling (Markus and Kitayama, 1991). Emotional advertising has consistently demonstrated its effectiveness across diverse cultural contexts, particularly when it draws on universal human experiences such as love, family, and the pursuit of happiness. These themes transcend cultural boundaries, creating a shared emotional resonance that enhances the impact of advertising campaigns.

However, the cultural expression of emotions and the symbols employed in storytelling vary significantly. For instance, individualistic cultures often emphasize personal achievements and self-expression, while collectivist cultures highlight themes of community and familial harmony. Effective cross-cultural advertising must therefore adapt its emotional appeals and narratives to align with the cultural norms and values of its target audience, ensuring that the message remains both relatable and impactful.

The rapid evolution of digital platforms and social media has fundamentally transformed cross-cultural advertising (Okazaki and Taylor 2013). Advertisers increasingly leverage data analytics and artificial intelligence to craft highly targeted campaigns that cater to the unique preferences and cultural sensitivities of their audiences. Personalization, enabled by advanced algorithms, has become a cornerstone of modern cross-cultural advertising, allowing brands to deliver messages tailored to individual consumers while respecting cultural nuances.

Social media influencers have emerged as powerful intermediaries in cross-cultural advertising. By creating authentic and relatable content, influencers bridge cultural gaps and build trust with their followers. Their ability to communicate in culturally resonant ways makes them particularly effective in promoting brands across diverse markets. For example, influencers often adapt their content to reflect local traditions and preferences, ensuring that their messaging aligns with the expectations of their audience. This trend highlights the importance of authenticity and cultural adaptability in leveraging social media for cross-cultural advertising.

Sustainability and social responsibility have become critical themes in cross-cultural advertising as consumers worldwide increasingly prioritize ethical business practices, environmental stewardship, and social justice. Brands that effectively communicate their commitment to these values through culturally relevant messages are better positioned to build trust and loyalty among global consumers.

Cross-cultural advertising research is now exploring how brands can localize their sustainability narratives to resonate with specific cultural expectations (Han, 2024). For example, in collectivist cultures, sustainability messaging might emphasize communal benefits and collective well-being, while in individualistic cultures, it may focus on personal contributions to environmental conservation. This localized approach ensures that sustainability efforts are perceived as authentic and aligned with the cultural values of the target audience.

These emerging trends underscore the dynamic nature of cross-cultural advertising research. The integration of emotional appeals, digital innovation, and sustainability narratives reflects the evolving priorities of both consumers and advertisers in a globalized marketplace. As these trends continue to develop, future research should focus on deepening our understanding of cultural nuances, ethical considerations, and technological advancements to create advertising strategies that are not only effective but also culturally sensitive and socially responsible.

Table 2 New Trends in Cross-Cultural Advertising Research

Key Trend	Description	Key References
Emotional Appeals & Storytelling	Emotional advertising leverages universal themes like love and family, but cultural variations exist in emotional expression and storytelling styles.	Markus & Kitayama (1991)
Personalization & AI-Driven Advertising	Data analytics and AI enhance personalized advertising, allowing culturally adaptive messaging tailored to specific audiences.	Okazaki & Taylor (2013)

Key Trend	Description	Key References
Role of Social Media Influencers	Influencers act as cultural intermediaries, adapting content to local traditions and building trust through authenticity.	Influencer marketing case studies
Sustainability & Social Responsibility	Consumers prioritize ethical business practices; localized sustainability messaging ensures cultural relevance and authenticity.	Gao et al. (2023)

Directions for Future Research: Insights and Perspectives

The integration of artificial intelligence (AI) into various facets of human life has not only enhanced efficiency but also challenged traditional notions of creativity, decision-making, and cultural norms. While AI systems are increasingly capable of producing innovative and creative outputs, societal biases against AI-driven creativity remain pervasive (Magni, Park and Chao, 2024). These biases reflect a deeper tension between human-centric creativity and the perceived limitations of machine-generated outputs.

Magni, Park, and Chao (2024) highlight this phenomenon, suggesting that humans often serve as gatekeepers of creativity, imposing subjective judgments on AI-generated content. Their study reveals a persistent skepticism regarding AI's ability to produce creative work comparable to human standards, particularly in fields traditionally dominated by human ingenuity. For instance, while AI can compose music, write stories, or design visual art, audiences frequently question the authenticity and emotional depth of such outputs. This skepticism is rooted in cultural and psychological perceptions, which frame creativity as inherently human.

Future research should explore the psychological and cultural factors driving this bias and investigate strategies to foster a more inclusive perspective on AI-generated creativity (Barnes, Zhang and Valenzuela, 2024) . Understanding how these biases vary across cultures is particularly crucial, as perceptions of AI may differ based on societal values, technological familiarity, and cultural openness to innovation. By addressing these biases, scholars can provide actionable insights for improving the acceptance and integration of AI-driven creativity in global contexts.

Artificial intelligence (AI) has revolutionized how cultural insights are generated, analyzed, and applied, but its role in cross-cultural research remains an underexplored domain with immense potential. AI's ability to process vast datasets and detect nuanced patterns offers researchers an unprecedented opportunity to deepen their understanding of cultural differences, similarities, and dynamics in globalized contexts. However, as noted by Barnes, Zhang, and Valenzuela (2024), cultural responses to AI systems themselves are deeply shaped by existing cultural norms, values, and beliefs.

Barnes et al. (2024) argue that perceptions of and interactions with AI vary significantly across cultures, depending on dimensions such as power distance, individualism versus collectivism, and uncertainty avoidance. For example, in high power-distance cultures, users may be more inclined to trust and accept recommendations provided by AI systems due to an inherent respect for authority figures and hierarchical structures. Conversely, in low power-distance cultures, skepticism toward AI's role in decision-making may be higher, with users preferring human input over algorithmic advice.

This intersection between cultural dimensions and AI adoption provides a fertile ground for future research. Scholars should investigate how cultural variables influence the effectiveness of AI-driven solutions, such as personalized marketing strategies or automated customer interactions. Moreover, understanding how cultural contexts shape trust in AI systems can inform the design of adaptive AI technologies that cater to the unique expectations of diverse cultural groups (Efthymiou, Hildebrand, Bellis and Hampton, 2024).

Another critical research avenue is the role of cultural hybridization in shaping AI development and deployment. As globalization fosters the blending of cultural elements, researchers must examine how hybrid identities influence interactions with AI systems. For instance, do individuals who navigate both collectivist and individualist cultural frameworks approach AI differently compared to those embedded within a single cultural paradigm? Addressing such questions will not only enhance our understanding of AI's role in cross-cultural contexts but also provide actionable insights for designing culturally responsive AI systems.

Artificial intelligence (AI) has transformed the advertising industry, introducing unprecedented opportunities for personalization, automation, and cultural relevance (Efthymiou, Hildebrand, Bellis and Hampton, 2024). In the realm of cross-cultural advertising, AI-powered technologies such as machine learning, natural language processing, and voice synthesis enable advertisers to tailor their messages to diverse audiences with unparalleled precision. Yet, these advancements also raise important challenges related to cultural sensitivity, ethical considerations, and the risk of homogenization in global advertising.

Back, Kim and Kim (2024) emphasize that disclosing the use of AI-generated content in advertising can significantly influence consumer perceptions. Their findings suggest that transparency about AI's involvement enhances the credibility of prosocial advertising campaigns, provided the content aligns with cultural values. However, when AI-generated advertisements fail to resonate with cultural norms, they risk being perceived as impersonal or tone-deaf, potentially alienating consumers. This highlights the dual challenge of leveraging AI's capabilities while ensuring cultural relevance and emotional resonance.

AI technologies also enable advertisers to create more interactive and engaging campaigns. For instance, Sun, Chen and Sundar (2024) explored the role of anthropomorphism, interactivity, and narrativity in chatbot advertisements, finding that human-like chatbots significantly improve consumer engagement and ad effectiveness. By integrating culturally adaptive narratives and interactive elements, AI-driven advertising can foster deeper connections with global audiences. Future research should examine how these human-AI interactions vary across cultures and how advertisers can design culturally adaptive chatbots that cater to diverse consumer preferences.

One of the most intriguing advancements in AI advertising is the use of AI-generated voices, as highlighted by Efthymiou, Hildebrand, Bellis and Hampton (2024). Their research demonstrates how digital vocal tract length and tonal features influence ad performance and product congruency. For instance, consumers in collectivist cultures may respond more favorably to warm, communal tones, while individualistic cultures might prefer assertive, confident vocal styles. These findings underscore the importance of considering cultural preferences in the design and deployment of AI-generated content, particularly in audio-based advertising.

Despite these opportunities, the ethical implications of AI in advertising demand careful consideration. Gao et al. (2023) warn of the risks associated with AI-driven hyper-personalization, including the potential to reinforce cultural stereotypes and exploit consumer vulnerabilities. They advocate for the development of ethical guidelines and algorithms that prioritize inclusivity and cultural respect, ensuring that AI technologies are used to empower rather than manipulate consumers.

The intersection of AI, cross-cultural research, and

advertising is an emerging frontier that holds immense potential for both academic inquiry and practical application. Despite the growing prevalence of AI-driven tools in advertising, limited research explicitly addresses the convergence of these domains. Current findings suggest that AI's capabilities in analyzing cultural nuances and generating culturally adaptive content remain underexplored. This gap presents an opportunity for future research to investigate how AI can effectively bridge cultural differences in advertising while maintaining a balance between global consistency and local relevance.

AI offers unprecedented opportunities to enhance cultural adaptability in advertising. For instance, algorithms powered by natural language processing (NLP) can analyze linguistic and semantic variations across cultures, enabling the creation of advertisements that resonate with specific audiences. However, as Barnes, Zhang, and Valenzuela (2024) emphasize, cultural responses to AI-generated content can vary significantly. Their study demonstrates that individuals from collectivist cultures may perceive AI-generated messages as less authentic compared to those from individualist cultures, highlighting the need for nuanced strategies in deploying AI across diverse cultural settings. This underscores the importance of embedding cultural sensitivity into AI algorithms to ensure that content aligns with local values and preferences.

Moreover, the integration of AI into cross-cultural advertising raises critical questions about ethics and consumer trust. Baek, Kim and Kim (2024) found that disclosing the use of AI in generating prosocial advertisements significantly influenced consumer perceptions, with transparency enhancing trust and engagement. This finding has implications for how brands position AI-driven campaigns in culturally diverse markets. For instance, while Western cultures may appreciate the technological innovation behind AI, other cultures may value the human touch and authenticity in storytelling. Future research should investigate how to balance these preferences, ensuring that AI applications in advertising are both effective and ethically sound.

A promising avenue for exploration is the use of AI in creating dynamic, culturally adaptive storytelling. Advances in machine learning and interactive media have opened up new possibilities for personalized narratives that cater to cultural contexts. Sun, Chen, and Sundar (2024) highlight the role of anthropomorphism and interactivity in chatbot-based advertisements, demonstrating that human-like features can enhance consumer engagement. This finding suggests that combining AI with culturally specific storytelling elements could create more impactful advertisements, especially in markets where narrative traditions hold cultural significance.

Another critical area for investigation is the role of AI-generated audio and visual elements in shaping cultural perceptions. Efthymiou et al. (2024) explore how AI-generated voices can influence product congruency and ad performance, finding that digital vocal characteristics tailored to cultural expectations significantly enhance consumer responses. These findings pave the way for further research into how AI-generated media can adapt to cultural aesthetics and auditory preferences, enabling brands to connect with audiences in more immersive and culturally resonant ways.

The challenge of integrating AI, cross-cultural research, and advertising lies not only in the technological execution but also in addressing broader societal implications. Xia et al. (2024) emphasize the importance of user experience in driving engagement with AI-powered mobile advertising, highlighting the need for seamless, intuitive designs that respect cultural preferences. This suggests that AI technologies must be developed with a comprehensive understanding of cultural contexts to avoid alienating users or reinforcing stereotypes.

Future research should focus on several key areas to

maximize the potential of AI in cross-cultural advertising. First, studies should explore how AI can better capture the evolving nature of cultural identities in an interconnected world. This includes investigating how AI can dynamically adapt advertisements to reflect cultural hybridization and the interplay of global and local influences. Second, researchers should examine the ethical implications of using AI in culturally diverse settings, ensuring that algorithms are designed to respect cultural integrity and avoid biases. Lastly, interdisciplinary collaborations between AI developers, cultural psychologists, and marketing scholars are essential to create holistic frameworks for implementing AI in cross-cultural advertising.

In conclusion, bridging AI, cross-cultural research, and advertising represents an exciting and transformative avenue for future inquiry. By leveraging AI's analytical capabilities while maintaining cultural sensitivity and ethical responsibility, researchers and practitioners can unlock new possibilities for creating impactful, culturally resonant advertising campaigns in an increasingly globalized marketplace.

Table 3 **Future Research Directions in AI and Cross-Cultural Advertising**

Future Research Direction	Description	Key References
Bias & Perceptions of AI-Generated Creativity	Investigate societal biases against AI-driven creativity and explore cultural differences in perceptions of AI-generated content.	Magni, Park & Chao (2024); Barnes, Zhang & Valenzuela (2024)
Cultural Variability in AI Adoption	Examine how cultural dimensions (e.g., power distance, individualism) influence trust and acceptance of AI in different societies.	Barnes, Zhang & Valenzuela (2024); Efthymiou et al. (2024)
AI-Driven Personalization & Cross-Cultural Sensitivity	Analyze how AI can balance personalization with cultural sensitivity to avoid misalignment with consumer expectations.	Baek, Kim & Kim (2024); Sun, Chen & Sundar (2024)
AI-Generated Audio & Visual Elements	Explore how AI-generated voices and visual elements impact advertising effectiveness in different cultural contexts.	Efthymiou et al. (2024); Xia et al. (2024)
Ethical Considerations in AI Advertising	Study the ethical challenges of AI in advertising, including data privacy, consumer trust, and potential reinforcement of cultural stereotypes.	Gao et al. (2023); Baek, Kim & Kim (2024)

REFERENCES

Abuhashesh, M., Alshurideh, M., Ahmed, A., Sumadi, M., and Masa'deh, R. (2021). The effect of culture on customers' attitudes toward Facebook advertising : the moderating role of gender. Review of International Business and Strategy, 31(3), 416-437.

Albaum, G., Erickson, R., and Strandskov, J. (1989). Questionnaire design in Iiternational and cross-cultural research: Is translation necessary?. In Proceedings of the Society for Consumer Psychology, American Psychological Association 1989 Annual Convention, New Orleans, LO, USA.

Advertising Age (2021). Advertising Marketing Fact Book.

Advertising Age (2024). Advertising Marketing Fact Book.

Akaka, M., and Alden, D. (2010). Global brand positioning and perceptions: international advertising and global consumer culture. International Journal of Advertising, 29(1), 37-49.

Al-Sharafi, M., Al-Emran, M., Arpaci, I., Iahad, N., AlQudah, A., Iranmanesh, M., and Al-Qaysi, N. (2023). Generation Z use of artificial intelligence products and its impact on environmental sustainability: A cross-cultural comparison. Computers in Human Behavior, 143, 107708.

Appadurai, A. (1996). Modernity at large: Cultural dimensions of globalization. Minneapolis, MN, USA : University of Minnesota Press.

Baek, T., Kim, J., and Kim, J. (2024). Effect of disclosing AI-generated content on prosocial advertising evaluation. International Journal of Advertising, 43 (Published online 11 Sep 2024), 1-22.

Barnes, A. J., Zhang, Y., and Valenzuela, A. (2024). AI and culture: culturally dependent responses to AI systems. Current Opinion in Psychology, 58 (Published online), 101838.

Barton, R. (1970). Handbook of Advertising Management, New York, USA : McGraw-Hill, Inc.

Berry, J. (1969). On cross-cultural comparability. International Journal of Psychology, 4, 119-128.

Berry, J. (1980). Introduction to methodology, In H. Triandis and J. Berry (Eds.), Handbook of Cross-Cultural Psychology, V.2, Boston, MA, USA : Allyn and Bacon.

Bond, M., and Hofstede, G. (1989). The cash value of Confucian values. Human systems management, 8(3), 195-199.

Briñol, P., Rucker, D., and Petty, R. (2015). Naïve theories about persuasion: implications for information processing and consumer attitude change. International Journal of Advertising, 34(1), 1-22.

Brislin, R. (1970). Back-translation for cross-cultural research. Journal of Cross-Cultural Psychology, 1, 185-216.

Brislin, R. (1980). Translation and content analysis of oral and written material. In H. Triandis and J. Berry (Eds.), Handbook of Cross-Cultural Psychology, V.2, Boston, MA, USA : Allyn and Bacon, 389-444.

Brislin, R. (1983). Cross-cultural research in psychology. Annal Review of Psychology, 34, 363-400.

Brislin, R., and Baumgardner, S. (1971). Non-random sampling of individuals in cross-cultural research. Journal of Cross-Cultural Psychology, 2(4), 397-400.

Buzeta, C., De Keyzer, F., Dens, N., and De Pelsmacker, P. (2024). Branded content and motivations for social media use as drivers of brand outcomes on social media: a cross-cultural study. International Journal of Advertising, 43(4), 637-671.

Byun, H., et al. (2024). AI Era, Advertising Industry Development Plan, Korea Broadcasting Advertising Corporation Research Report.

Cavallone, M. (2013). From adaptation to standardization: the positive cycle of cross-culturally customized communication. Southern

Business Review, 38(2), 1-21.
Cheil Worldwide (2021). 2021 Advertising Yearbook.
Cheil Worldwide (2024). 2024 Advertising Yearbook.
Cheng, H. (Ed.). (2014). The handbook of international advertising research. New York, USA : John Wiley and Sons.
Cheon, H., Cho, C., and Sutherland, J. (2007). A meta-analysis of studies on the determinants of standardization and localization of international marketing and advertising strategies. Journal of International Consumer Marketing, 19(4), 109-147.
Cho, B. (1991). Characteristics and Influence of Transnational Advertising Agencies in the World. Seoul, Korea : Korean Press Foundation.
Cho, B., and Jang, H. (1987). Study on Response Strategies to the Opening of the Korean Advertising Market. Seoul, Korea : Korea Broadcasting Advertising Corporation.
Choudhry, Y. (1986). Pitfalls in international marketing research: are you speaking French like a spanish cow?. Arkon Business and Economic Review, 17(4), 18-28.
Czarnecka, B., and Schivinski, B. (2022). Individualism/collectivism and perceived consumer effectiveness: the moderating role of global–local identities in a post-transitional European economy. Journal of Consumer Behavior, 21(2), 180-196.
Davidson, A., Faccard, J., Triandis, H., Morales, M., and Diaz-Guerrero, R. (1976). Cross-cultural model testing: toward a solution of the Etic-Emic dilemma. International Journal of Psychology, 11(1), 1-13.
Decker, C. (2001). The New Landscape of the Advertising Industry. in Proceedings of the 2001 Seoul International Advertising Seminar, Korea Federation of Advertising Associations.
Desmarais, F. (2017). Who is the athlete endorser : cross-cultural exploration of advertising practitioners' views. Journal of Global Marketing, 30(1), 12-30.
Diehl, S., and Terlutter, R. (Eds.). (2006). International advertising and communication: Current insights and empirical findings. New

York, USA : Springer Science & Business Media.

Douglas, S., and Craig, C. (1983). International Marketing Research, Englewood Cliffs, NJ, USA : Prentice-Hall.

Down, J. (2000). 21st century advertising agency management strategy: focusing on brand building and media planning value enhancement. Advertising Information, March issue, 46–47.

Efthymiou, F., Hildebrand, C., de Bellis, E., and Hampton, W. (2024). The power of AI-generated voices How digital vocal tract length shapes product congruency and ad performance. Journal of Interactive Marketing, 59(2), 117-134.

Ford, J., Mueller, B., and Mueller, S. (2023). Forty years of cross-cultural advertising research in the International Journal of Advertising: a Bibliometric Analysis. International Journal of Advertising, 42(1), 119-127.

Frijda, N., and Jahoda, G. (1966). On the scope and methods of cross-cultural research. International Journal of Psychology, 1(2), 109-127.

Gao, B., Wang, Y., Xie, H., Hu, Y., and Hu, Y. (2023). Artificial intelligence in advertising: advancements, challenges, and ethical considerations in targeting, personalization, content creation, and ad optimization. Sage Open, 13(4), 21582440231210759.

Geng, C., Xiaoyan, Y., Wang, H., and Liu, H. (2012). Culturally incongruent messages in international advertising. International Journal of Advertising, 31(2), 355–376.

Glenn, E., Witmeyer, D., and Stevenson, K. (1977). Cultural styles of persuasion, International Journal of Intercultural Relations, 3, 52-65.

Green, R., and Langeard, E. (1975). A cross-national comparison of consumer habits and innovator characteristics. Journal of Marketing, 49, 34-41.

Green, R., and White, R. (1976). Methodological considerations in cross-national consumer research. Journal of International Business Studies, 7, 81-87.

Guang, T., and Trotter, D. (2012). Key issues in cross-cultural business communication: anthropological approaches to international business. African Journal of Business Management, 22, 6456-6463.

Gudykunst, W., and Ting-Toomey, S. (1988). Culture and Interpersonal Communication. CA, USA : Sage Publication.

Han, S. (1990). Individualism and Collectivism : Its implications for cross-cultural advertising. Ph. D. Dissertation, University of Illinois at Urbana-Champaign.

Han, S. (1997). Survey on practitioners' perceptions of the internationalization of the advertising industry. Journal of Korean Advertising, 8(1), 101–127.

Han, H. (1998). Empirical analysis of the effects of market opening on the advertising industry. Journal of Korean Advertising, 9(2), 9–29.

Han, S. (2016). Advertisements that reflect culture, advertisements that create culture. Journal of Korean Advertising, 27(2), 29-54.

Han, S. (2021). A comparison of government and public institutions advertising appeals in collectivistic and individualistic cultures. Journal of the Korean Convergence Society, 12(7), 153-158,

Han, S. (2024). Advertising strategies according to product type and advertising appeal type: focusing on individualism and collectivism. Journal of Business Convergence, 9(1), 18 – 28.

Han, S., Choi, Y., and Yu, S. (2106). Reflection of Culture : An analysis of Korean advertising appeals from 1980's to 2010's. Indian Journal of Science and Technology, 3(4), 16-29.

Han, S., and Shavitt, S. (1994). Persuasion and culture: advertising appeals in individualistic and collectivisitic societies. Journal of Experimental Social Psychology, 30, 326-350.

Han, S., and Shavitt, S. (2005). Westernization of cultural values in Korean advertising: a longitudinal content analysis of magazine ads, Advances in Consumer Research, 32(1), 110 – 112.

Hilton, M. (2022). West, Sally. I shop in Moscow: advertising and the creation of consumer culture in late Tsarist Russia. Slavonic and East European Review. 92(1), 155-157.

Hofstede, G. (2001). Culture's consequences: Comparing values, behaviors, institutions, and organizations across nations.

International Educational and Professional Eds. New York, USA : Sage Publication.

Hofstede, G., and Hofstede, G. (2004). Cultures and Organizations: Software of the Mind. 2nd ed rev. and expanded. New York, USA : Sage Publication.

Hollensen, S. (2017). Global Marketing. New York, USA : Pearson.

Hornik, J. (1980). Comparative evaluation of international vs. national advertising strategies. Columbia Journal of World Business, 15(1), 36-45.

Hornikx, J., and Groot, E. (2017). Cultural values adapted to individualism–collectivism in advertising in Western Europe: an experimental and meta-analytical approach. International Communication, 79(3), 298–316.

Hsu, S., and Barker, G. (2013). Individualism and collectivism in Chinese and American television advertising. International Communication, 75(8), 695–714.

Hui, C., and Triandis, H. (1985). Measurement in cross-cultural psychology: a review and comparison of strategies. Journal of Cross-Cultural Psychology, 16(2), 131-152.

Hui, C., and Triandis, H. (1989). Effects of culture and response format of extreme response style. Journal of Cross-Cultural Psychology, 20(3), 296-309.

Irvine, S., and Carroll, W. (1980). Testing and assessment across cultures: issues in methodology and theory. In H. Triandis (Ed.), Handbook of Cross-Cultural Research, Vol. 2, 181-244.

Irwin, M., Klein, R., Engle, P., Yarbrough, C., and Nerlove, S. (1977). The problem of establishing validity in cross-cultural measurements. In L. Loeb Adler (Ed.), Issues in Cross-Cultural Research, Annals of the New York Academy of Sciences, 285, 308-325.

Jenkins, H. (2006). Convergence Culture : Where Old and New Media Collide. New York, USA : New York University Press.

Jung, J. (2004). Acquisitions or joint ventures: Foreign market entry strategy of US advertising agencies. The Journal of Media

Economics, 17(1), 35-50.

Kanso, A., and Nelson, R. (2002). Advertising localization overshadows standardization. Journal of Advertising Research, January/ February, 79-89.

Kaplan, A., and Haenlcin, M. (2010). Users of the World, Unite! The Challenges and Opportunities of Social Media. Business Horizons, 53(1), 59-68.

Kim, M. (2016). Individualism collectivism revisited: analysis of self-other perceptions in Korea and the U.S. Asian Communication Research, 13(1), 58-79.

Kim, J. (2020). National culture and advertising sensitivity to business cycles: a reexamination. Journal of International Marketing, 28(4), 41-57.

Kim, S. (1990). Measures to Enhance International Competitiveness of Advertising Following the Uruguay Round Negotiations and Market Opening, in Development Directions of the Korean Advertising Industry during Transition. Korean Ministry of Public Information.

Kim, S. and Lee, S. (2001). A Study on the Market Entry Strategies of Multinational Advertising Agencies in Korea. Paper published in Spring Advertising Seminar, Korean Advertising Society.

Kim, Y., and Kim, J. (2020). Korean Advertising and Consumer Culture. New York, USA : Routledge, Inc.

Kline, P. (1988). The cross-cultural measurement of personality. In G. K. Verma et al. (Eds.), Cross-Cultural Studies of Personality, Attitudes, and Cognition, London, UK : MacMillan Press, 3-40.

Korea Broadcasting Advertising Corporation (1995). Survey on Strategies to Activate Overseas Advertising. Korea Broadcasting Advertising Corporation: Seoul, Korea.

Korea Broadcasting Advertising Corporation (1996). Globalization of the Advertising Industry,. Korea Broadcasting Advertising Corporation: Seoul.

Korea Commercial Film Production Association (1995). Challenges for Advertising Production Following the Opening of the Advertising

Market. Korea Commercial Film Production Association: Seoul, Korea.
Korea Federation of Advertising Associations (2000). Handbook of Korean Advertising Industry in Recent Years.
Korea Federation of Advertising Associations (2001). Seoul International Advertising Seminar, Seoul, Korea.
Kotler, P., and Keller, K. (2016). Marketing Management. New York, USA : Pearson Publishing.
Kumkang Planning and Hyundai Research Institute for Economic and Social Studies (1991). A study on the impact of the Uruguay round on the advertising industry, Kumkang Planning, Seoul, Korea.
Laczniak, G. (1979). Information content in print advertising. Journalism Quarterly, 54, 482-491.
Lau-Gesk, M. and G. Loraine (2023). Activating culture through persuasion appeals: an examination of the bicultural consumer. Journal of Consumer Psychology, 13(3), 301-315.
Lee, J. (2001). Becoming a Marketing Partner to Foster Strong Brands. Advertising Trends, February issue.
Lee, M. (2002). Utilizing Multinational Agencies for Korean Companies' Overseas Expansion. Advertising Trends, February issue.
Leslie, D. (1995). Global scan: The globalization of advertising agencies, concepts, and campaigns. Economic Geography, 71(4), 402-426.
Liamputtong, P. (2008). Doing cross-cultural research: Ethical and methodological perspectives (Vol. 34). New York, USA : Springer Science & Business Media..
Lim, D. (2001). Significant Progress by Foreign Advertising Agencies. Seoul Economic Daily, Distribution Section, November 6.
Lonner, W., and Berry, J. (1986). Field Methods in Cross-Cultural Research, Beverly Hills, CA, USA : SAGE.
Madden, C., Caballero, M., and Matsukubo, S. (1986). Analysis of information content in U.S. and Japanese magazine advertising. Journal of Advertising, 15(3), 38-45.
Magni, F., Park, J., and Chao, M. (2024). Humans as creativity

gatekeepers: Are we biased against AI creativity?. Journal of Business and Psychology, 39(3), 643-656.
Maheswaran, D., and Shavitt, S. (2014). Issues and new directions in global consumer psychology. Journal of Consumer Psychology, 9(2), 59-66.
Mai, S, Ketron, S., and Yang, J. (2020). How individualism-collectivism influences consumer responses to the sharing economy: consociality and promotional type. Psychology and Marketing, 37(5), 677-688.
Malpass, R. (1977). Theory and method in cross-cultural psychology. American Psychologist, December, 1069-1079.
Manrai, A. (2018). New research on cross-cultural and cross-national comparisons in advertising and consumer behavior. Journal of Global Marketing, 31(1), 1-3.
Markus, H., and Kitayama, S. (1991). Culture and the self: Implications for cognition, emotion, and motivation. Psychological Review, 98(2), 224–253.
Martenson, R. (1987). Advertising strategies and information content in American and Swedish advertising. International Journal of Advertising, 6, 133-144.
Martinez, F., and Fieulaine, N. (2015). Time and the misfits: temporal framing and priming in persuasive communication. In Time Perspective Theory; Review, Research and Application (pp. 385-402). New York, USA : Springer International Publishing.
Mazze, E. (1964). How to push a body abroad without making it a corpse. Business Abroad, August 10, 15.
Mele, E., Kerkhof, P., and Cantoni, L. (2021). Analyzing cultural tourism promotion on Instagram: a cross-cultural perspective. Journal of Travel and Tourism Marketing, 38(3), 326-340.
Mehra, A. (1986). Free Flow of Information : a New Paradigm. New York, USA : Greenwood Press.
Min, K. (1993a). Comprehensive Study on the Opening of the Advertising Market. Seoul, Korea : Korea Broadcasting Advertising Corporation.

Min, K. (1993b). A Study on the Service Strategies of Foreign Advertising Companies Entering the Domestic Market. Seoul, Korea : Korea Broadcasting Advertising Corporation.

Min, K. (1994). Study on Structural Changes and Countermeasures for the Advertising Industry after the UR Agreement. Seoul, Korea : Korea Broadcasting Advertising Corporation.

Ministry of Public Information (1995). Advertising Administration White Paper. Seoul, Korea : Ministry of Public Information.

Ministry of Public Information (1997). Advertising Administration White Paper. Seoul, Korea : Ministry of Public Information.

Miracle, G. (1990). Research methodological problems of equivalency in cross-cultural advertising research. In Proceedings of the 1990 Conference of the American Academy of Advertising, P. Stout (Ed.), American Academy of Advertising, RTS197-198.

Monthly Advertising (1999). Interview with CEOs of Multinational Advertising Agencies: Trends and Prospects for Agencies and Advertisers. Monthly Advertising, May issue.

Mooij, M. (1994). Advertising Worldwide : Concepts, Theories, and Practice of International, Multinational, and Global Advertising. Englewood Cliffs, NJ, USA : Prentice Hall.

Mooij, M. (2019). Global Marketing and Advertising: Understanding Cultural Paradoxes. New York, USA : Sage Publications.

Mooij, M. (2022). Global Marketing and Advertising: Understanding Cultural Paradoxes (2nd Ed.). London, UK : Sage Publications.

Mooij, M., and Hofstede, G. (2010). The Hofstede model: applications to global branding and advertising strategy and research. International Journal of Advertising, 29(1), 85-110.

Mooij, M., and Hofstede, G. (2011). Cross-cultural consumer behavior: A review of research findings. Journal of international consumer marketing, 23(3-4), 181-192.

Mowlana, H. (1986). Global Information and World Communication : New Frontiers in International Relations. New York, USA : Longman Press.

Mueller, A. (1987). Reflections of culture: an analysis of Japanese and

American advertising appeals. Journal of Advertising Research, 27, 51-59.
Mueller, A. (1990). Cultural pitfalls in international advertising research. In Proceedings of the 1990 Conference of the American Academy of Advertising, P. Stout (Ed.), American Academy of Advertising, RTS194-197.
Norris, V. (1980). Advertising history – according to the textbook. Journal of Advertising, 9(3), 3-11.
O'Guinn, T. (1990). International Advertising, Department of Advertising, University of Illinois, unpublished paper.
Okazaki, S., Barbara M., and Diehl, S. (2013). A multi-country examination Of hard-Sell and soft-Sell advertising comparing global consumer positioning In holistic- and analytic-thinking cultures. Journal of Advertising, 53(3). 258-272.
Okazaki S., and Taylor, C. (2006). Towards an understanding advertising standardisation in the European Union: a theoretical framework and research propositions, in International advertising and communication: Current insights and empirical findings. Diehl, S., and Terlutter, R. (Eds.). New York, USA : Springer Science & Business Media.
Okazaki, S., and Taylor, C. (2013). Social media and international advertising: theoretical challenges and future directions. International Marketing Review, 30(1), 56-71.
Osgood, C. (1967). Cross-cultural comparability in attitude measurement via multilingual semantic differentials. In M. Fishbein (Ed.), Readings in Attitude Theory and Measurement, New York: John Wiley.
Pareek, U., and Rao, V. (1980). Cross-cultural surveys and interviewing. In H. Triandis (Ed.), Handbook of Cross-Cultural Research. New York, USA : Sage Publications, 127-180.
Park J., and et al. (2021). Korea Broadcast Advertising Promotion Corporation Research Report.
Park, Y. (1989). Study on Response Strategies to the Opening of the Korean Advertising Market. Market Opening Strategy Committee.

Seoul, Korea : Korea Advertising Federation.

Peck, R., and Daiz-Guerrero, R. (1967). Two core-culture patterns and the diffusion of Values across their border. International Journal of Psychology, 2, 175-182.

Pike, R. (1966). Language in Relation to a Unified Theory of the Structure of Human Behavior. New York, USA : The Hague Mouton.

Poortinga, Y. (1989). Equivalence of cross-cultural date: an overview of basic issues. International Journal of Psychology, 24(6), 737-756.

Renforth, W., and Raveed, S. (1983). Consumer information cues in television advertising: a cross country analysis. Journal of the Academy of Marketing Science, 11(3), 216-225.

Rhee, M., Alexandra, V., and Powell, K. (2020). Individualism-collectivism cultural differences in performance feedback theory. Cross Cultural and Strategic Management, 27(3), 343-364.

Rice, M., and Lu, Z. (1988). A content analysis of Chinese magazine advertisements. Journal of Advertising, 17(4), 43-48.

Ricks, D. (2009). Blunders in International Business. New York, USA : Wiley Publication.

Ricks, D., Ju, M., and Arpan, F. (1974). International Business Blunders, Columbus. Columbus, OH, USA : Grid Publishing.

Robertson, R. (1995). Glocalization: Time-space and homogeneity-heterogeneity. New York, USA : Sage Publication.

Rodgers, W., and Nguyen, T. (2022). Advertising benefits from ethical artificial intelligence algorithmic purchase decision pathways. Journal of business ethics, 178(4), 1043-1061.

Sampson, H. (2014). A History of Advertising from the Earliest Times: Illustrated by Anecdotes, Curious Specimens and Biographical Notes.New York, USA : Nabu Press.

Shapiro, A. Rosenblood, L., and Berlyne, B. (1976). The relationship of test familiarity to extreme response styles in Bedouin and Moroccan boys. Journal of Cross-Cultural Psychology, 7, 357-364.

Sharma, S., and Bumb, A. (2020). Culture in advertising: model for indian markets. Journal for Cultural Research, 24(2), 145-158.

Shavitt, S., Ashok K., Shang, J., and Torelli, C. (2006). The horizontal/ vertical distinction in Ccoss-cultural consumer research, Journal of Consumer Psychology, 16(4), 325–356.

Shaw, A. (2006). Convergence Culture: Where Old and New Media Collide. New York, USA : Sage Publication.

Shen, G. (2022). AI-enabled talent training for the cross-cultural news communication talent. Technological Forecasting and Social Change, 185, 122031.

Shin, H. (2001). Survey on Advertising Professionals' Perceptions of Market Opening in the Korean Advertising Industry. Master's Thesis, Graduate School of Media and Information, Hanyang University.

Silver, I. (1993). Marketing authenticity in third world countries. Annals of tourism research, 20(2), 302-318.

Slater, J. (1984). The hazards of cross-cultural advertising, Business America, April 2, 20-23.

Salzberger, T., and Sinkovics, R. (2006). Reconsidering the problem of data equivalence in international marketing research. International Marketing Review, 23(4), 390-417.

Snyder, M., and DeBono, K. (1985). Appeals to image and claims about quality: understanding the psychology of advertising. Journal of Personality and Social Psychology, 49, 586-597.

Steenkamp, J., and Baumgartner, H. (1998). Assessing measurement invariance in cross-national consumer research. Journal of consumer research, 25(1), 78-90.

Stening, B. and Everett, J. (1984). Response styles in a cross-cultural managerial study. Journal of Social Psychology, 122, 151-156.

Stern, B., Krugman, D., and Resnik, A. (1981). Magazine advertising: an analysis of its information content. Journal of Advertising Research, 21(2), 39-44.

Sun, Y., Chen, J., and Sundar, S. (2024). Chatbot ads with a human touch: A test of anthropomorphism, interactivity, and narrativity. Journal of Business Research, 172, 114403.

Taylor, C. (2023). Thoughts on cross-cultural advertising research in

2023. International Journal of Advertising, 42(6), 969-971.

Terpstra, V. (1980). International Dimensions of Marketing, New York, USA : Kent Publishing Co.

Triandis, H. (1972). The Analysis of Subjective Culture, New York, NY, USA : Wiley.

Triandis, H. (1974). Major theoretical and methodological issues in cross-cultural psychology. In J. W. Dawson and W. J. Lonner (Eds.), Readings in Cross-Cultural Psychology, Hang Kong : Hong Kong University Press.

Triandis, H. (1979). Cross-cultural psychology. in M. E. Meyer (Ed.), Foundations of Contemporary Psychology, 544-579.

Triandis, H. (1989). Unpublished Classroom Note, University of Illinois.

Triandis, H. (1995). Individualism and Collectivism. Boulder, CO, USA : Westview Press.

Triandis, H., and Berry, J. (1980). Handbook of Cross-Cultural Psychology, V.2, Boston, MA, USA : Allyn and Bacon.

Triandis, H., and Brislin, R. (1984). Cross-cultural psychology. American Psychologist, 39(9), 1008-1016.

Triandis, H., Bontempo, M., Villareal, M., and Lucca, N. (1988). Individualism and collectivism: cross-cultural perspectives on self-ingroup relationships. Journal of Personality and Social Psychology, 54, 323-338.

Triandis, H.., Brislin, R., and Hui, C. (1988). Cross-cultural training across the individualism collectivism divide. International Journal of Intercultural Relations, 12, 269- 289.

Triandis, H., Malpass, R., and Davidson, A. (1971). Cross-cultural psychology. In B. Siegel (Ed.), Biennial Review of Anthropology, Stanford, CA, USA : Stanford University Press.

Triandis, H., and Marin, G. (1983). Etic Plus emic Vs. pseudoetic: a test of a basic assumption of contemporary cross-cultural psychology. Journal of Cross-Cultural Psychology, 14(4), 489-500.

Usunier, J., and Lee, J. (2013). Marketing Across Cultures. New York, USA : Pearson Publication.

Van de Vijver, F., and Leung, K. (2021). Methods and Data Analysis for

Cross-cultural Research (Vol. 116). Cambridge, United Kingdom : Cambridge University Press.

Vignali, C. (2001). McDonald's think global, act local – the marketing mix. British food journal, 103(2), 97-111.

Walsh, G., Shiu, E., and Hassan, L. (2014). Cross-national advertising and behavioral intentions: A multilevel analysis. Journal of International Marketing, 22(1), 77-98.

Wang, R., Huang, S., and Natascha G. (2020). Multinational luxury brands' communication strategies on international and local social media: comparing Twitter and Weibo. Journal of International Consumer Marketing, 32(4), 313-323.

Wells, W., Burnett, J., and Moriarty, S. (1995). Advertising : Principles and Practice. Englewood Cliffs, NJ, USA : Prentice Hall.

Westjohn, S. Magnusson, P., Franke, G,, and Peng, Y, (2022). Trust propensity across cultures: the role of collectivism. Journal of International Marketing, 30(1), 1-17.

Wood, L. (2015). Brands and brand management: contemporary research perspectives. Journal of Marketing Management, 31(9-10), 1017-1039.

Xia, Y., Liu, Z., Wang, S., Huang, C., and Zhao, W. (2024). Unlocking the impact of user experience on AI-powered mobile advertising engagement. Journal of the Knowledge Economy, 15(2), 1-3.

Xu, K., and Li, J. (2021). Artificial intelligence in cross-cultural advertising: ooportunities and ethical considerations. Journal of Advertising, 50(4), 492-508.

Zafran, M., and Masud, S. (2023). Consumer's response to fear appeals and their effectiveness in advertising: cross-cultural comparison of Innish and Pakistani consumer's attitude towards threat appeals. Economy and Market Communication Review, 13(1), 95-112.

Zhu, L., and Wang, Y. (2024). Acting real: a cross-cultural investigation of finfluencer strategic authenticity. International Journal of Advertising, 43 (Published online), 1-20.

SANGPIL HAN Dr. Sang-Pil Han is Professor of Advertising and Public Relations at Hanyang University. He received his Ph.D. in Advertising from the University of Illinois at Urbana-Champaign. A leading scholar in cultural perspectives on advertising, Dr. Han has published widely in international and domestic journals and received numerous academic honors, including the Gallup Korea Academic Award and Hanyang University's HYU Academic Award. He has also served in major leadership roles in Korea's academic societies and contributed to advancing the global presence of the Korean advertising industry.

HANYANG UNIVERSITY PRESS

ADVERTISING AND CULTURE
: THEORETICAL CHALLENGES AND FUTURE DIRECTIONS

펴낸날 2026년 3월 10일 초판 1쇄
지은이 한상필 ● **펴낸이** 이기정
펴낸곳 한양대학교출판부 ● **출판등록** 제4-7호(1972.2.29)
주소 서울 성동구 왕십리로 222 ● **전화** 02.2220.1432-4 ● **팩스** 02.2220.1435
홈페이지 press.hanyang.ac.kr ● **이메일** presshy@hanyang.ac.kr
디자인 안광일 ● **편집** 김민지 ● **인쇄** 미르P&P

This work was supported by the Ministry of Education of the Republic of Korea and the National Research Foundation of Korea (NRF-2022S1A6A4045931).

ISBN 978.89.7218.859.9 (93320)